D1093842

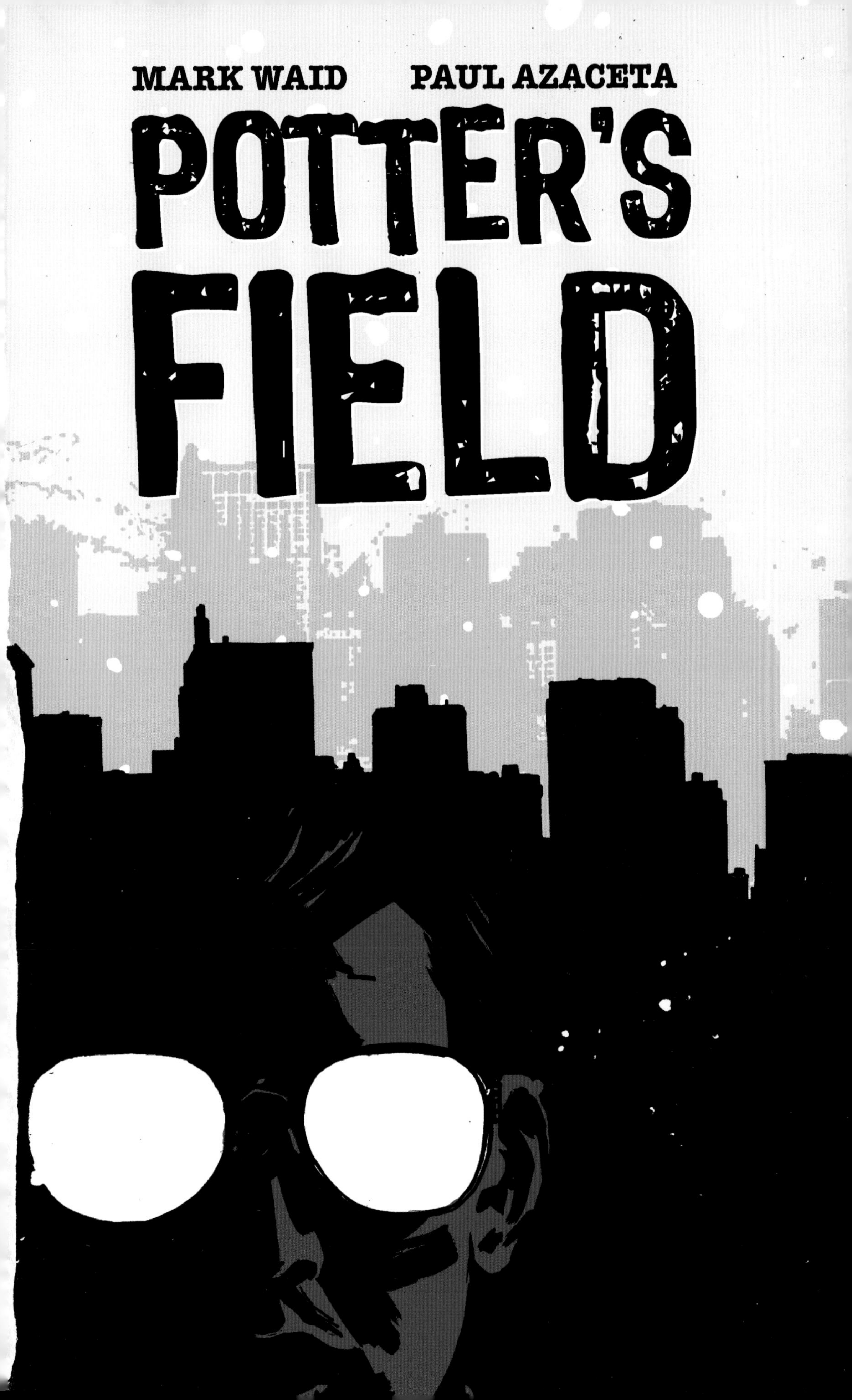
MARK WAID
PAUL AZACETA
POTTER'S
FIELD

ROSS RICHIE
chief executive officer

MARK WAID
editor-in-chief

ADAM FORTIER
vice president,
publishing

CHIP MOSHER
marketing director

MATT GAGNON
managing editor

JENNY CHRISTOPHER
sales director

Potter's Field — published by Boom! Studios. Potter's Field is copyright © 2009 Mark Waid. BOOM! Studios™ and the BOOM! logo are trademarks of Boom Entertainment, Inc., registered in various countries and categories. All rights reserved. The characters and events depicted herein are fictional. Any similarity to actual persons, demons, anti-Christs, aliens, vampires, face-suckers or political figures, whether living, dead or undead, or to any actual or supernatural events is coincidental and unintentional. So don't come whining to us. Office of publication: 6310 San Vicente Blvd, Ste 404, Los Angeles, CA 90048-5457.

First Edition: April 2009

10 9 8 7 6 5 4 3 2 1
PRINTED IN KOREA

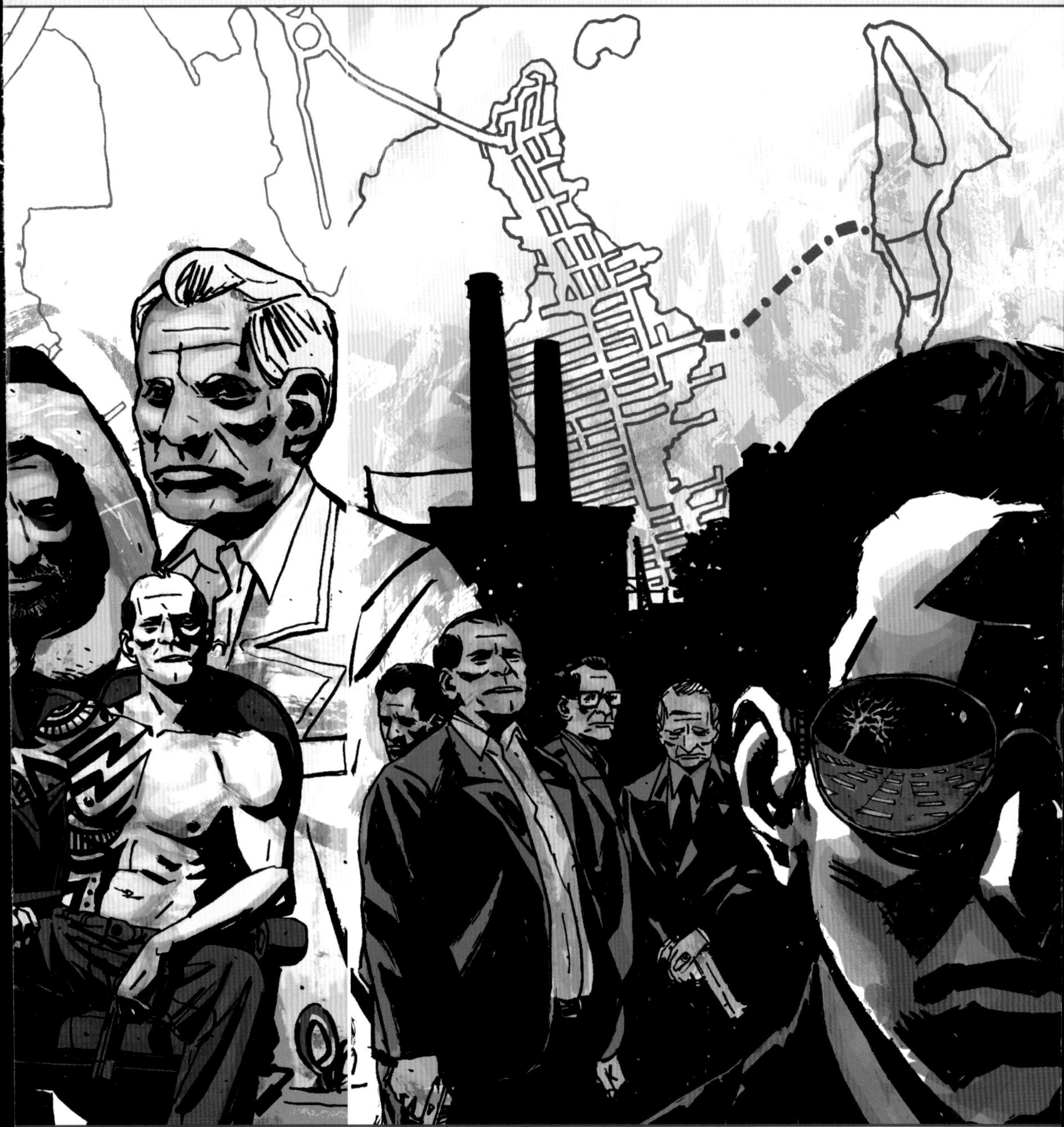

MARK WAID
WRITER

PAUL AZACETA
ARTIST

NICK FILARDI
COLORIST

J.G. JONES
COVER ARTIST

ED DUKESHIRE
LETTERER (chapter 1-3)

MARSHALL DILLON
LETTERER (chapter 4)

MATT GAGNON
EDITOR

DAFNA PLEBAN
COVER DESIGN

Foreword

Ah, the smell of freshly turned earth, the moist fall of dirt on a coffin-lid, the creep of the earthworm inching closer to its dinner. The sweet dramatic potential of death. Ashes to ashes, dust to dust, and the inexorable call of the grave. It's the terminus, our collective endpoint. Everyone dies.

Raymond Chandler, Patron Saint of the Private Investigator Story, argued that the only crime worth a damn to write about was murder. All mystery stories must lead to it or end with it, but at its heart, murder is what it's all about. The detective's quest to restore order from chaos, to solve the insoluble, to be a speaker for the dead in a world where no one will carry that burden, where society is content to let the dead stay buried.

I've known Mark Waid for several years now, and I've known him while he's worn a variety of hats. But if there's a consistent personality trait that has emerged, it's that Mark's looking for the Righteous. He's looking for the Right, and he's looking to fight the Wrong. It's what drives his ethic as a professional, and it's the fuel for his writing.

In *Potter's Field*, he's fighting the battle of the righteous again (and what could be more righteous than solving those crimes society has, quite literally, buried away, left to decompose behind a slate of anonymous numbers?), but in a new way, with a new twist.

What begins with a neo-noir feel, a story that looks – on its surface – to be post-modern comic-telling, quickly strips itself back to its roots. Yes, at first blush, John Doe has the trappings of a super-hero. But you look again, and you see something that is far more exciting, and far more admirable. You see a reaching back to the pulps, to the proto super-hero; images of Operator Number 9 and The Spider and The Shadow – stories of men hunting the darkness, in pursuit of a justice all others have abandoned. Stories of heroes who labored unsung against evil, both banal and grand, of which the rest of us lived in blissful ignorance.

The work that Waid and Azaceta have done here is inspired, remarkable for its depth and ambition. *Potter's Field* is a modern pulp told with an affectionate reverence for what has come before, all the while being imbued with an unmistakable sense of the now. Not just John Doe, but the entire world around him, is timeless, a sense that becomes all the more apparent in Paul Azaceta's art, the palpable layer of *darkness* that permeates every surface, from the sorrow of a lonely man's bedroom right to the sterility of the city morgue. This is a modern world of iPods and mobile phones, and yet, like the literal truth of Potter's Field itself, it is unchanged, and unchanging. It's stark, and it's abrupt, and it casts a hero's light on John Doe's self-appointed mission, to speak for the thousands upon thousands of unnamed dead.

An impossible task. One that is guaranteed to fail. And, as such, one that is inherently noble, all the more so in the world that Azaceta has drawn, a world that manages to be both energetic and oppressive, filled with energy even as his pen weighs the shoulders of every man and woman we meet with untold histories of pain, and loss, and suffering.

This is the first story, the introduction, the mission statement. First stories are oftentimes slow, and too often-times consumed with answering the reader's questions before they're even asked. Not so here – another testament to Waid's skill as a writer; nothing is wasted. My favorite mystery writers all have played, at one point or another, the same trick; that of solving their mystery in the first dozen or so pages, leaving the reader the rest of the story to figure out what they've already been shown. So a word of advice:

Don't blink, you'll miss it.

But if you do blink – and frankly, I wouldn't blame you if you did – and find yourself, instead, more in Dr. Paxtin's shoes than in John Doe's, trying to unravel the mystery of his crusading employer, that's as it should be. From the start, the mystery of John Doe is the real heart of *Potter's Field* – who is he? Even when this first case is solved, the question remains, and certainly that is also as it should be.

I have my theories. Pay close attention to John Doe's dialogue, what he says, *how* he says it. The turns of phrase are key. Just a small piece in a larger puzzle, but, perhaps, a telling one.

Of course, I could be wrong. I could be dead wrong.

John Doe, after all, is just another name for a body you'll find in Potter's Field.

Hope to see you there.

Greg Rucka
Portland, Oregon – February 2009

CHAPTER ONE

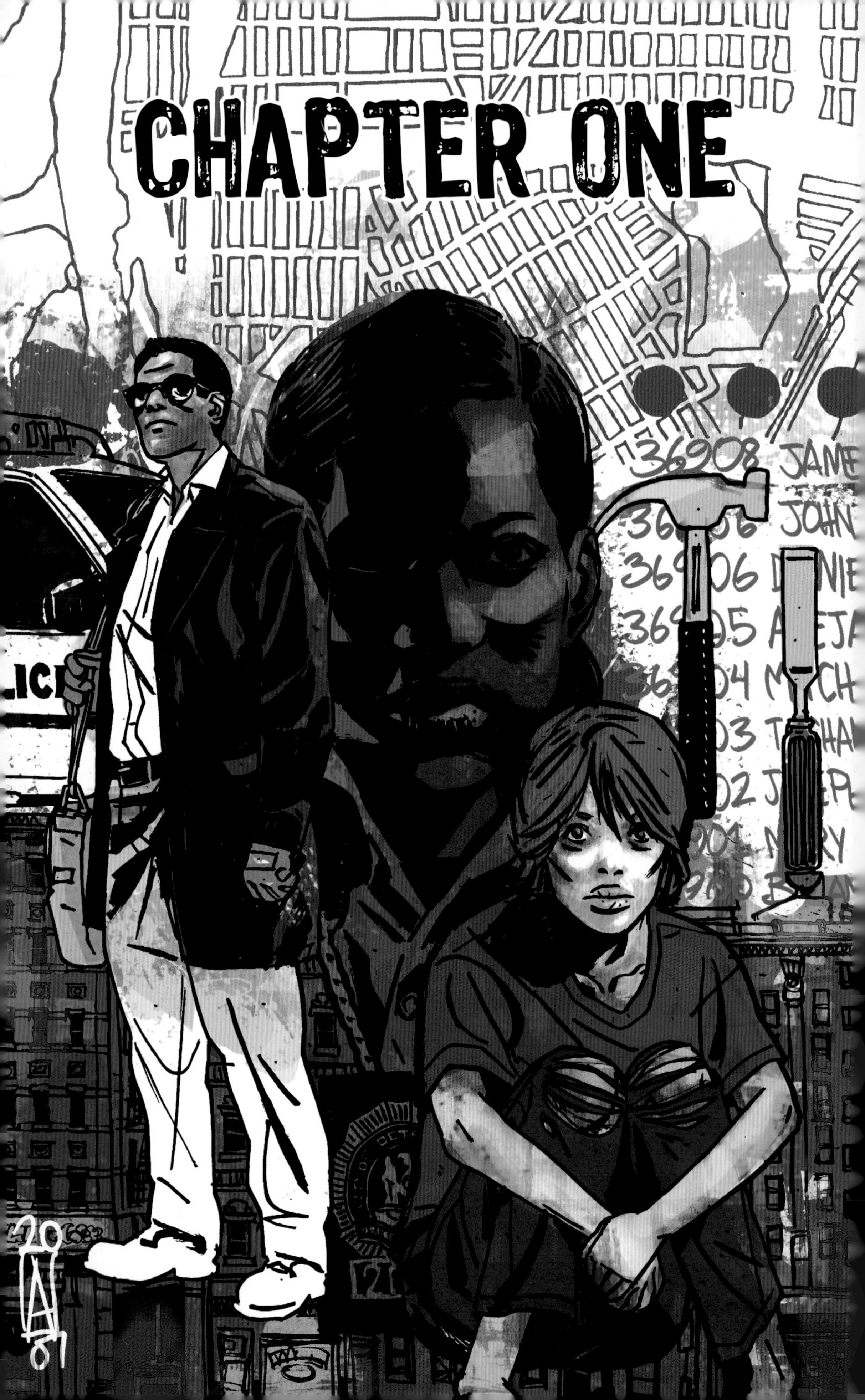

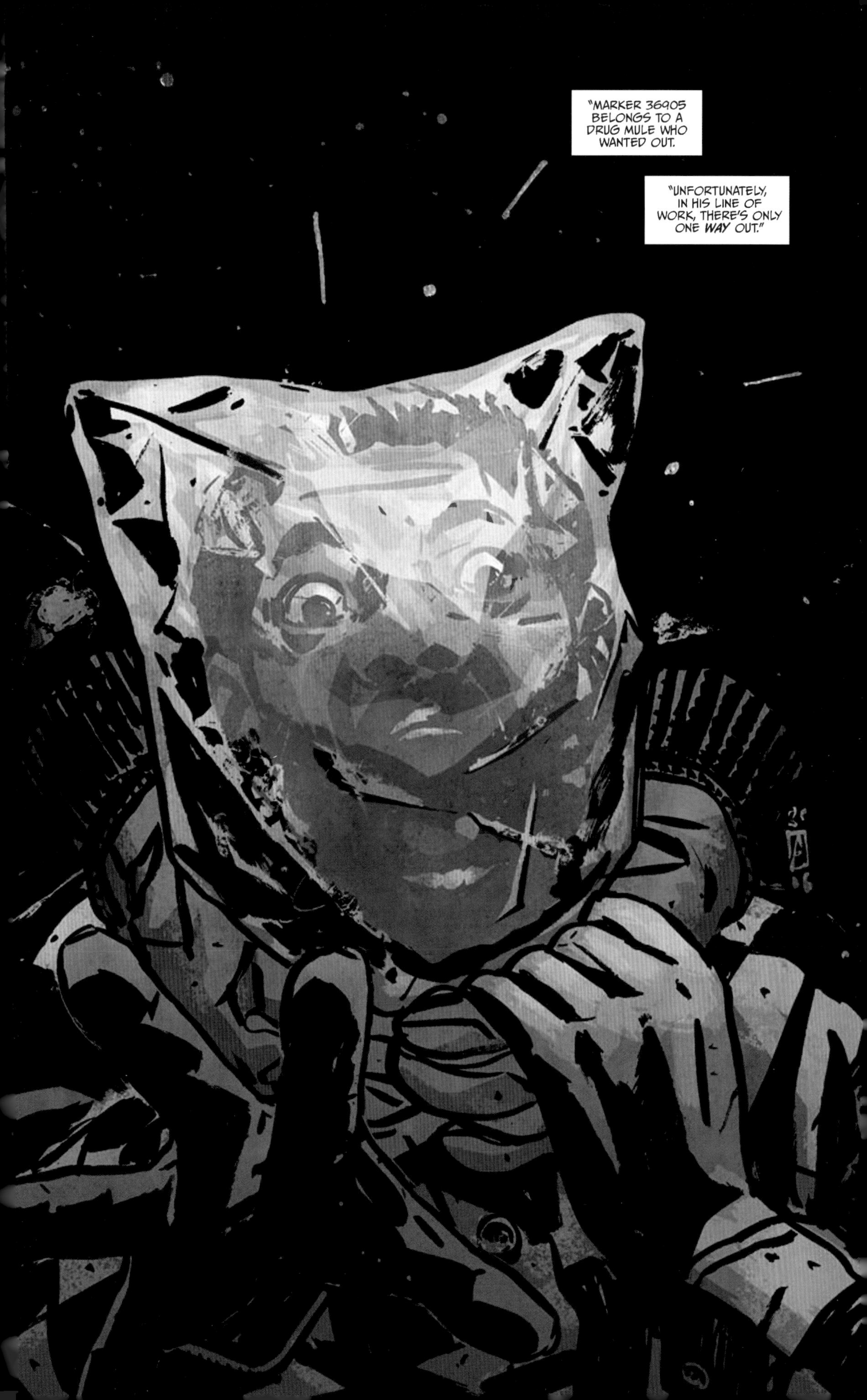
"MARKER 36905 BELONGS TO A DRUG MULE WHO WANTED OUT.
"UNFORTUNATELY, IN HIS LINE OF WORK, THERE'S ONLY ONE WAY OUT."

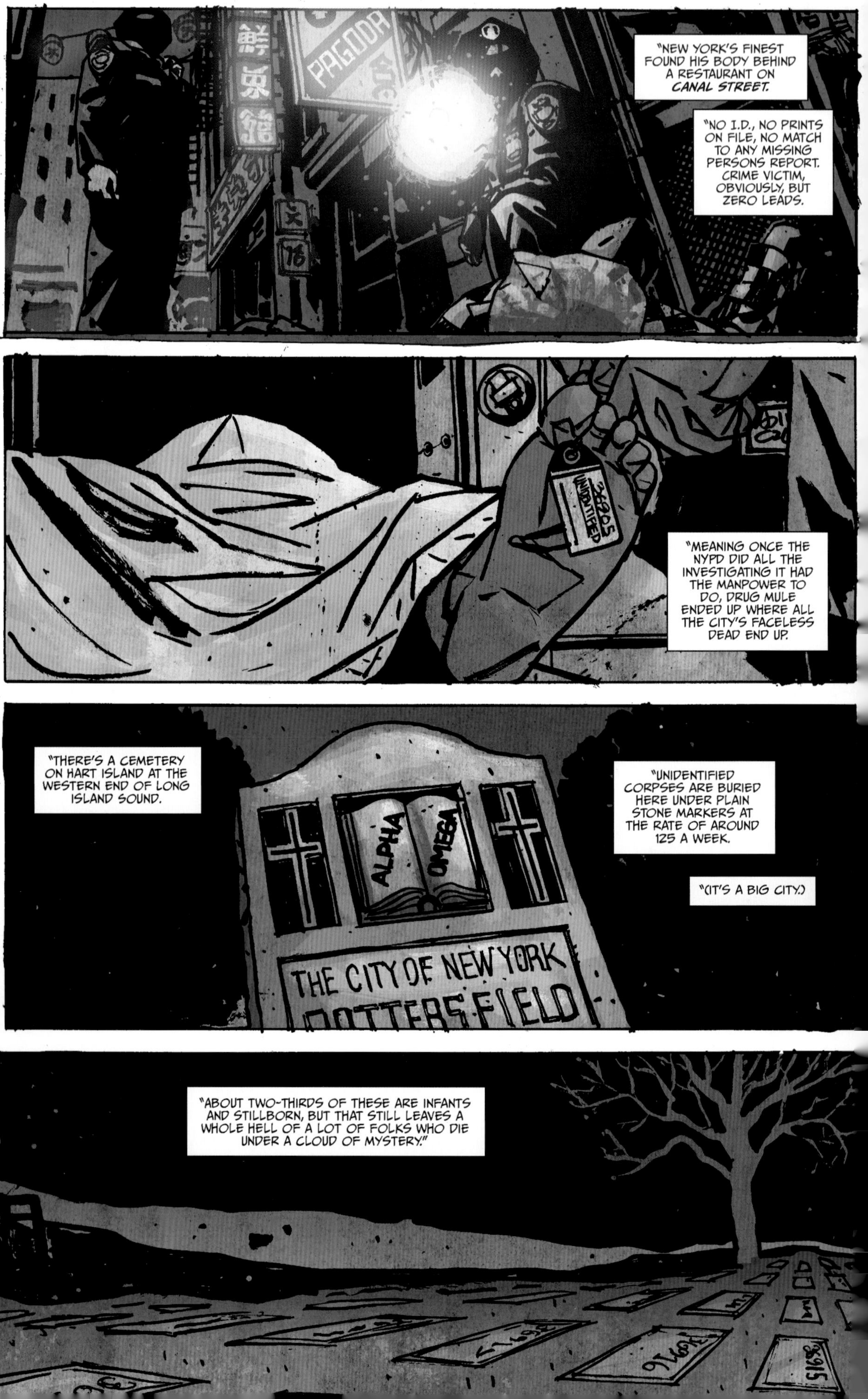
"NEW YORK'S FINEST FOUND HIS BODY BEHIND A RESTAURANT ON CANAL STREET.
"NO I.D., NO PRINTS ON FILE, NO MATCH TO ANY MISSING PERSONS REPORT. CRIME VICTIM, OBVIOUSLY, BUT ZERO LEADS.
PAGODA
3620S UNIDENTIFIED
"MEANING ONCE THE NYPD DID ALL THE INVESTIGATING IT HAD THE MANPOWER TO DO, DRUG MULE ENDED UP WHERE ALL THE CITY'S FACELESS DEAD END UP.
"THERE'S A CEMETERY ON HART ISLAND AT THE WESTERN END OF LONG ISLAND SOUND.
ALPHA
OMEGA
THE CITY OF NEW YORK
POTTERS FIELD
"UNIDENTIFIED CORPSES ARE BURIED HERE UNDER PLAIN STONE MARKERS AT THE RATE OF AROUND 125 A WEEK.
"(IT'S A BIG CITY.)
"ABOUT TWO-THIRDS OF THESE ARE INFANTS AND STILLBORN, BUT THAT STILL LEAVES A WHOLE HELL OF A LOT OF FOLKS WHO DIE UNDER A CLOUD OF MYSTERY."
9916
3915

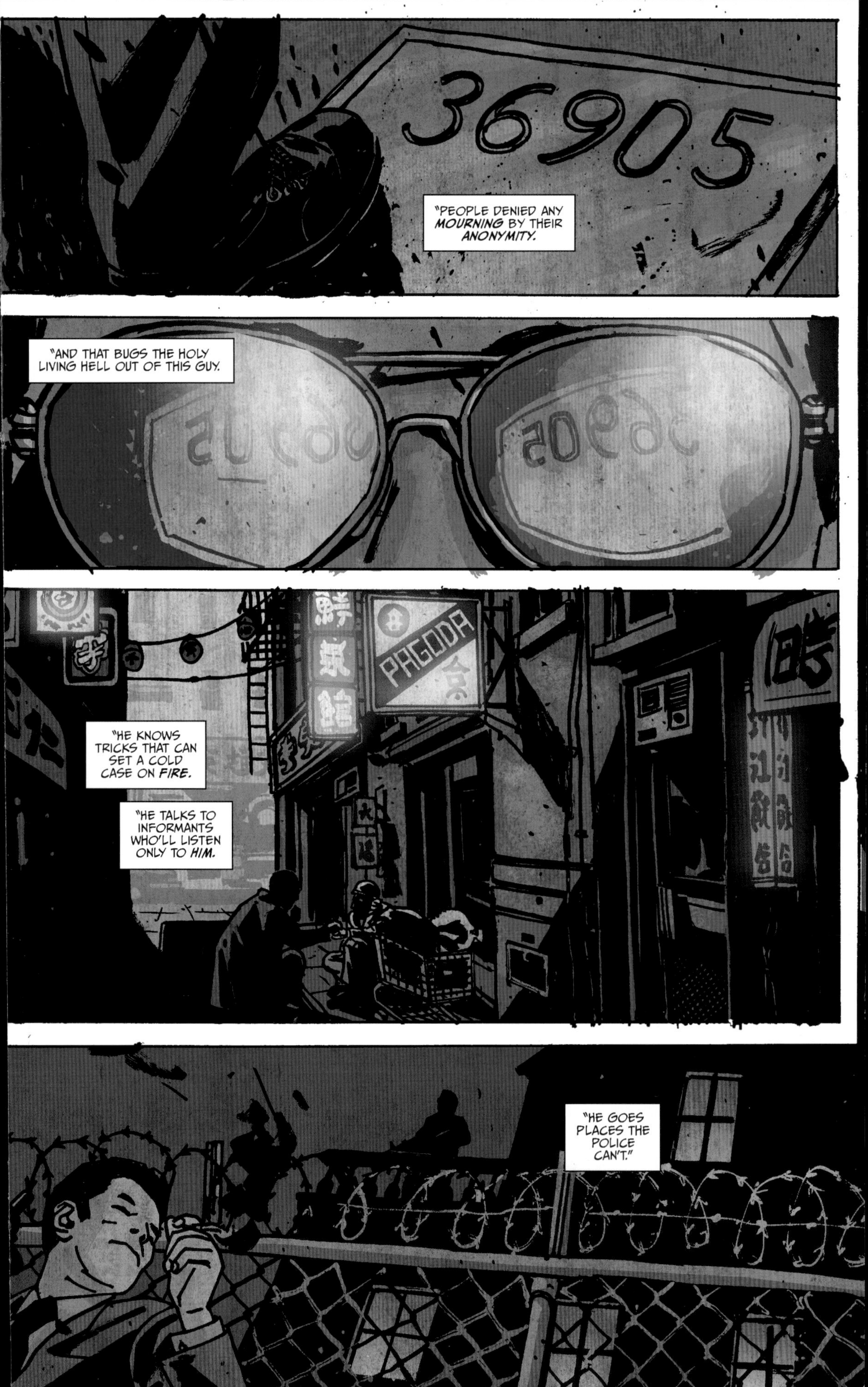
36905
"PEOPLE DENIED ANY MOURNING BY THEIR ANONYMITY.
"AND THAT BUGS THE HOLY LIVING HELL OUT OF THIS GUY.
PAGODA
"HE KNOWS TRICKS THAT CAN SET A COLD CASE ON FIRE.
"HE TALKS TO INFORMANTS WHO'LL LISTEN ONLY TO HIM.
"HE GOES PLACES THE POLICE CAN'T."

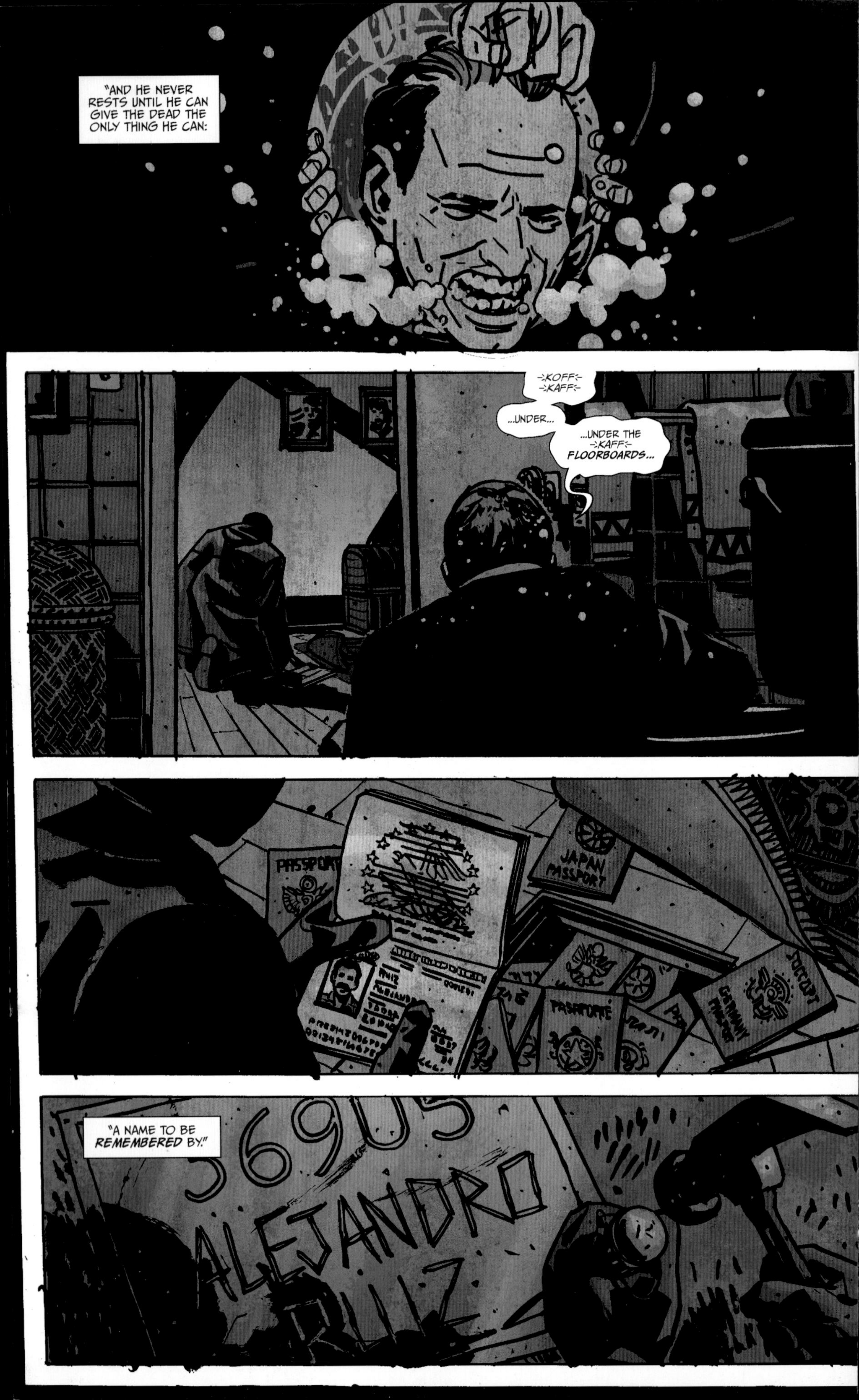
"AND HE NEVER RESTS UNTIL HE CAN GIVE THE DEAD THE ONLY THING HE CAN:
-KOFF- -KAFF-
...UNDER...
...UNDER THE -KAFF- FLOORBOARDS...
PASSPORT
JAPAN PASSPORT
PASSAPORTE
GERMANY PASSPORT
"A NAME TO BE *REMEMBERED* BY."
569US
ALEJANDRO
RUIZ

36901 MARY BEATTY
36902 JOSEPH LEE CARON
36903 INSHANA BROWN
36904 MICHAEL NELSON
36905 ALEJANDRO RUIZ
36906

"WHO IS THIS GUY? BEATS ME. I'VE BEEN WORKING FOR HIM FOR THREE YEARS, AND HE'S NEVER *SAID*."

"I CALL HIM *JOHN DOE*."

PEACE

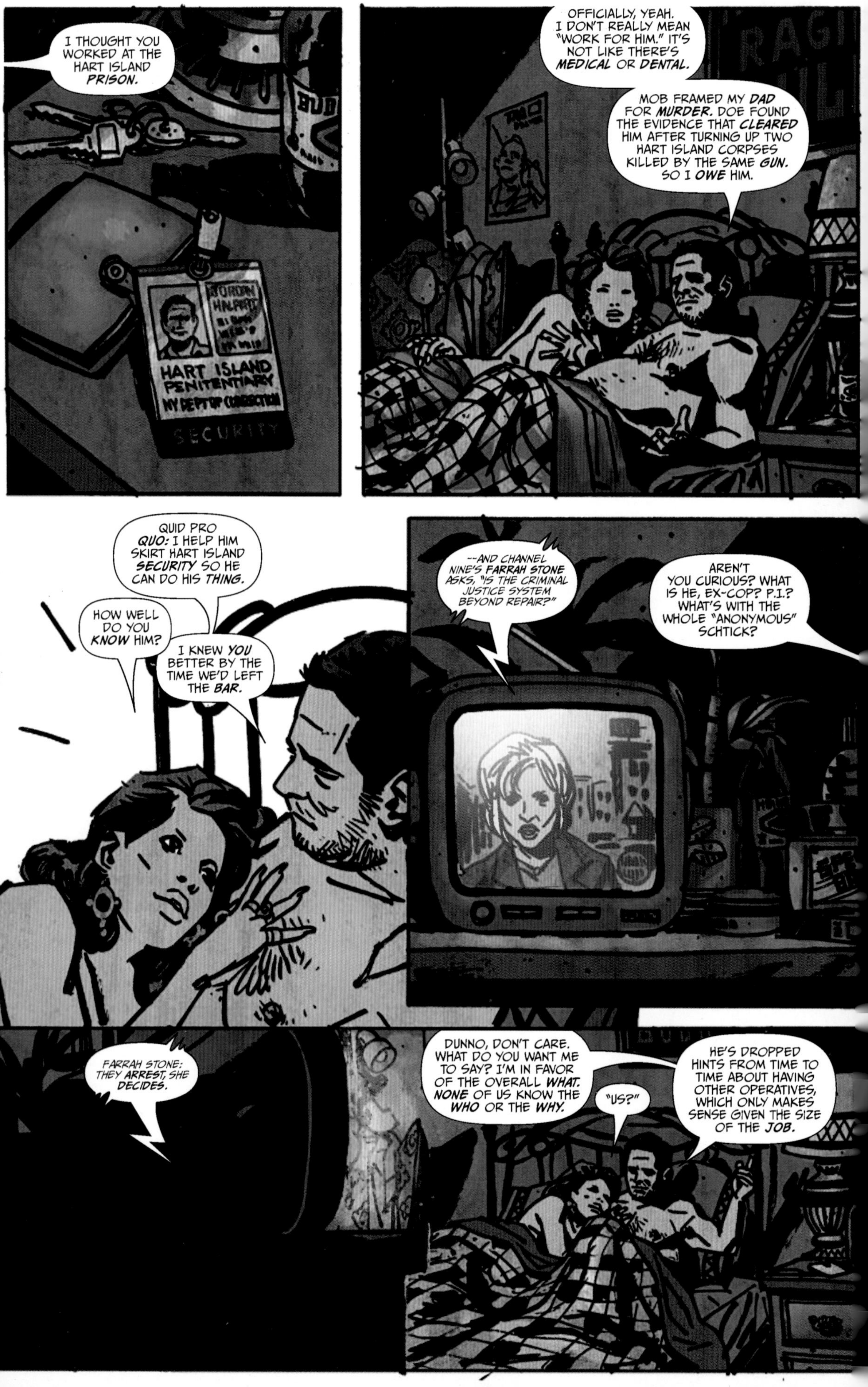

I THOUGHT YOU WORKED AT THE HART ISLAND PRISON.
HART ISLAND PENITENTIARY
NY DEPT OF CORRECTION
SECURITY
OFFICIALLY, YEAH. I DON'T REALLY MEAN "WORK FOR HIM." IT'S NOT LIKE THERE'S MEDICAL OR DENTAL.
MOB FRAMED MY DAD FOR MURDER. DOE FOUND THE EVIDENCE THAT CLEARED HIM AFTER TURNING UP TWO HART ISLAND CORPSES KILLED BY THE SAME GUN. SO I OWE HIM.
QUID PRO QUO: I HELP HIM SKIRT HART ISLAND SECURITY SO HE CAN DO HIS THING.
HOW WELL DO YOU KNOW HIM?
I KNEW YOU BETTER BY THE TIME WE'D LEFT THE BAR.
--AND CHANNEL NINE'S FARRAH STONE ASKS, "IS THE CRIMINAL JUSTICE SYSTEM BEYOND REPAIR?"
AREN'T YOU CURIOUS? WHAT IS HE, EX-COP? P.I.? WHAT'S WITH THE WHOLE "ANONYMOUS" SCHTICK?
FARRAH STONE: THEY ARREST, SHE DECIDES.
DUNNO, DON'T CARE. WHAT DO YOU WANT ME TO SAY? I'M IN FAVOR OF THE OVERALL WHAT. NONE OF US KNOW THE WHO OR THE WHY.
"US?"
HE'S DROPPED HINTS FROM TIME TO TIME ABOUT HAVING OTHER OPERATIVES, WHICH ONLY MAKES SENSE GIVEN THE SIZE OF THE JOB.

"I TAKE IT HE'S GOT INSIDE AGENTS ALL OVER THE *CITY.*"

AUTOPS ROOM

CORONER

PAXTIN, JAMES

--ACT MIGHTY *NERVOUS* FOR AN INNOCENT *MAN,* MR. TRENDLE. MAYBE THE D.A. BUYS YOUR STORY, BUT MY VIEWERS KNOW THE *TRUTH.*

WHY NOT JUST COME *CLEAN,* SIR?

BECAUSE HE'S NOT *GUILTY,* YOU SANCTIMONIOUS *HARRIDAN!*

SHE MAKES ME *ILL.* HOW DOES BEING A FORMER *CRIME VICTIM* GIVE YOU THE RIGHT TO PLAY JUDGE *AND* JURY ON THE PUBLIC AIRWAVES?

THIS IS *NEW YORK.* FIND ME SOMEONE WHO'S *NOT* A CRIME VICTIM! I'D CALL FARRAH STONE A *HARPY,* BUT THAT'S AN INSULT TO HARPIES *EVERYWH--*

WAIT. SHE AND I AREN'T IN THE SAME *FRATERNITY,* ARE WE?

CHK

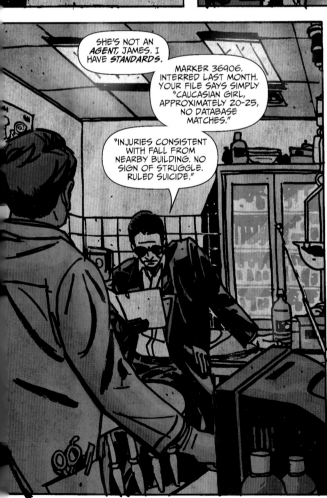

SHE'S NOT AN *AGENT,* JAMES. I HAVE *STANDARDS.*

MARKER 36906. INTERRED LAST MONTH. YOUR FILE SAYS SIMPLY "CAUCASIAN GIRL, APPROXIMATELY 20-25, NO DATABASE MATCHES."

"INJURIES CONSISTENT WITH FALL FROM NEARBY BUILDING. NO SIGN OF STRUGGLE. RULED SUICIDE."

THIS IS A PHOTO OF HER PERSONAL EFFECTS?

SUCH AS THEY *WERE,* BOSS. NO WALLET, NO I.D.

WHAT DID YOU MAKE OF THE *WALKMAN?*

WE CALL THEM *IPODS* NOW, GRAMPA.

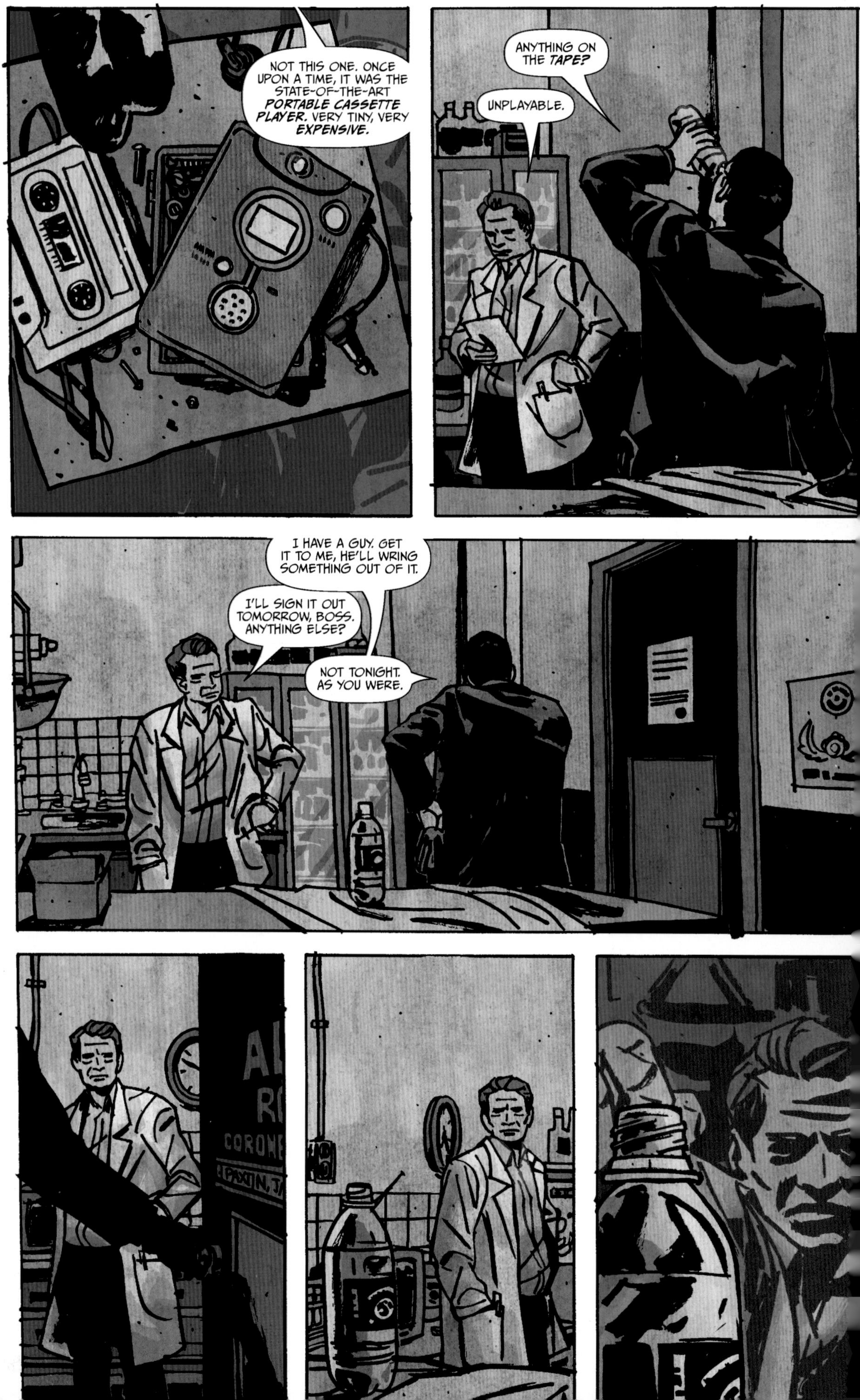
NOT THIS ONE. ONCE UPON A TIME, IT WAS THE STATE-OF-THE-ART ***PORTABLE CASSETTE PLAYER.*** VERY TINY, VERY ***EXPENSIVE.***
ANYTHING ON THE *TAPE?*
UNPLAYABLE.
I HAVE A GUY. GET IT TO ME, HE'LL WRING SOMETHING OUT OF IT.
I'LL SIGN IT OUT TOMORROW, BOSS. ANYTHING ELSE?
NOT TONIGHT. AS YOU WERE.

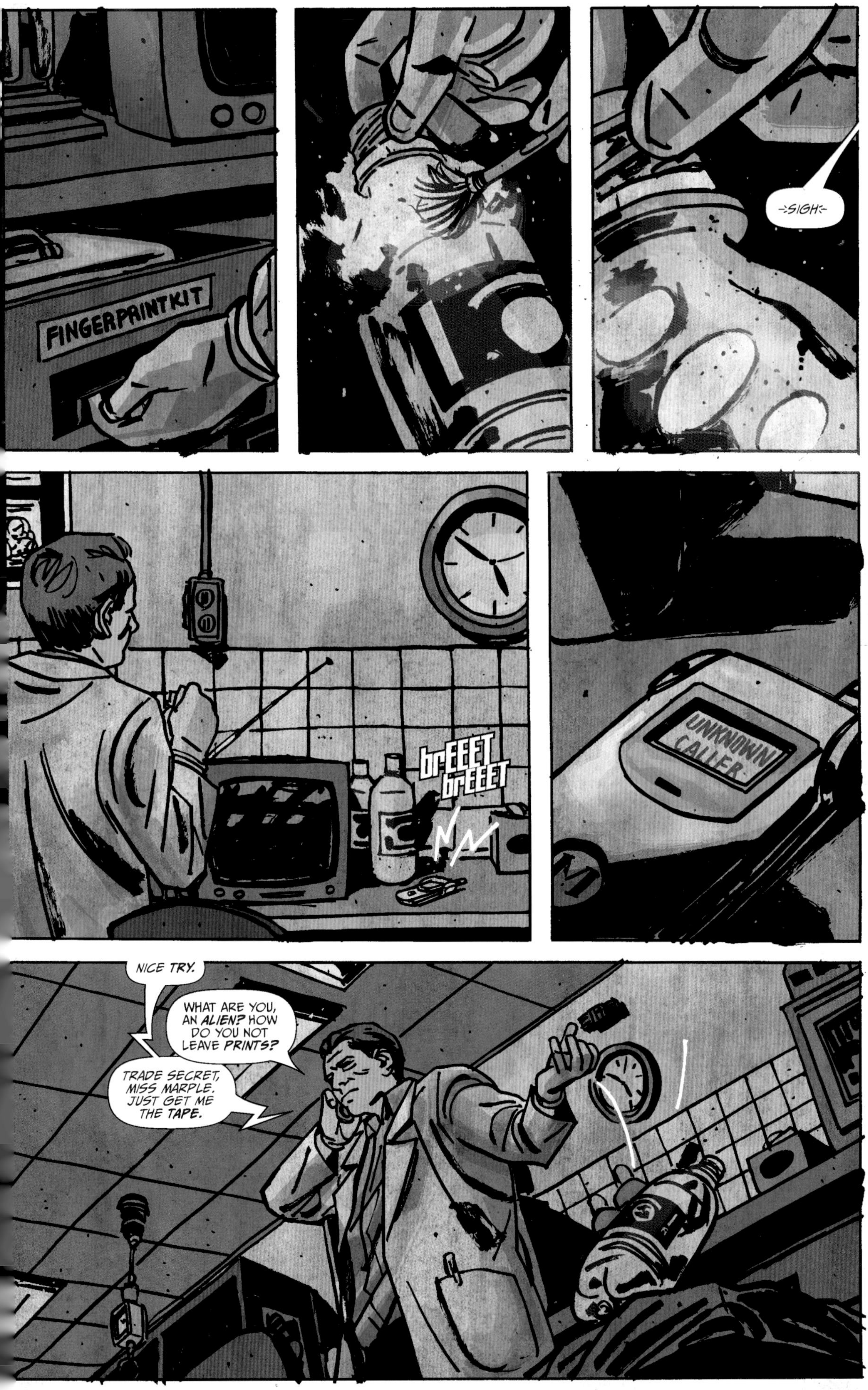
FINGERPRINT KIT
-SIGH-
brEEET brEEET
UNKNOWN CALLER
NICE TRY.
WHAT ARE YOU, AN ALIEN? HOW DO YOU NOT LEAVE PRINTS?
TRADE SECRET, MISS MARPLE. JUST GET ME THE TAPE.

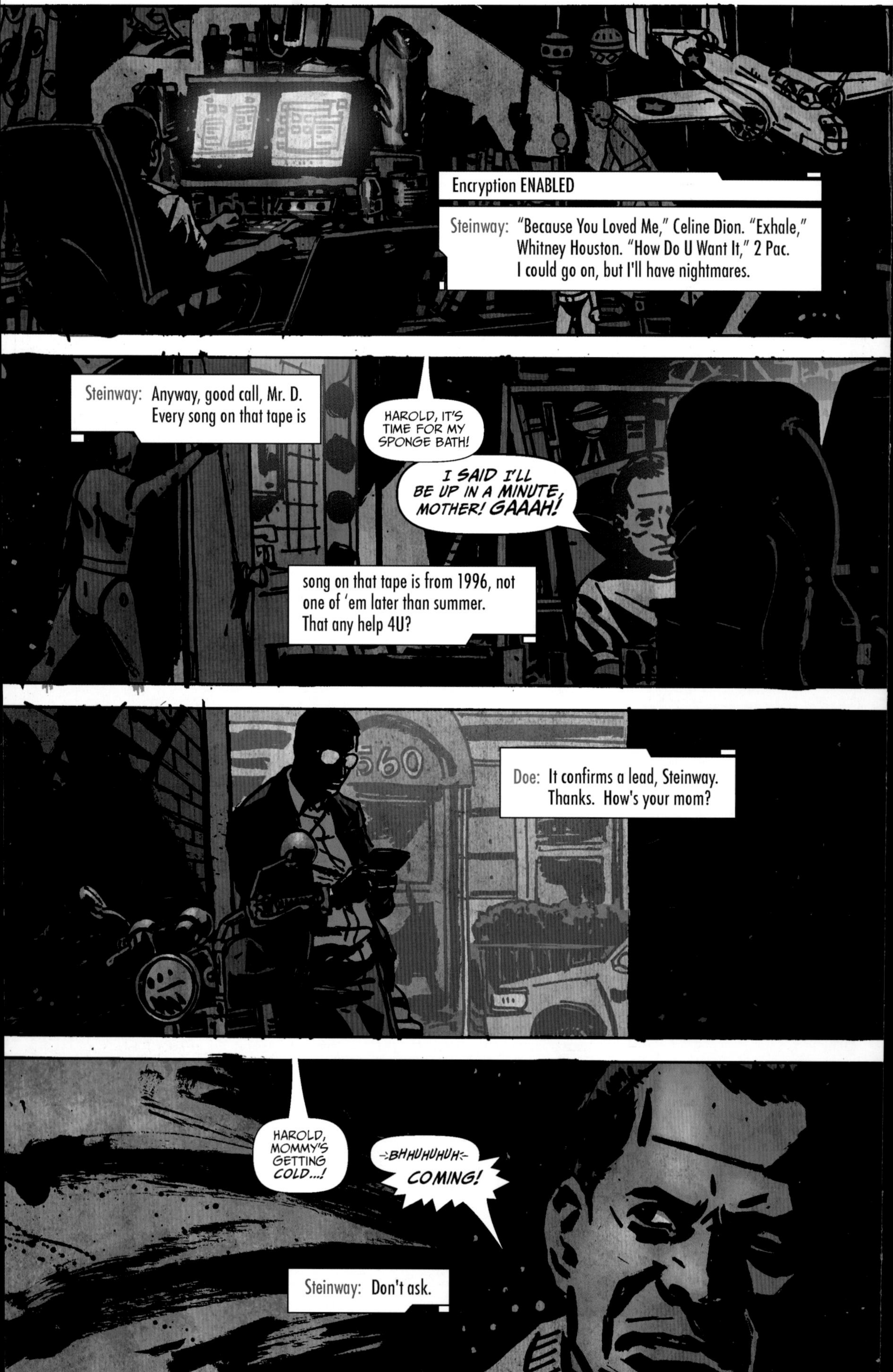
Encryption ENABLED
Steinway: "Because You Loved Me," Celine Dion. "Exhale," Whitney Houston. "How Do U Want It," 2 Pac. I could go on, but I'll have nightmares.
Steinway: Anyway, good call, Mr. D. Every song on that tape is
HAROLD, IT'S TIME FOR MY SPONGE BATH!
I SAID I'LL BE UP IN A MINUTE, MOTHER! GAAAH!
song on that tape is from 1996, not one of 'em later than summer. That any help 4U?
Doe: It confirms a lead, Steinway. Thanks. How's your mom?
HAROLD, MOMMY'S GETTING COLD...!
-BHHUHUHUH- COMING!
Steinway: Don't ask.

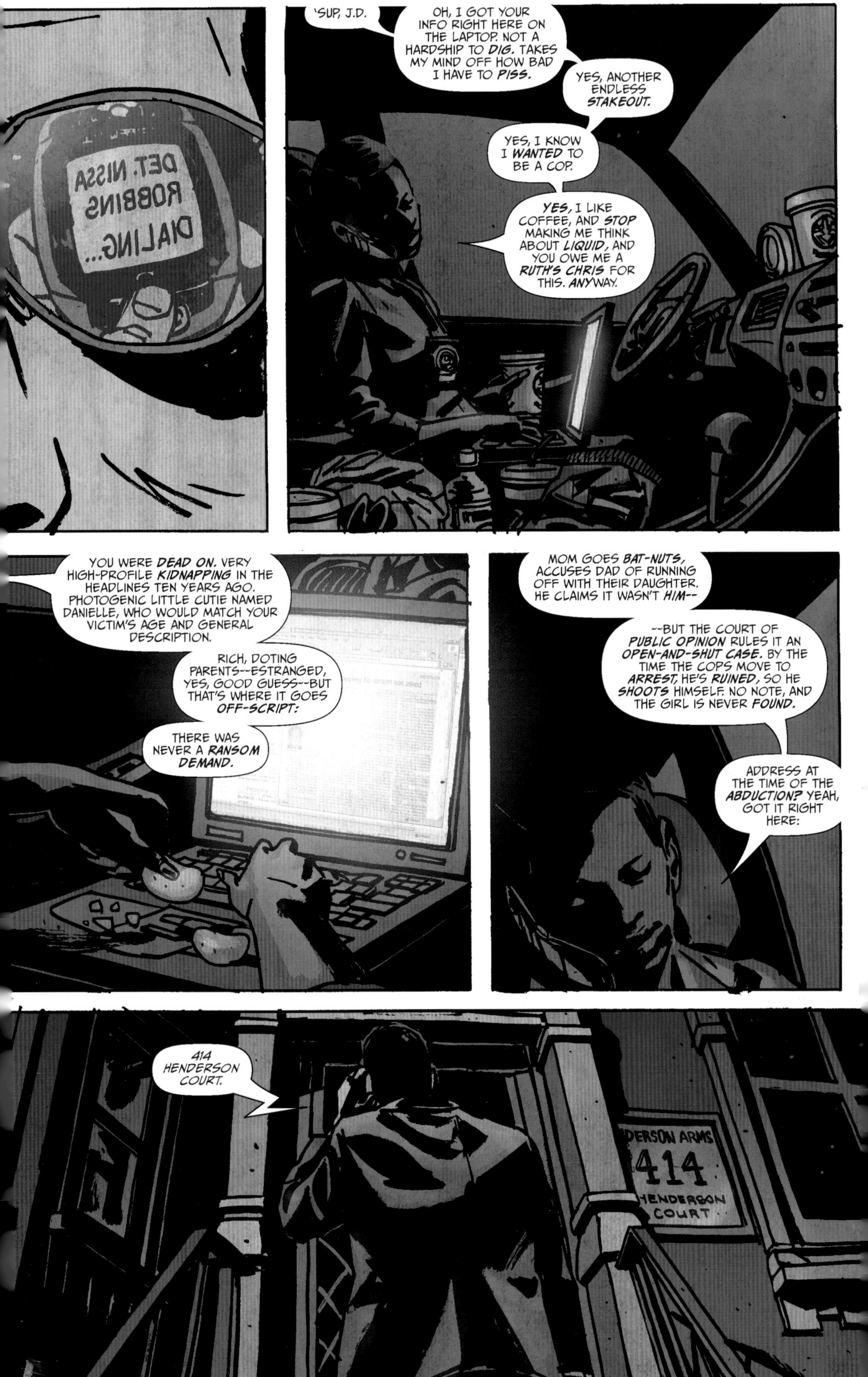

DET. NISSA ROBBINS DIALING...
'SUP, J.D.
OH, I GOT YOUR INFO RIGHT HERE ON THE LAPTOP. NOT A HARDSHIP TO DIG. TAKES MY MIND OFF HOW BAD I HAVE TO PISS.
YES, ANOTHER ENDLESS STAKEOUT.
YES, I KNOW I WANTED TO BE A COP.
YES, I LIKE COFFEE, AND STOP MAKING ME THINK ABOUT LIQUID, AND YOU OWE ME A RUTH'S CHRIS FOR THIS. ANYWAY.
YOU WERE DEAD ON. VERY HIGH-PROFILE KIDNAPPING IN THE HEADLINES TEN YEARS AGO. PHOTOGENIC LITTLE CUTIE NAMED DANIELLE, WHO WOULD MATCH YOUR VICTIM'S AGE AND GENERAL DESCRIPTION.
RICH, DOTING PARENTS--ESTRANGED, YES, GOOD GUESS--BUT THAT'S WHERE IT GOES OFF-SCRIPT:
THERE WAS NEVER A RANSOM DEMAND.
MOM GOES BAT-NUTS, ACCUSES DAD OF RUNNING OFF WITH THEIR DAUGHTER. HE CLAIMS IT WASN'T HIM--
--BUT THE COURT OF PUBLIC OPINION RULES IT AN OPEN-AND-SHUT CASE. BY THE TIME THE COPS MOVE TO ARREST, HE'S RUINED, SO HE SHOOTS HIMSELF. NO NOTE, AND THE GIRL IS NEVER FOUND.
ADDRESS AT THE TIME OF THE ABDUCTION? YEAH, GOT IT RIGHT HERE:
414 HENDERSON COURT.
DERSON ARMS
414
HENDERSON COURT

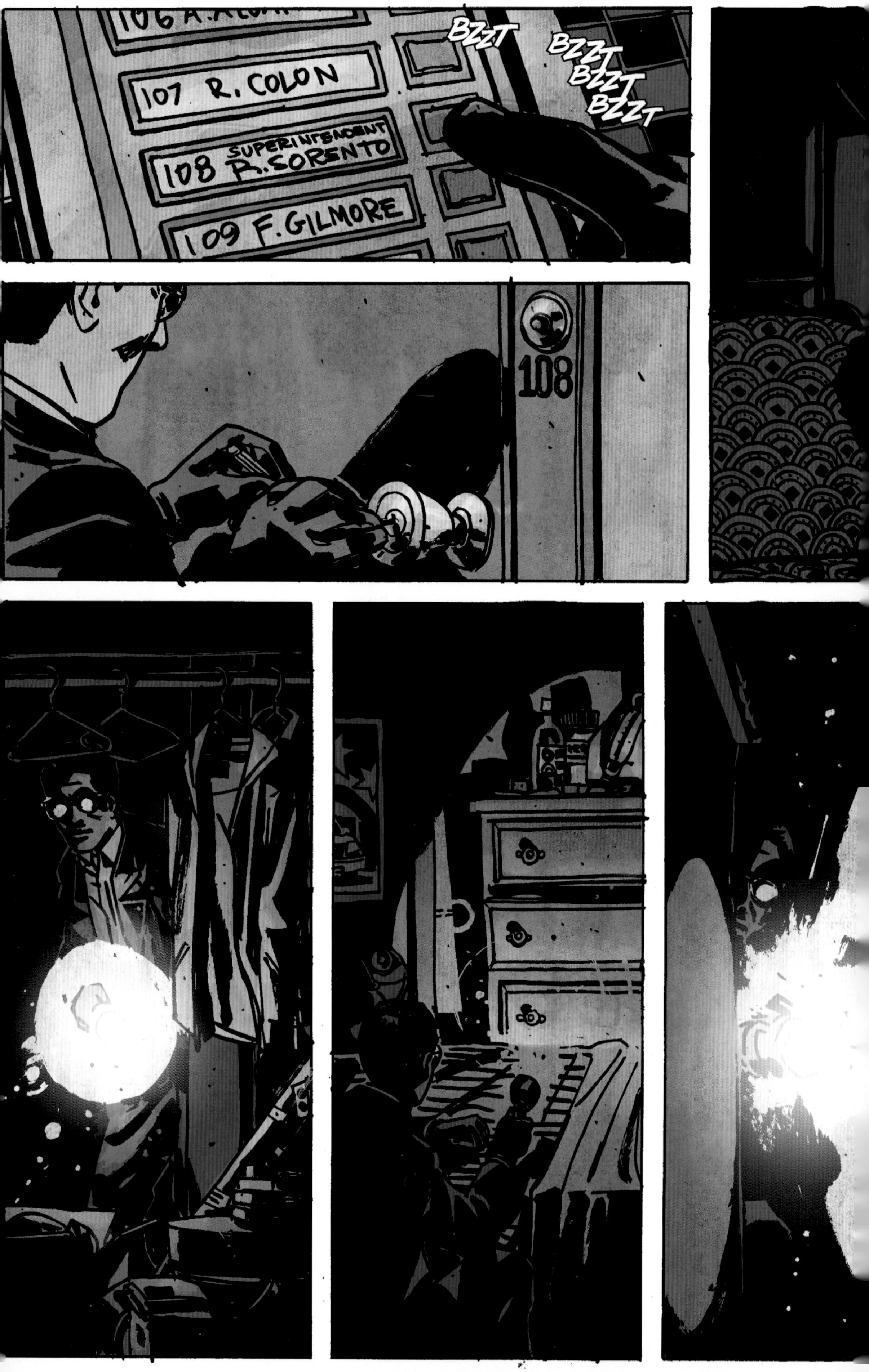
107 R. COLON
SUPERINTENDENT
108 R. SORENTO
109 F. GILMORE
BZZT
BZZT
BZZT
BZZT
108

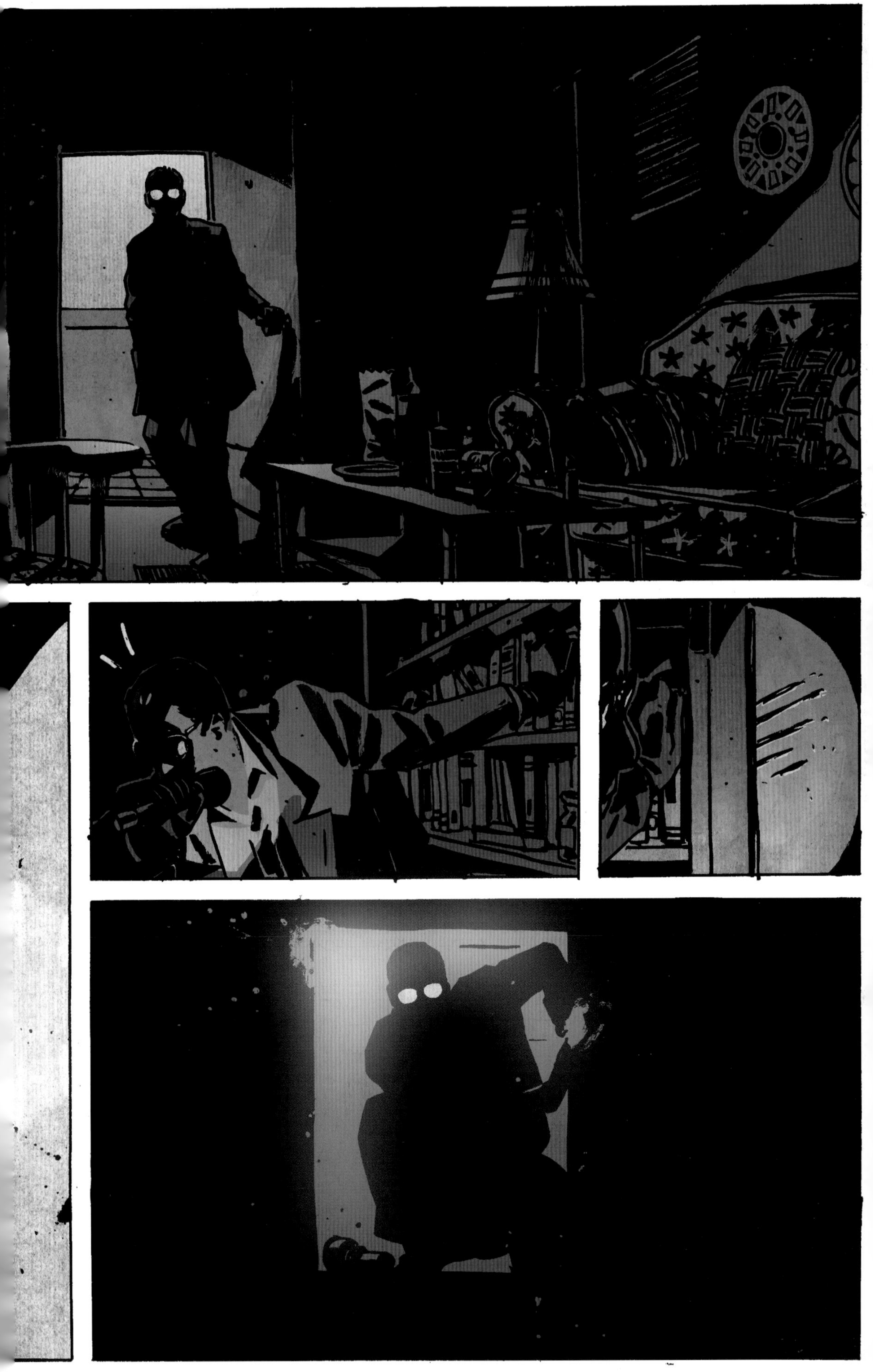

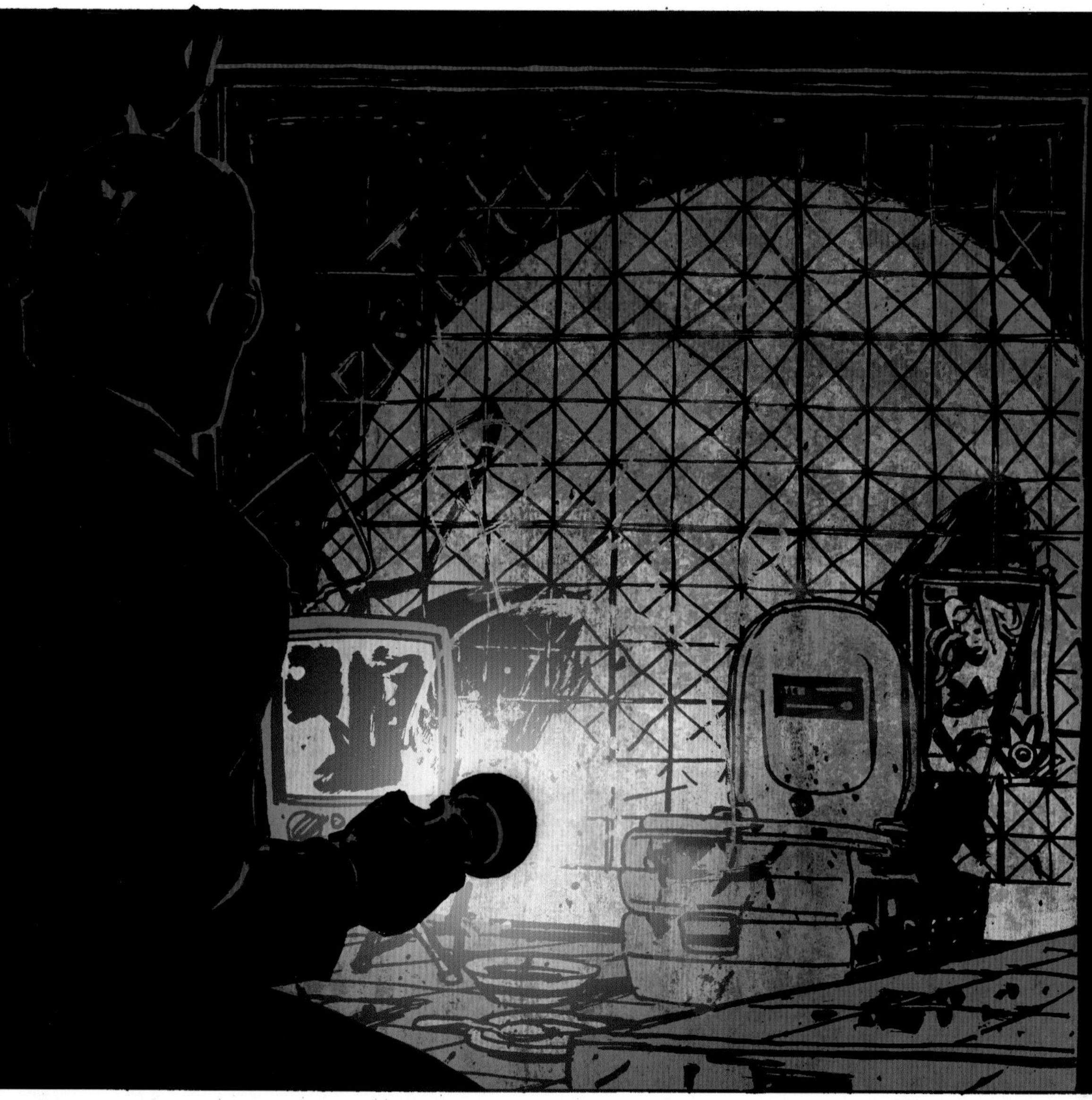
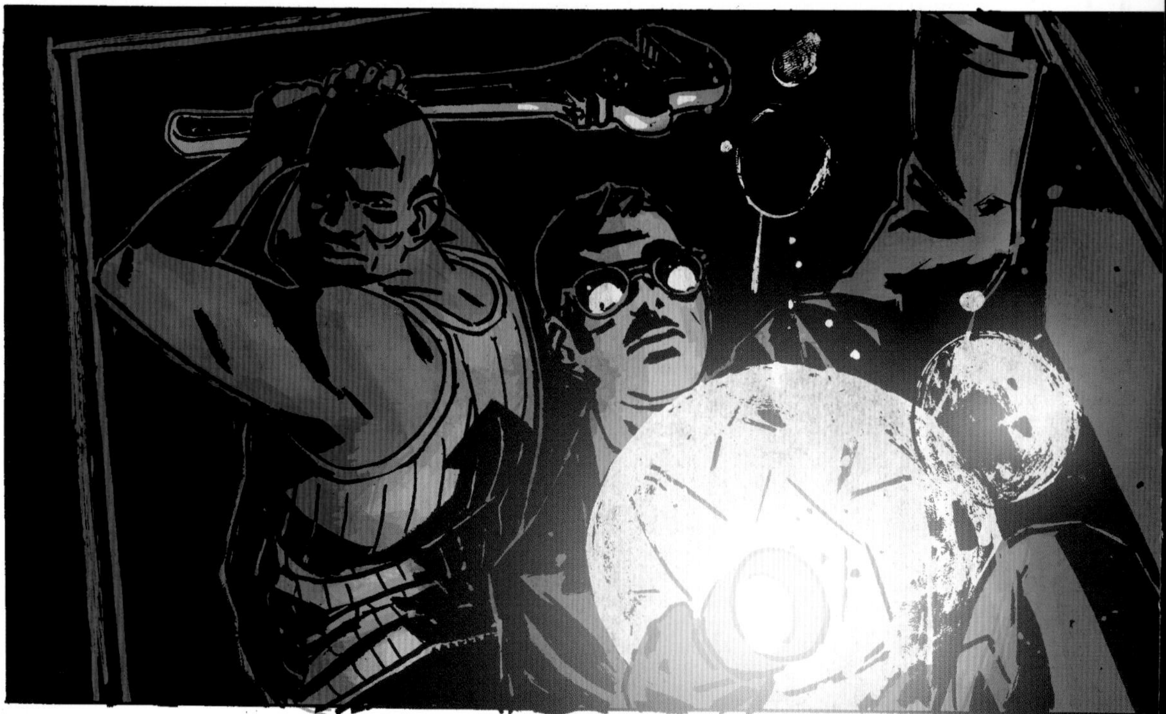

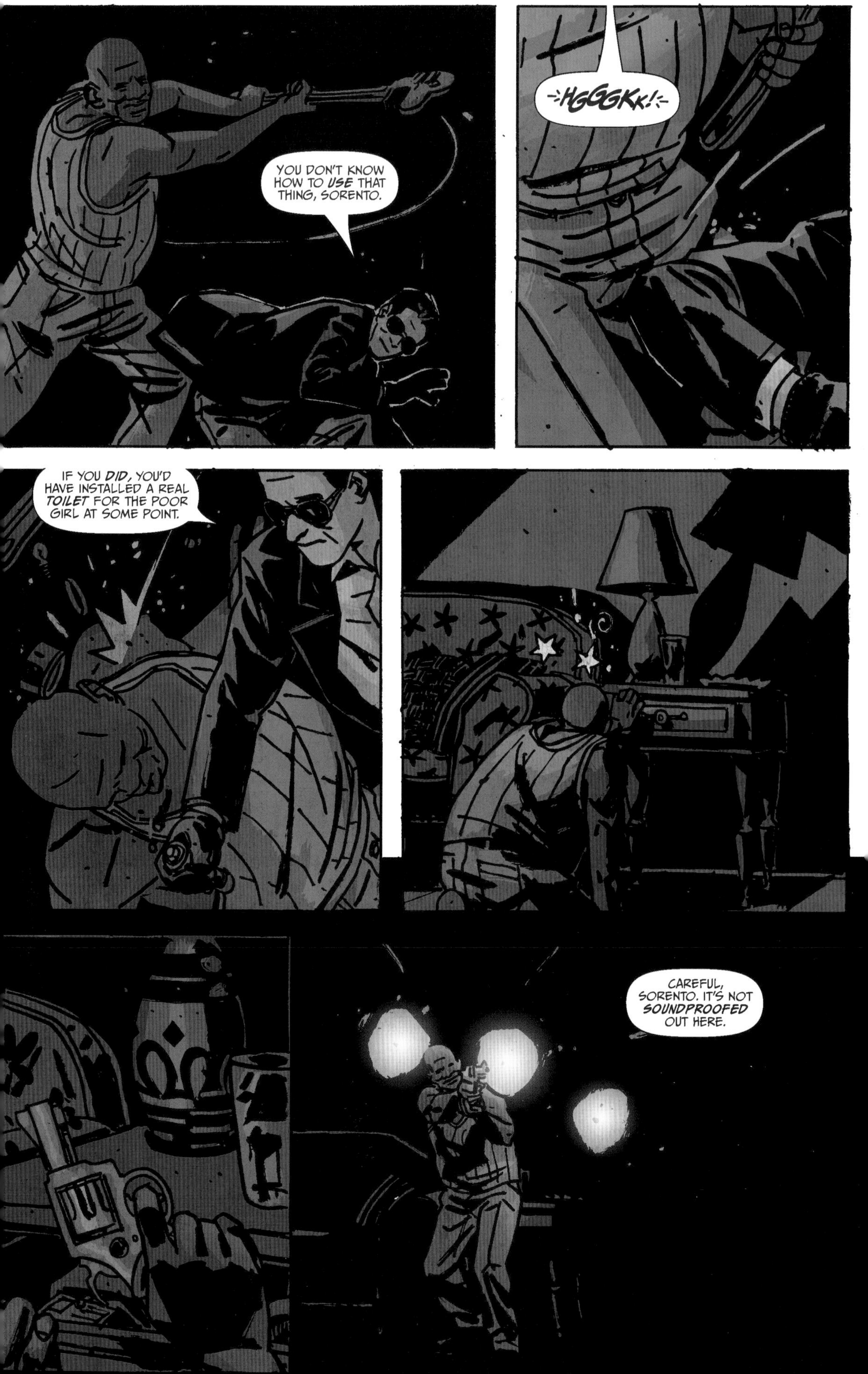
YOU DON'T KNOW HOW TO USE THAT THING, SORENTO.
-HGGGKK!-
IF YOU DID, YOU'D HAVE INSTALLED A REAL TOILET FOR THE POOR GIRL AT SOME POINT.
CAREFUL, SORENTO. IT'S NOT SOUNDPROOFED OUT HERE.

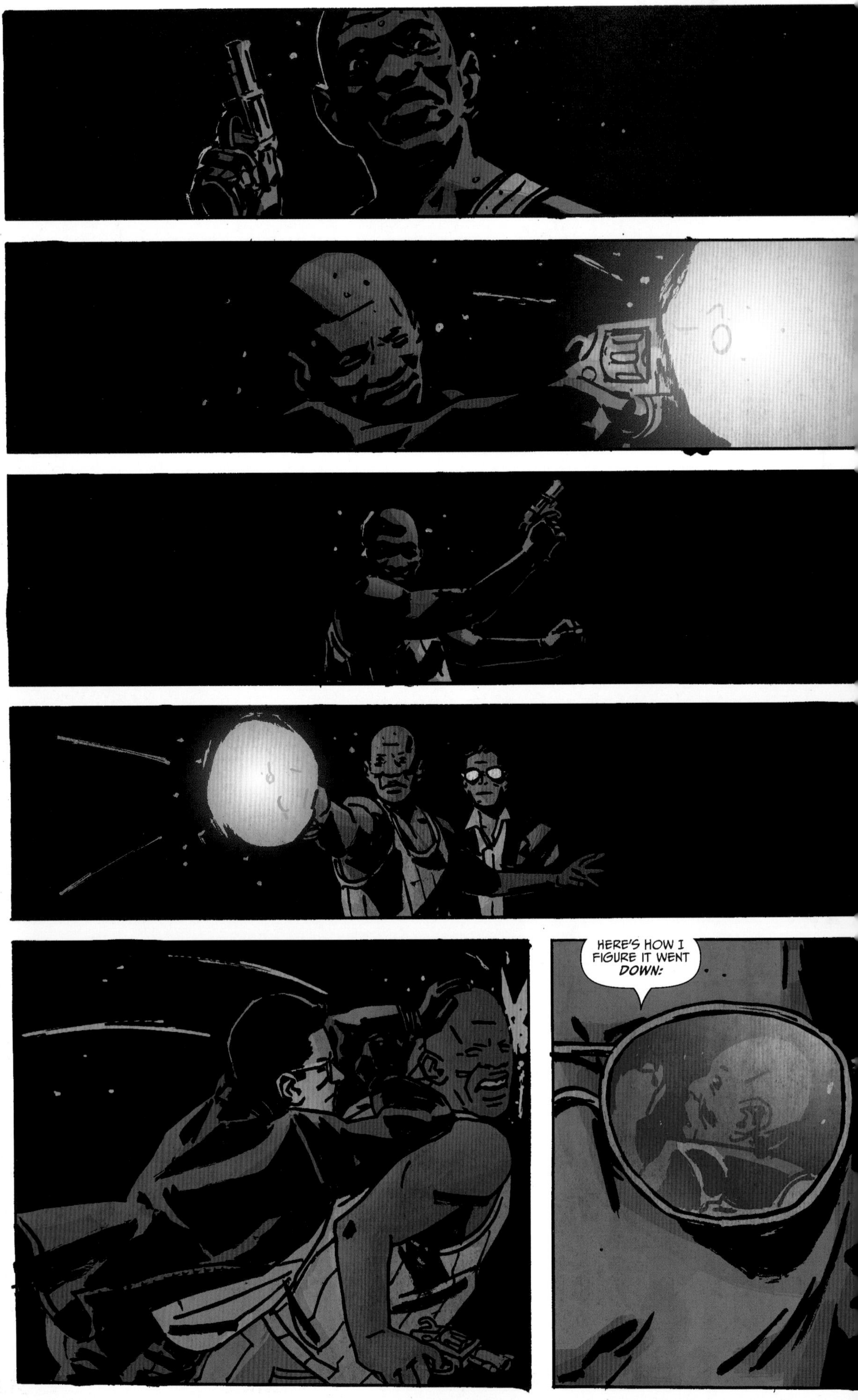
HERE'S HOW I FIGURE IT WENT DOWN:

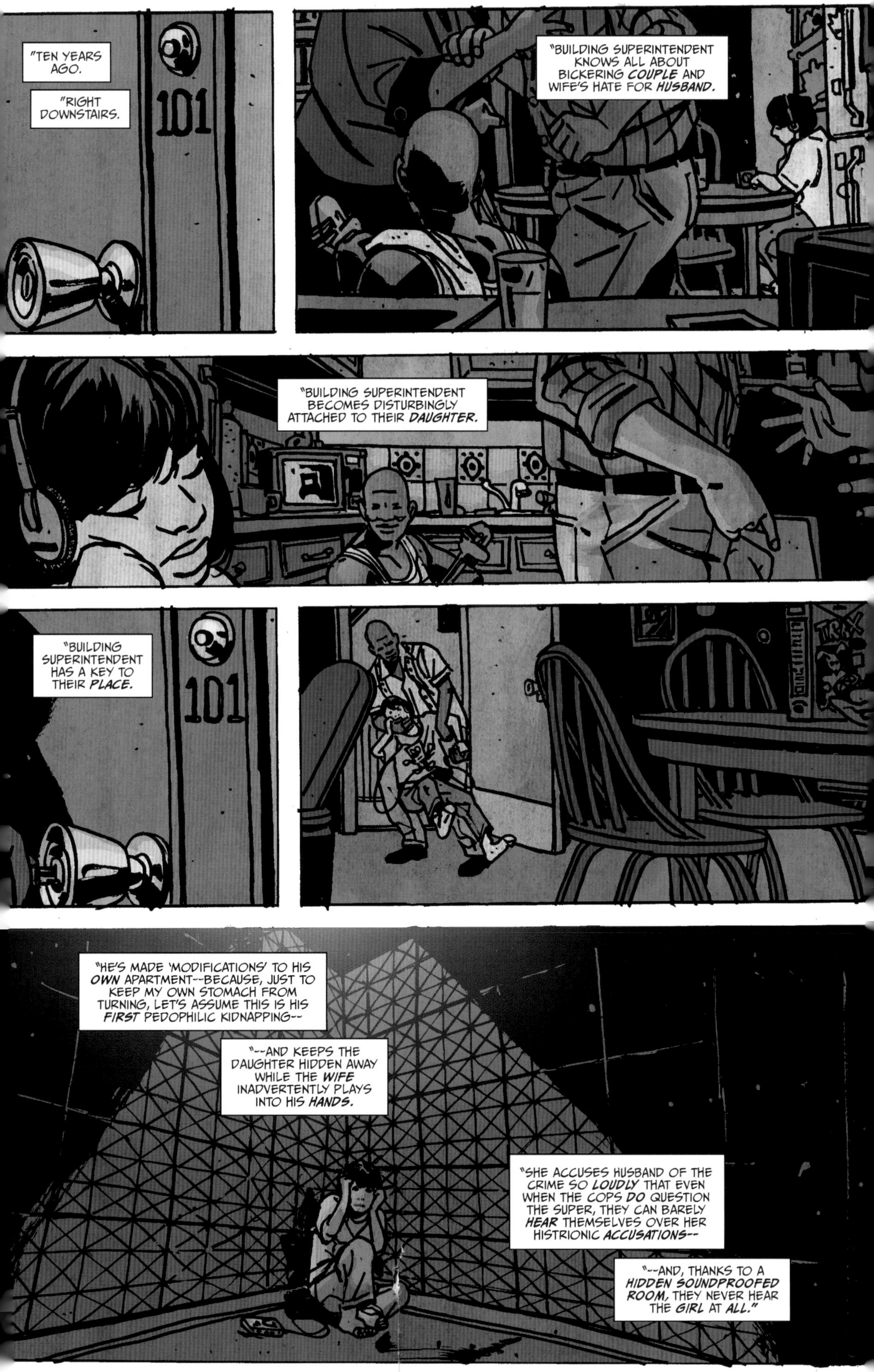
"TEN YEARS AGO.
"RIGHT DOWNSTAIRS.
101
"BUILDING SUPERINTENDENT KNOWS ALL ABOUT BICKERING COUPLE AND WIFE'S HATE FOR HUSBAND.
"BUILDING SUPERINTENDENT BECOMES DISTURBINGLY ATTACHED TO THEIR DAUGHTER.
"BUILDING SUPERINTENDENT HAS A KEY TO THEIR PLACE.
101
"HE'S MADE 'MODIFICATIONS' TO HIS OWN APARTMENT--BECAUSE, JUST TO KEEP MY OWN STOMACH FROM TURNING, LET'S ASSUME THIS IS HIS FIRST PEDOPHILIC KIDNAPPING--
"--AND KEEPS THE DAUGHTER HIDDEN AWAY WHILE THE WIFE INADVERTENTLY PLAYS INTO HIS HANDS.
"SHE ACCUSES HUSBAND OF THE CRIME SO LOUDLY THAT EVEN WHEN THE COPS DO QUESTION THE SUPER, THEY CAN BARELY HEAR THEMSELVES OVER HER HISTRIONIC ACCUSATIONS--
"--AND, THANKS TO A HIDDEN SOUNDPROOFED ROOM, THEY NEVER HEAR THE GIRL AT ALL."

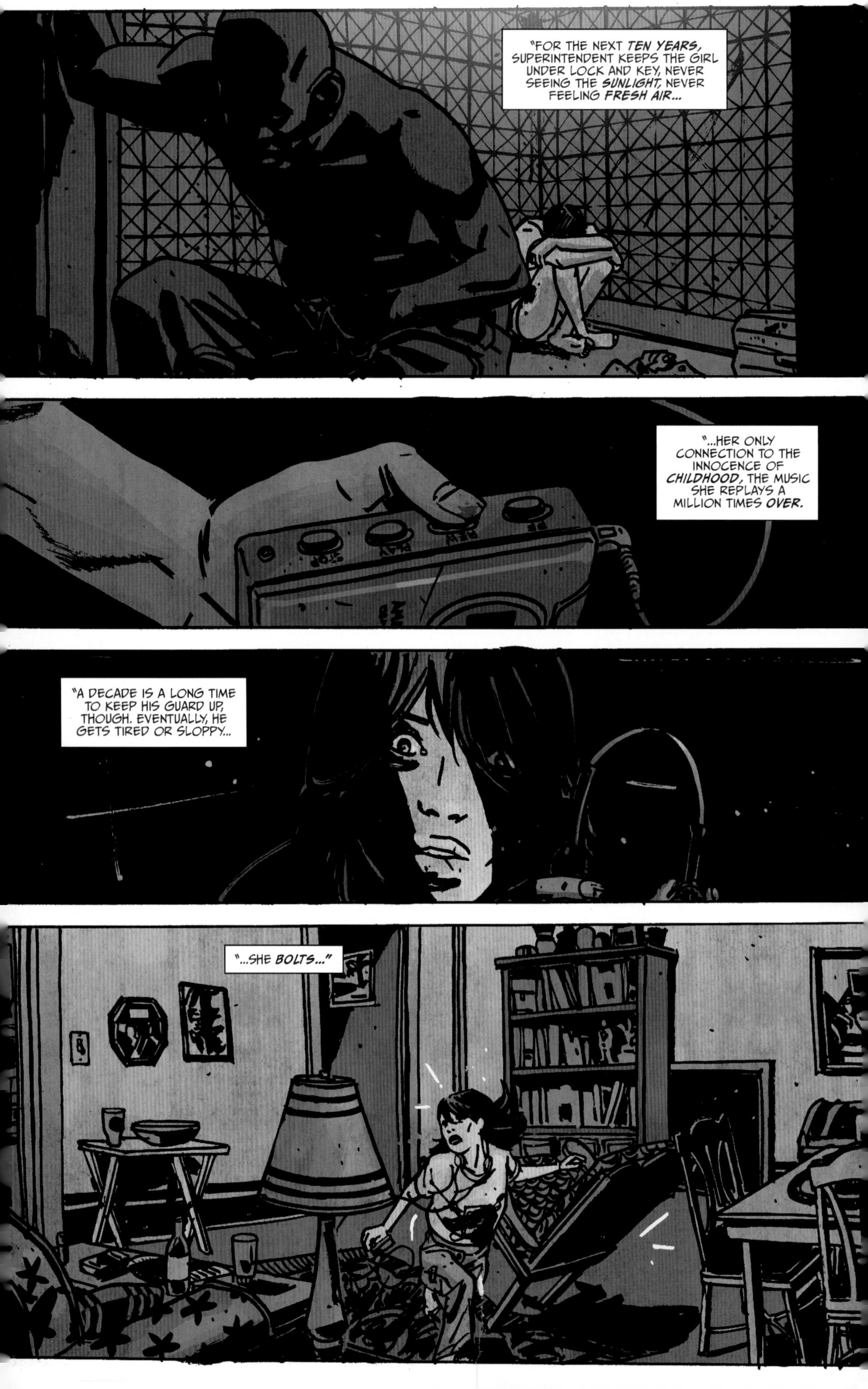
"FOR THE NEXT TEN YEARS, SUPERINTENDENT KEEPS THE GIRL UNDER LOCK AND KEY, NEVER SEEING THE SUNLIGHT, NEVER FEELING FRESH AIR...
"...HER ONLY CONNECTION TO THE INNOCENCE OF CHILDHOOD, THE MUSIC SHE REPLAYS A MILLION TIMES OVER.
"A DECADE IS A LONG TIME TO KEEP HIS GUARD UP, THOUGH. EVENTUALLY, HE GETS TIRED OR SLOPPY...
"...SHE BOLTS..."

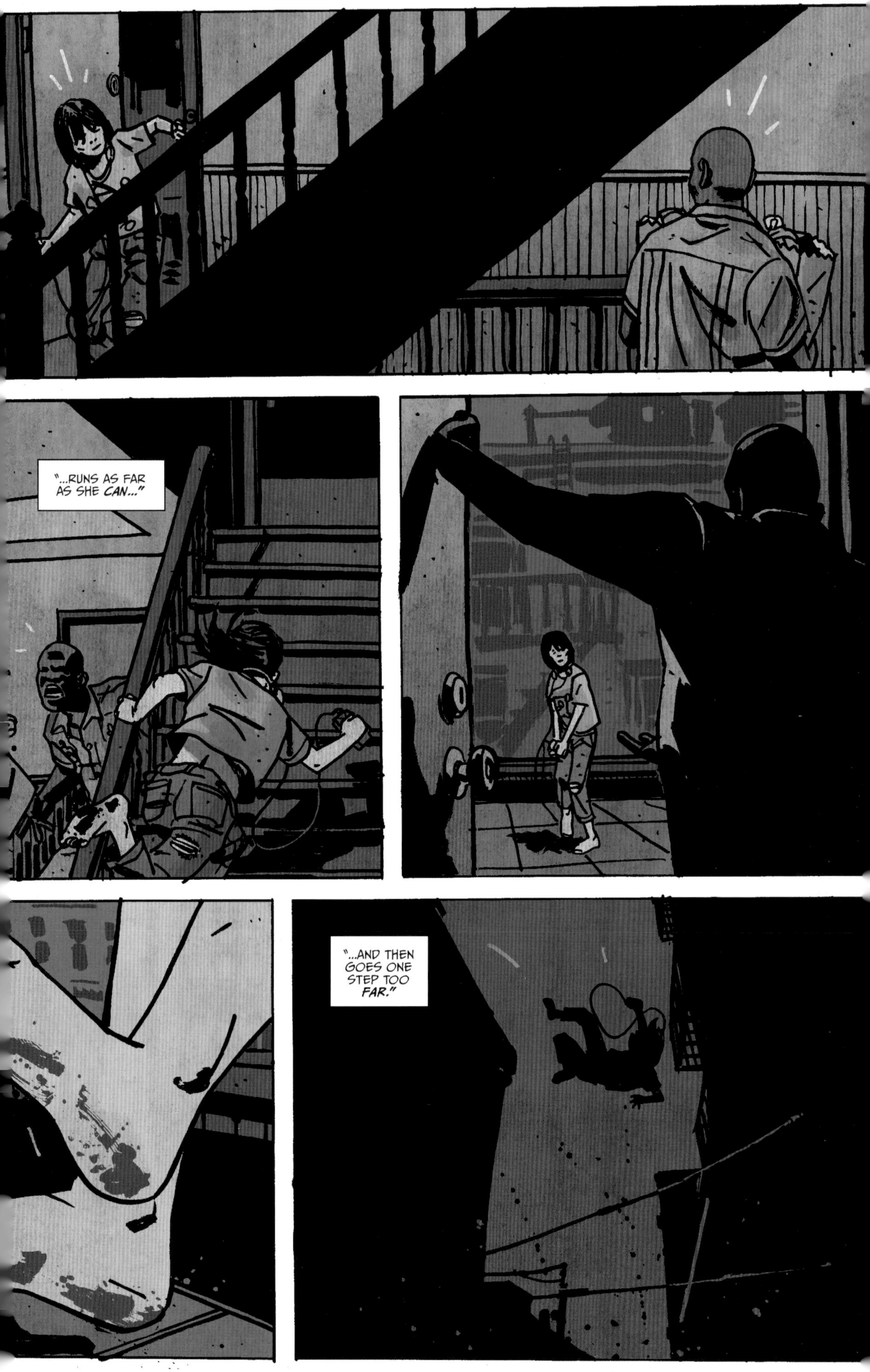
"...RUNS AS FAR AS SHE CAN..."
"...AND THEN GOES ONE STEP TOO FAR."

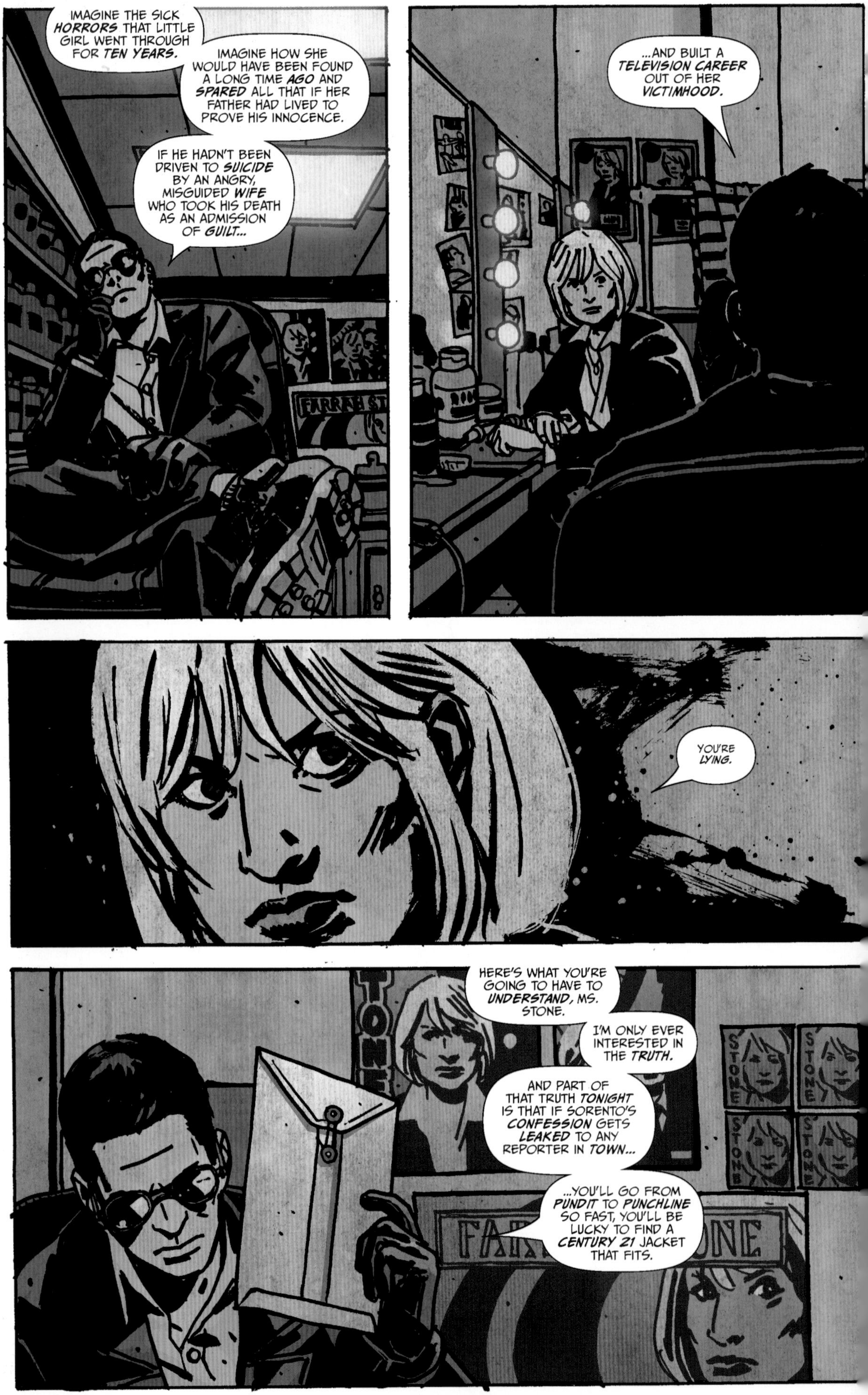
IMAGINE THE SICK HORRORS THAT LITTLE GIRL WENT THROUGH FOR TEN YEARS.
IMAGINE HOW SHE WOULD HAVE BEEN FOUND A LONG TIME AGO AND SPARED ALL THAT IF HER FATHER HAD LIVED TO PROVE HIS INNOCENCE.
IF HE HADN'T BEEN DRIVEN TO SUICIDE BY AN ANGRY, MISGUIDED WIFE WHO TOOK HIS DEATH AS AN ADMISSION OF GUILT...
...AND BUILT A TELEVISION CAREER OUT OF HER VICTIMHOOD.
YOU'RE LYING.
HERE'S WHAT YOU'RE GOING TO HAVE TO UNDERSTAND, MS. STONE.
I'M ONLY EVER INTERESTED IN THE TRUTH.
AND PART OF THAT TRUTH TONIGHT IS THAT IF SORENTO'S CONFESSION GETS LEAKED TO ANY REPORTER IN TOWN...
...YOU'LL GO FROM PUNDIT TO PUNCHLINE SO FAST, YOU'LL BE LUCKY TO FIND A CENTURY 21 JACKET THAT FITS.

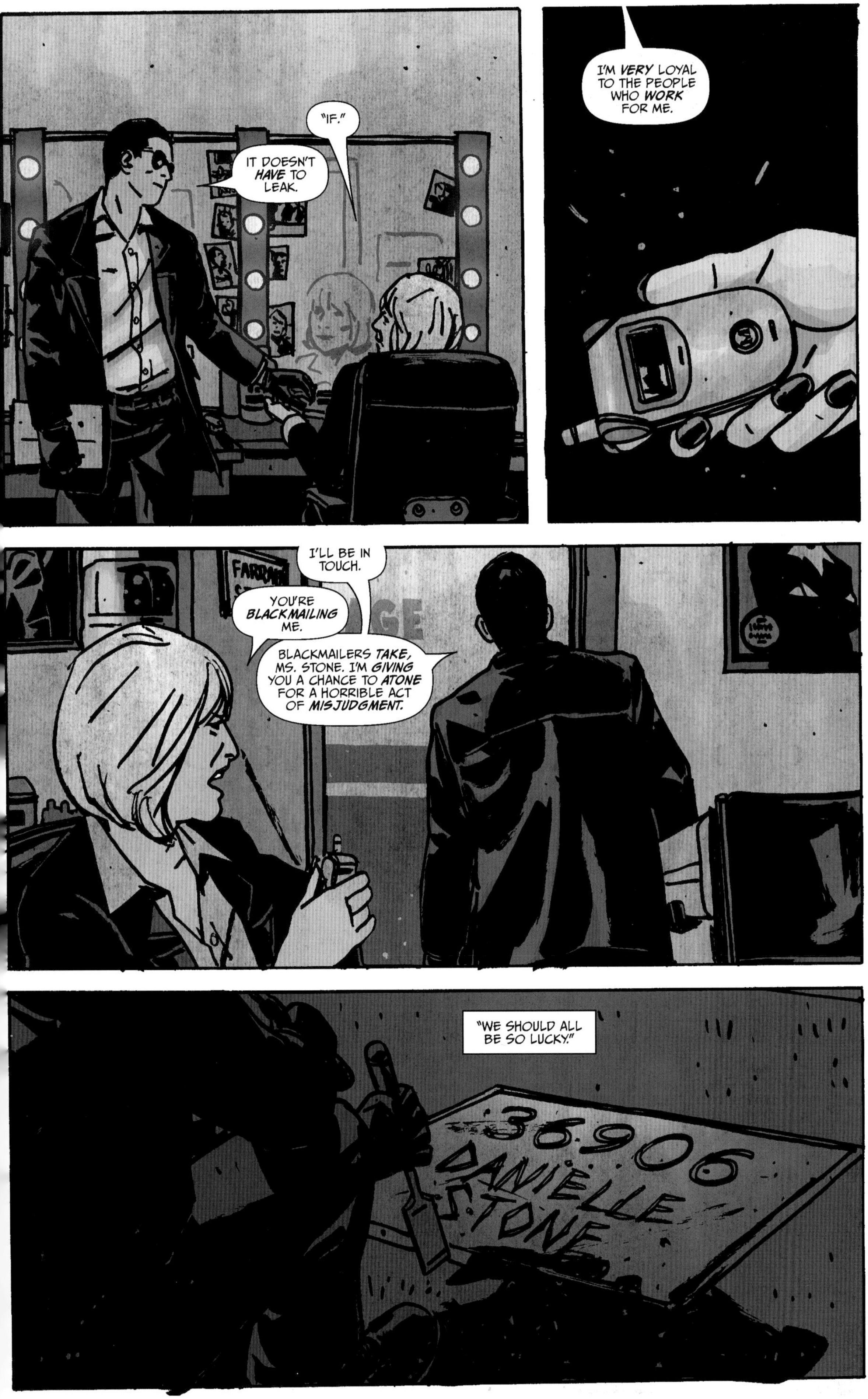
"IF."
IT DOESN'T HAVE TO LEAK.
I'M VERY LOYAL TO THE PEOPLE WHO WORK FOR ME.
I'LL BE IN TOUCH.
YOU'RE BLACKMAILING ME.
BLACKMAILERS TAKE, MS. STONE. I'M GIVING YOU A CHANCE TO ATONE FOR A HORRIBLE ACT OF MISJUDGMENT.
"WE SHOULD ALL BE SO LUCKY."
36.906
DANIELLE STONE

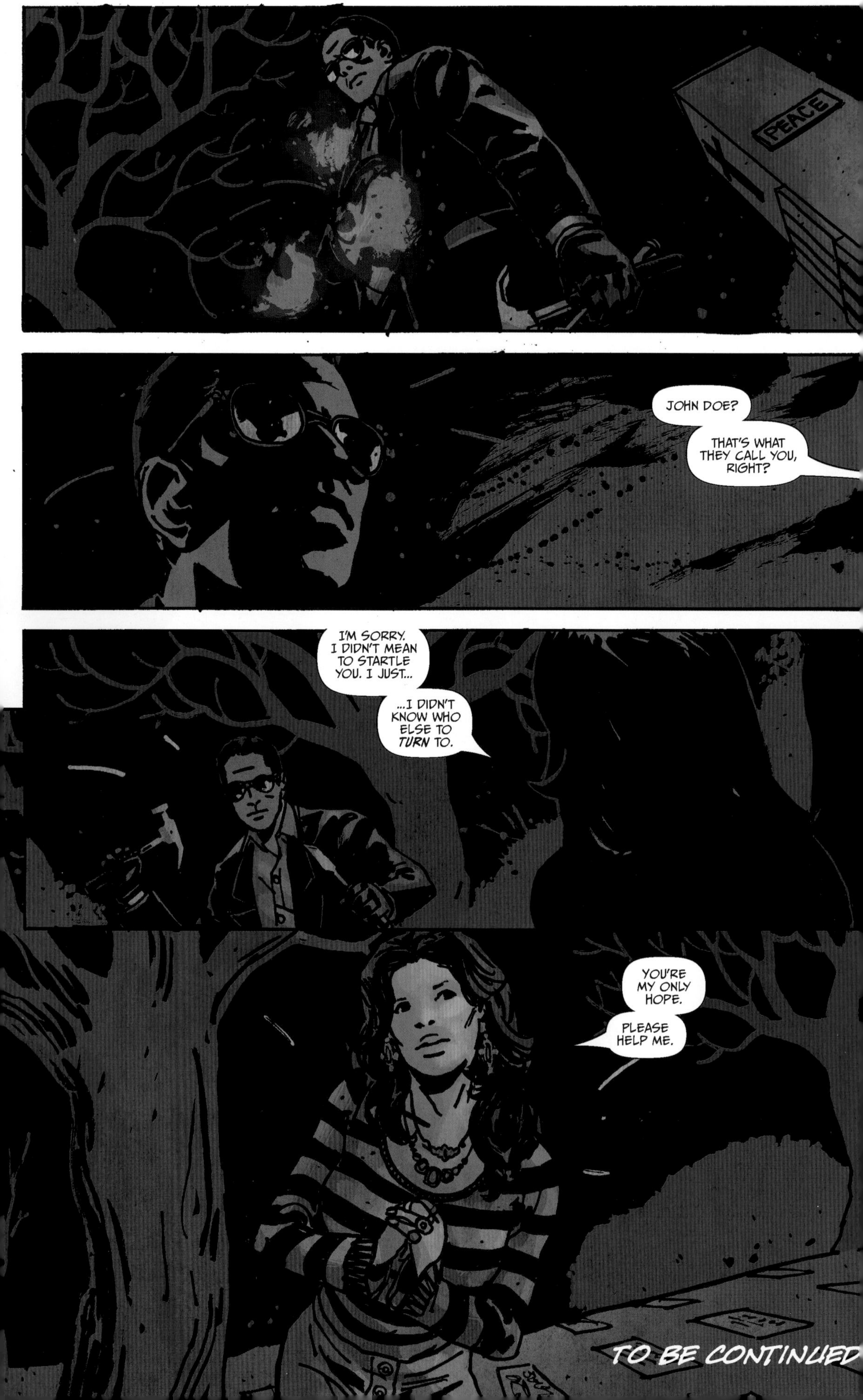
PEACE
JOHN DOE?
THAT'S WHAT THEY CALL YOU, RIGHT?
I'M SORRY. I DIDN'T MEAN TO STARTLE YOU. I JUST...
...I DIDN'T KNOW WHO ELSE TO TURN TO.
YOU'RE MY ONLY HOPE.
PLEASE HELP ME.
TO BE CONTINUED

CHAPTER TWO

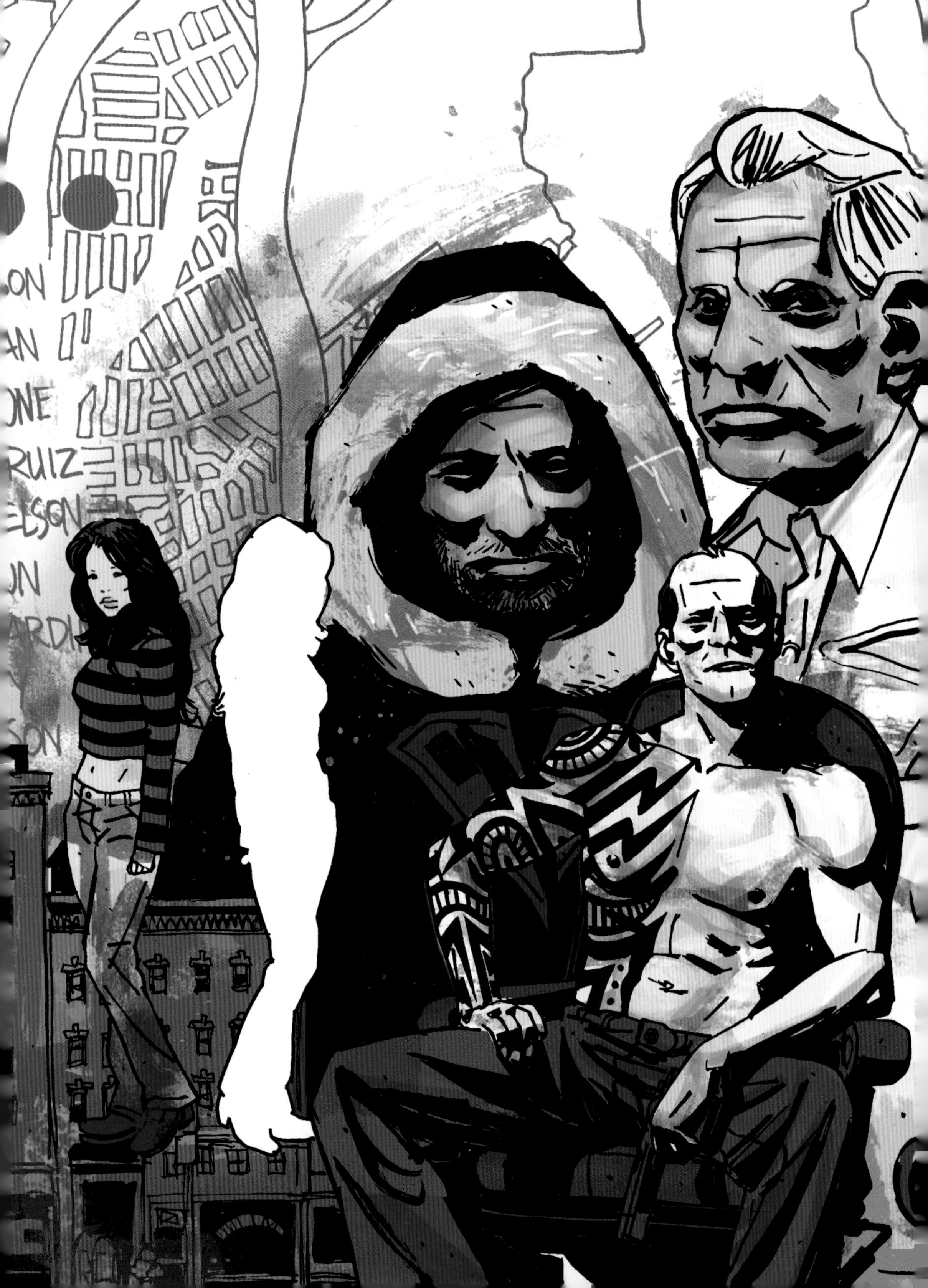

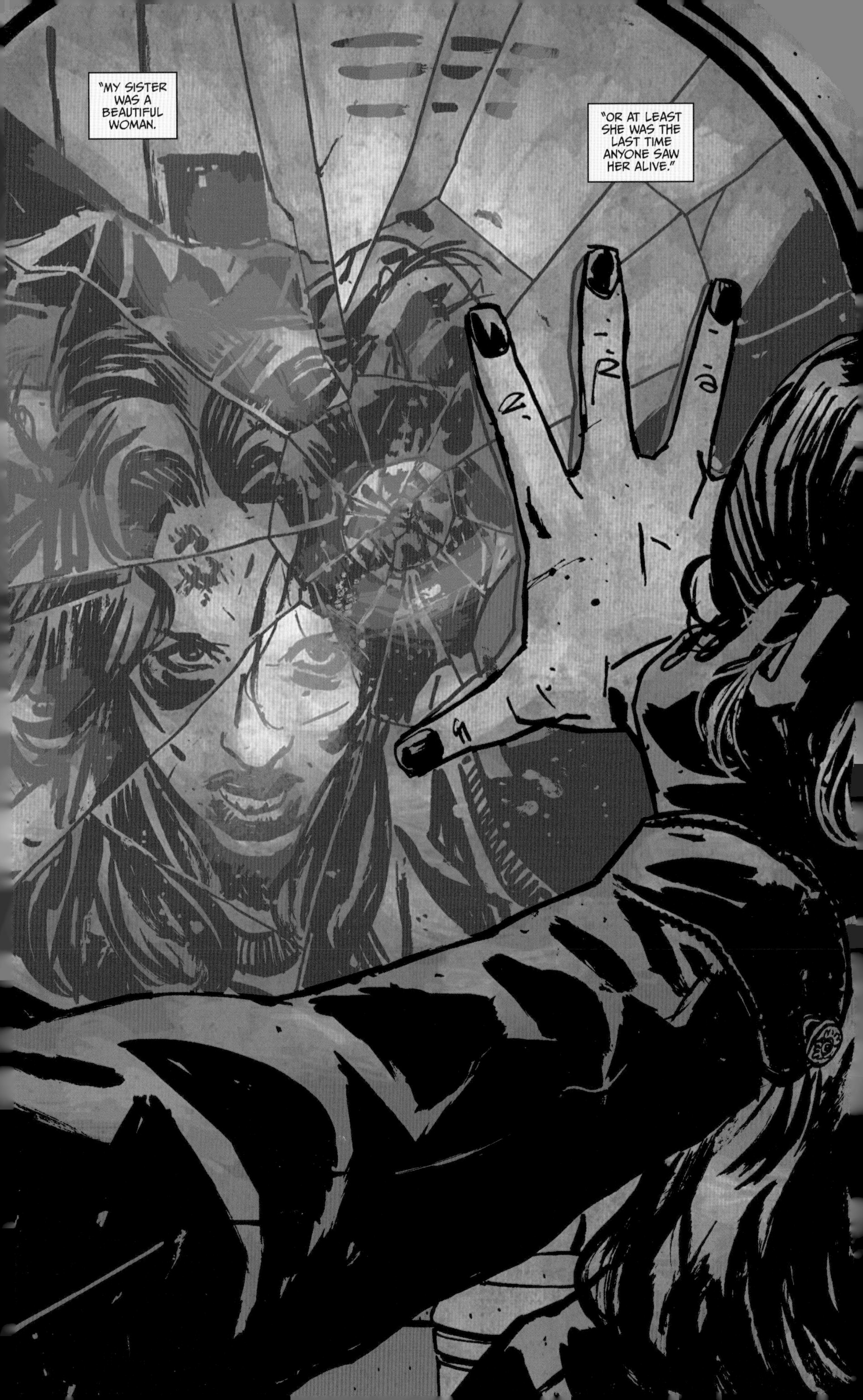
"MY SISTER WAS A BEAUTIFUL WOMAN.
"OR AT LEAST SHE WAS THE LAST TIME ANYONE SAW HER ALIVE."

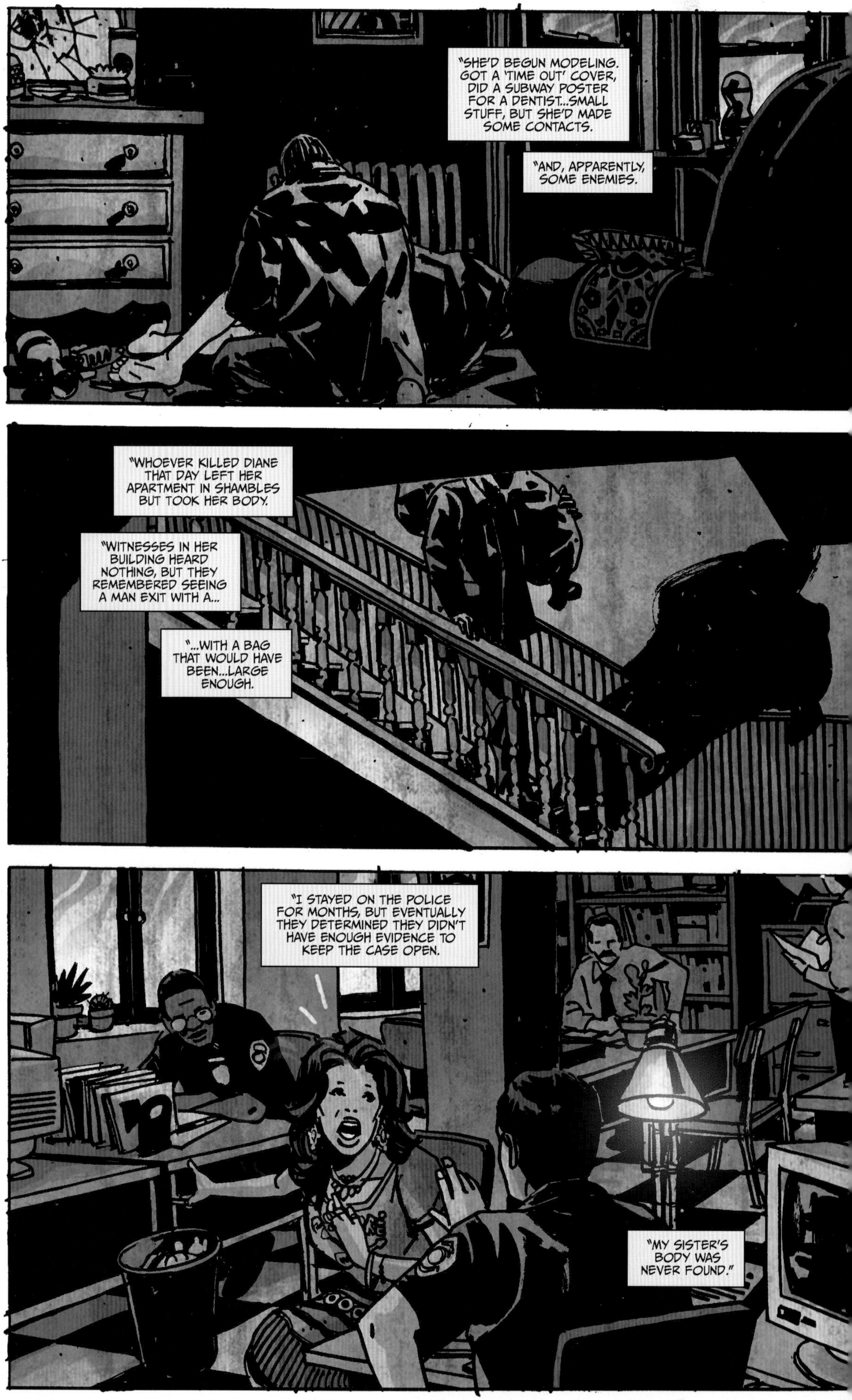
"SHE'D BEGUN MODELING. GOT A 'TIME OUT' COVER, DID A SUBWAY POSTER FOR A DENTIST...SMALL STUFF, BUT SHE'D MADE SOME CONTACTS.
"AND, APPARENTLY, SOME ENEMIES.
"WHOEVER KILLED DIANE THAT DAY LEFT HER APARTMENT IN SHAMBLES BUT TOOK HER BODY.
"WITNESSES IN HER BUILDING HEARD NOTHING, BUT THEY REMEMBERED SEEING A MAN EXIT WITH A...
"...WITH A BAG THAT WOULD HAVE BEEN...LARGE ENOUGH.
"I STAYED ON THE POLICE FOR MONTHS, BUT EVENTUALLY THEY DETERMINED THEY DIDN'T HAVE ENOUGH EVIDENCE TO KEEP THE CASE OPEN.
"MY SISTER'S BODY WAS NEVER FOUND."

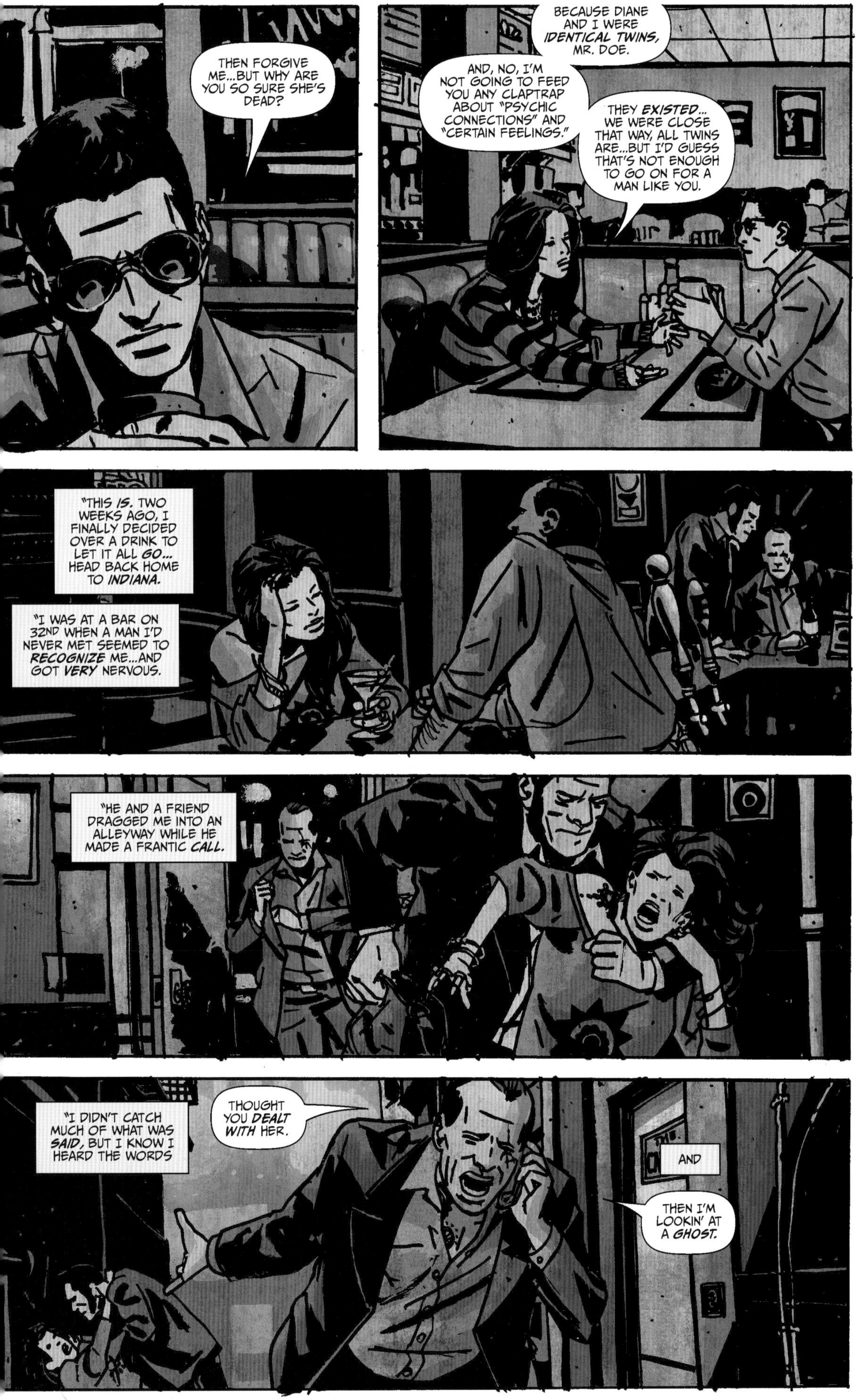
THEN FORGIVE ME...BUT WHY ARE YOU SO SURE SHE'S DEAD?
BECAUSE DIANE AND I WERE IDENTICAL TWINS, MR. DOE.
AND, NO, I'M NOT GOING TO FEED YOU ANY CLAPTRAP ABOUT "PSYCHIC CONNECTIONS" AND "CERTAIN FEELINGS."
THEY EXISTED... WE WERE CLOSE THAT WAY, ALL TWINS ARE...BUT I'D GUESS THAT'S NOT ENOUGH TO GO ON FOR A MAN LIKE YOU.
"THIS IS. TWO WEEKS AGO, I FINALLY DECIDED OVER A DRINK TO LET IT ALL GO... HEAD BACK HOME TO INDIANA.
"I WAS AT A BAR ON 32ND WHEN A MAN I'D NEVER MET SEEMED TO RECOGNIZE ME...AND GOT VERY NERVOUS.
"HE AND A FRIEND DRAGGED ME INTO AN ALLEYWAY WHILE HE MADE A FRANTIC CALL.
"I DIDN'T CATCH MUCH OF WHAT WAS SAID, BUT I KNOW I HEARD THE WORDS
THOUGHT YOU DEALT WITH HER.
AND
THEN I'M LOOKIN' AT A GHOST.

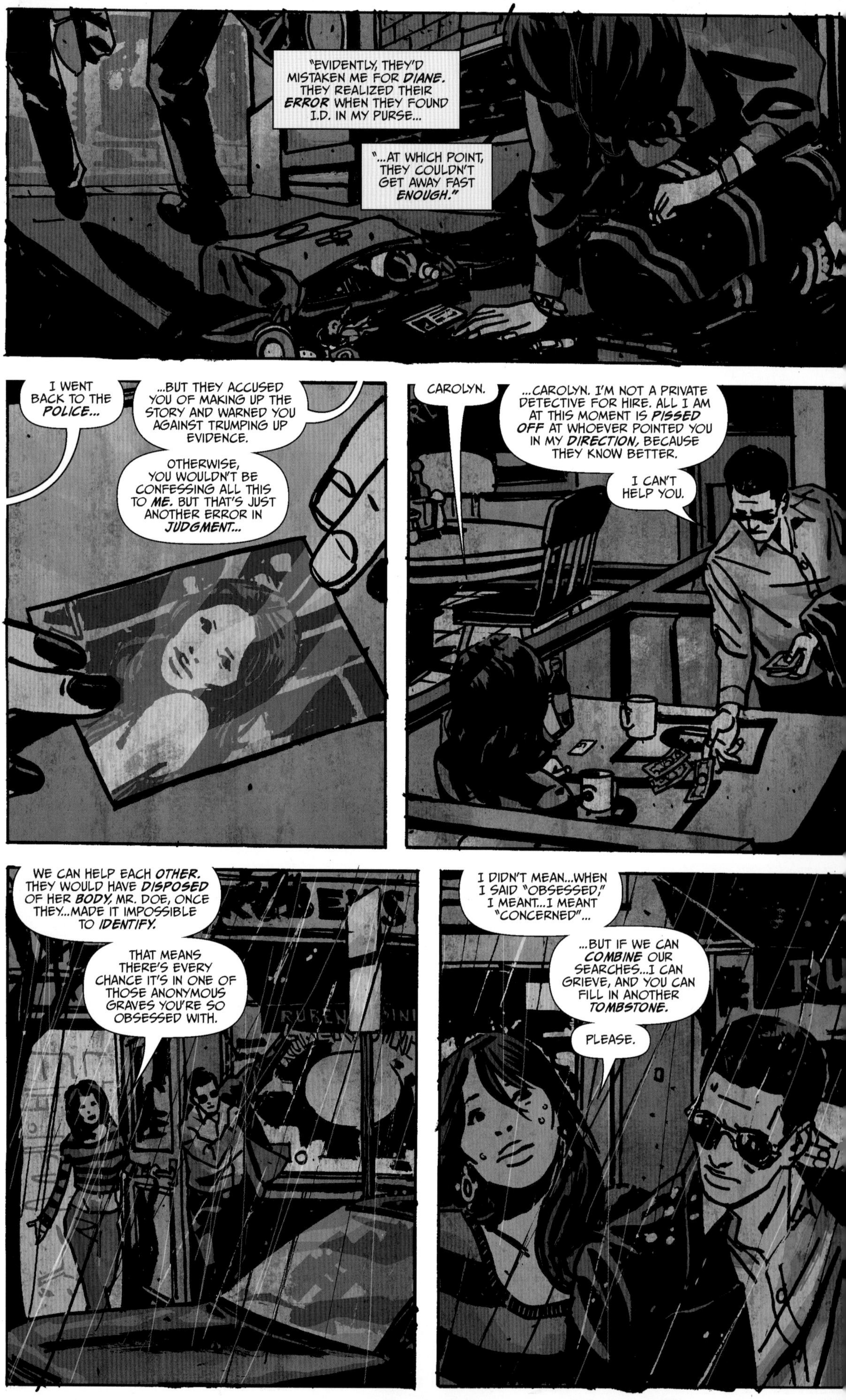
"EVIDENTLY, THEY'D MISTAKEN ME FOR DIANE. THEY REALIZED THEIR ERROR WHEN THEY FOUND I.D. IN MY PURSE...
"...AT WHICH POINT, THEY COULDN'T GET AWAY FAST ENOUGH."
I WENT BACK TO THE POLICE...
...BUT THEY ACCUSED YOU OF MAKING UP THE STORY AND WARNED YOU AGAINST TRUMPING UP EVIDENCE.
OTHERWISE, YOU WOULDN'T BE CONFESSING ALL THIS TO ME. BUT THAT'S JUST ANOTHER ERROR IN JUDGMENT...
CAROLYN.
...CAROLYN. I'M NOT A PRIVATE DETECTIVE FOR HIRE. ALL I AM AT THIS MOMENT IS PISSED OFF AT WHOEVER POINTED YOU IN MY DIRECTION, BECAUSE THEY KNOW BETTER.
I CAN'T HELP YOU.
WE CAN HELP EACH OTHER. THEY WOULD HAVE DISPOSED OF HER BODY, MR. DOE, ONCE THEY...MADE IT IMPOSSIBLE TO IDENTIFY.
THAT MEANS THERE'S EVERY CHANCE IT'S IN ONE OF THOSE ANONYMOUS GRAVES YOU'RE SO OBSESSED WITH.
I DIDN'T MEAN...WHEN I SAID "OBSESSED," I MEANT...I MEANT "CONCERNED"...
...BUT IF WE CAN COMBINE OUR SEARCHES...I CAN GRIEVE, AND YOU CAN FILL IN ANOTHER TOMBSTONE.
PLEASE.

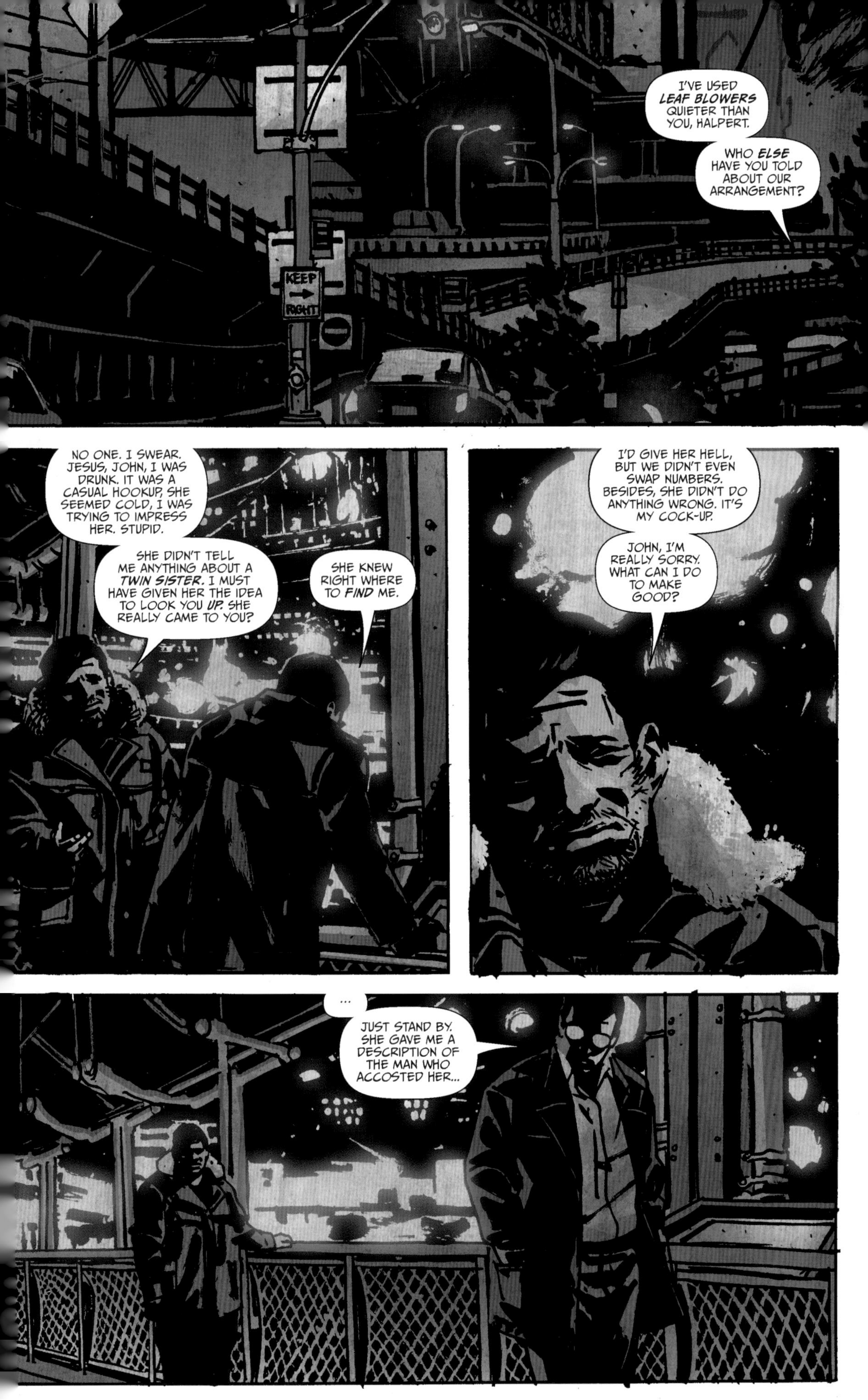
I'VE USED LEAF BLOWERS QUIETER THAN YOU, HALPERT.
WHO ELSE HAVE YOU TOLD ABOUT OUR ARRANGEMENT?
KEEP RIGHT
NO ONE. I SWEAR. JESUS, JOHN, I WAS DRUNK. IT WAS A CASUAL HOOKUP, SHE SEEMED COLD, I WAS TRYING TO IMPRESS HER. STUPID.
SHE DIDN'T TELL ME ANYTHING ABOUT A TWIN SISTER. I MUST HAVE GIVEN HER THE IDEA TO LOOK YOU UP. SHE REALLY CAME TO YOU?
SHE KNEW RIGHT WHERE TO FIND ME.
I'D GIVE HER HELL, BUT WE DIDN'T EVEN SWAP NUMBERS. BESIDES, SHE DIDN'T DO ANYTHING WRONG. IT'S MY COCK-UP.
JOHN, I'M REALLY SORRY. WHAT CAN I DO TO MAKE GOOD?
...
JUST STAND BY. SHE GAVE ME A DESCRIPTION OF THE MAN WHO ACCOSTED HER...

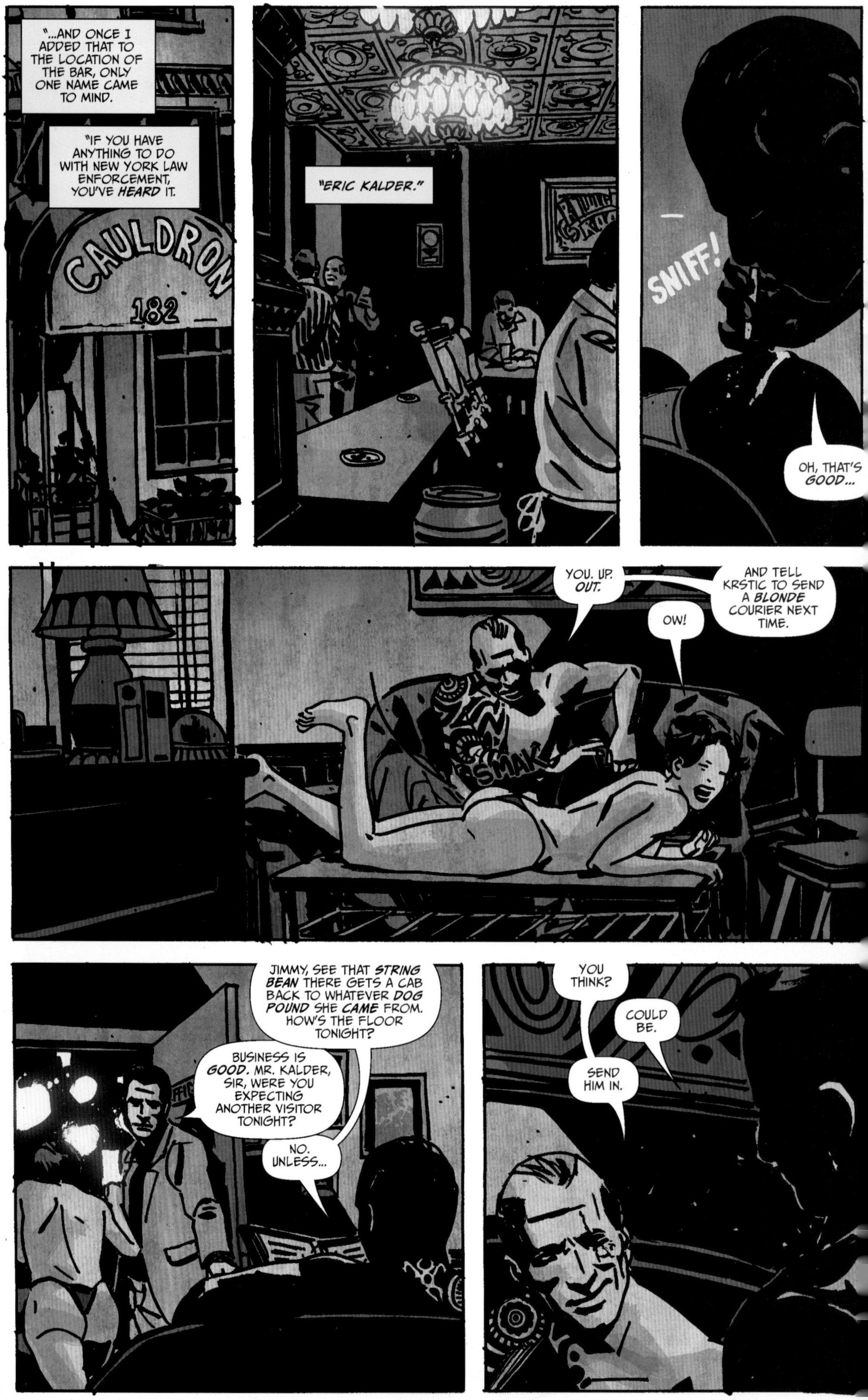
"...AND ONCE I ADDED THAT TO THE LOCATION OF THE BAR, ONLY ONE NAME CAME TO MIND.
"IF YOU HAVE ANYTHING TO DO WITH NEW YORK LAW ENFORCEMENT, YOU'VE HEARD IT.
CAULDRON
182
"ERIC KALDER."
SNIFF!
OH, THAT'S GOOD...
YOU. UP. OUT.
AND TELL KRSTIC TO SEND A BLONDE COURIER NEXT TIME.
OW!
SMAK
JIMMY, SEE THAT STRING BEAN THERE GETS A CAB BACK TO WHATEVER DOG POUND SHE CAME FROM. HOW'S THE FLOOR TONIGHT?
BUSINESS IS GOOD. MR. KALDER, SIR, WERE YOU EXPECTING ANOTHER VISITOR TONIGHT?
NO. UNLESS...
YOU THINK?
COULD BE.
SEND HIM IN.

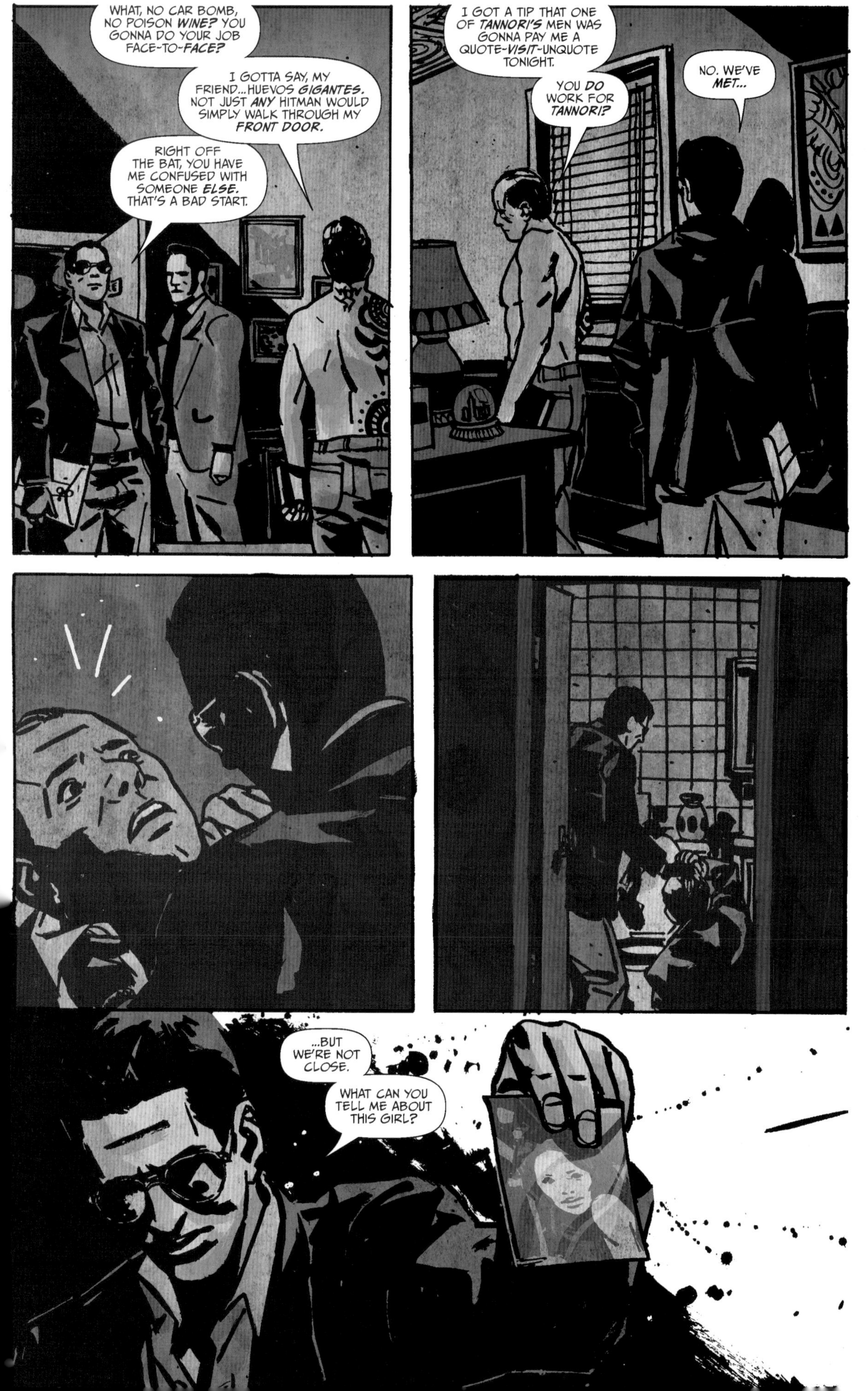
WHAT, NO CAR BOMB, NO POISON WINE? YOU GONNA DO YOUR JOB FACE-TO-FACE?
I GOTTA SAY, MY FRIEND...HUEVOS GIGANTES. NOT JUST ANY HITMAN WOULD SIMPLY WALK THROUGH MY FRONT DOOR.
RIGHT OFF THE BAT, YOU HAVE ME CONFUSED WITH SOMEONE ELSE. THAT'S A BAD START.
I GOT A TIP THAT ONE OF TANNORI'S MEN WAS GONNA PAY ME A QUOTE-VISIT-UNQUOTE TONIGHT.
YOU DO WORK FOR TANNORI?
NO. WE'VE MET...
...BUT WE'RE NOT CLOSE.
WHAT CAN YOU TELL ME ABOUT THIS GIRL?

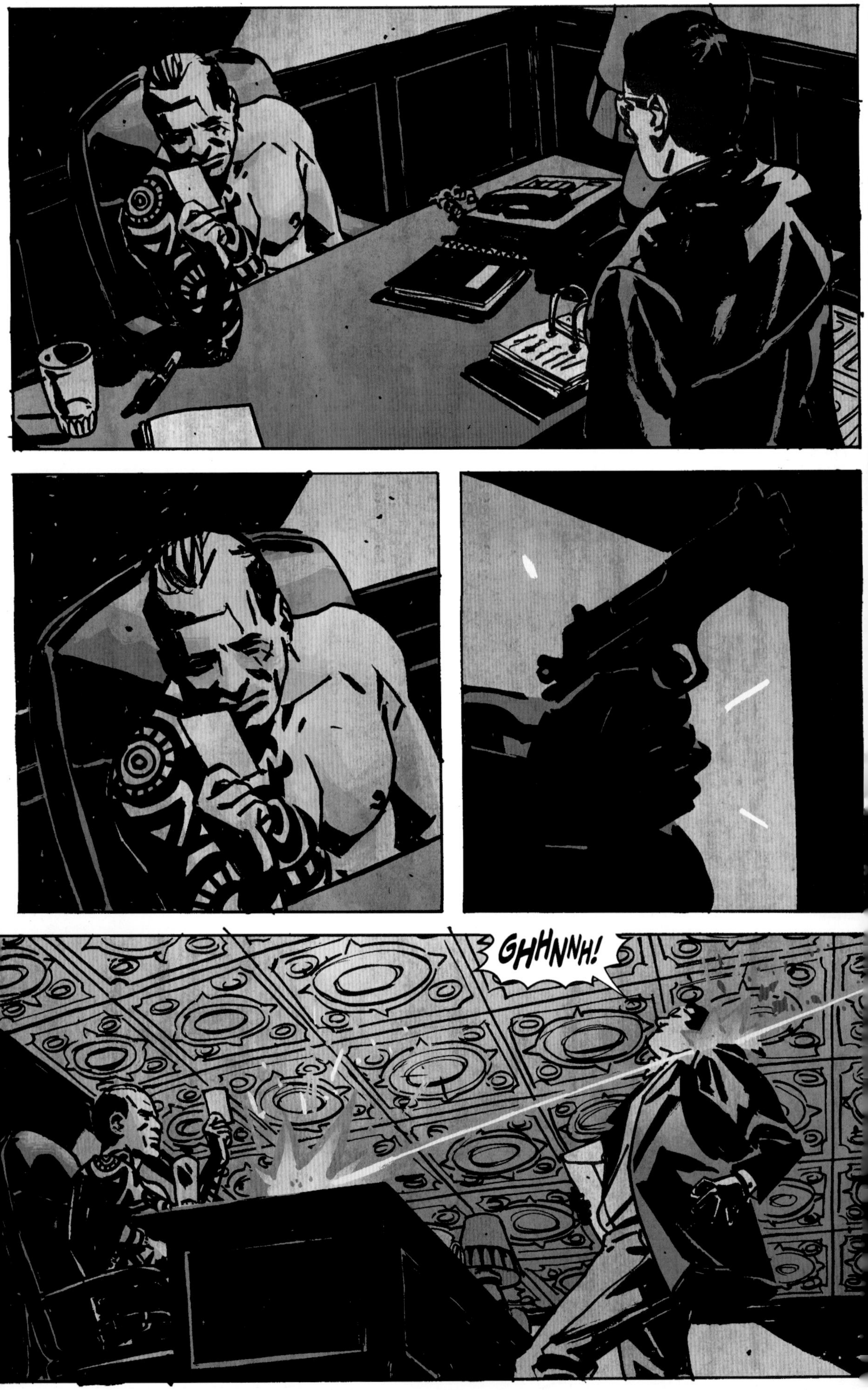
GHHNNH!

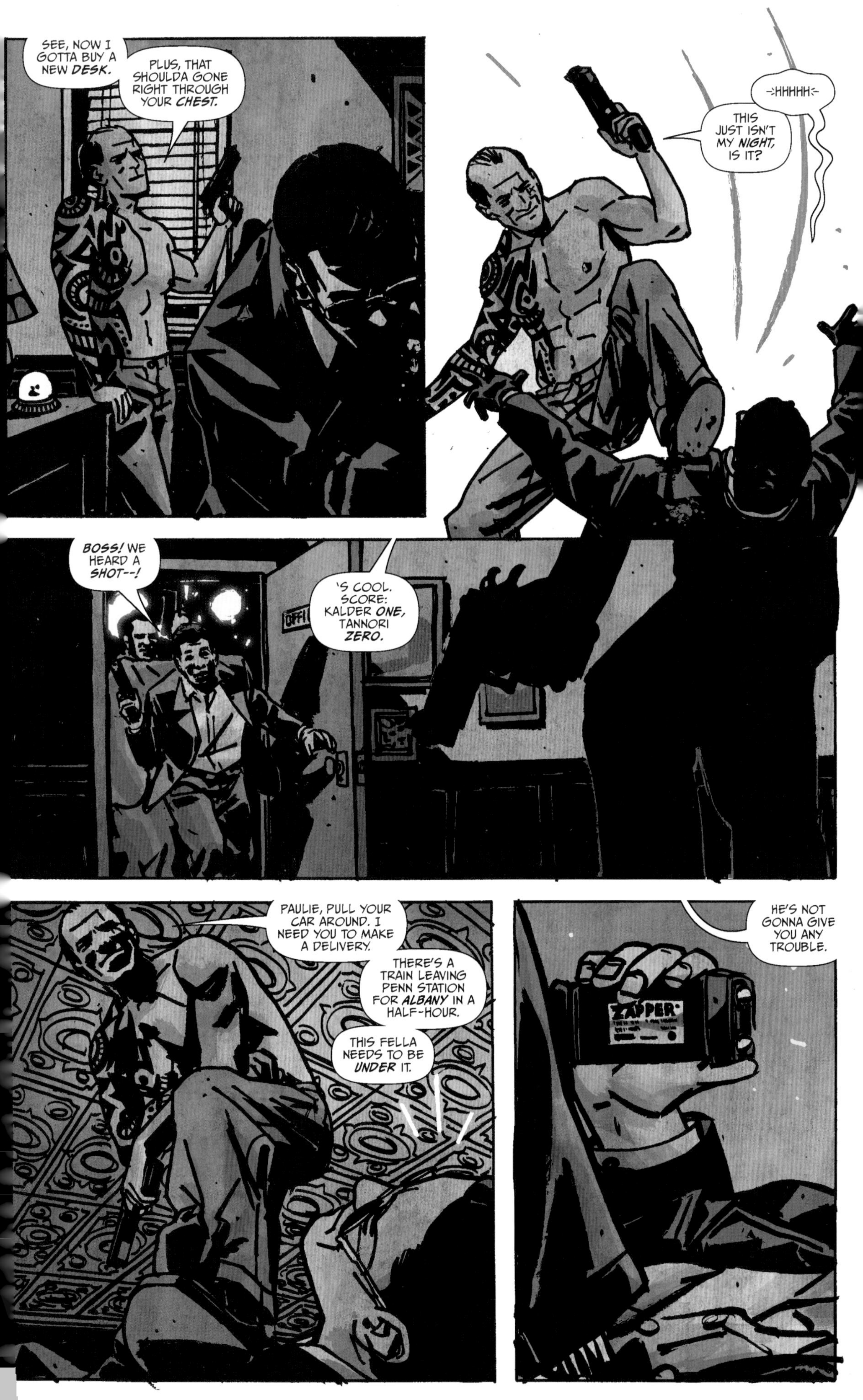
SEE, NOW I GOTTA BUY A NEW DESK.
PLUS, THAT SHOULDA GONE RIGHT THROUGH YOUR CHEST.
-HHHHH-
THIS JUST ISN'T MY NIGHT, IS IT?
BOSS! WE HEARD A SHOT--!
'S COOL. SCORE: KALDER ONE, TANNORI ZERO.
PAULIE, PULL YOUR CAR AROUND. I NEED YOU TO MAKE A DELIVERY.
THERE'S A TRAIN LEAVING PENN STATION FOR ALBANY IN A HALF-HOUR.
THIS FELLA NEEDS TO BE UNDER IT.
HE'S NOT GONNA GIVE YOU ANY TROUBLE.
ZAPPER

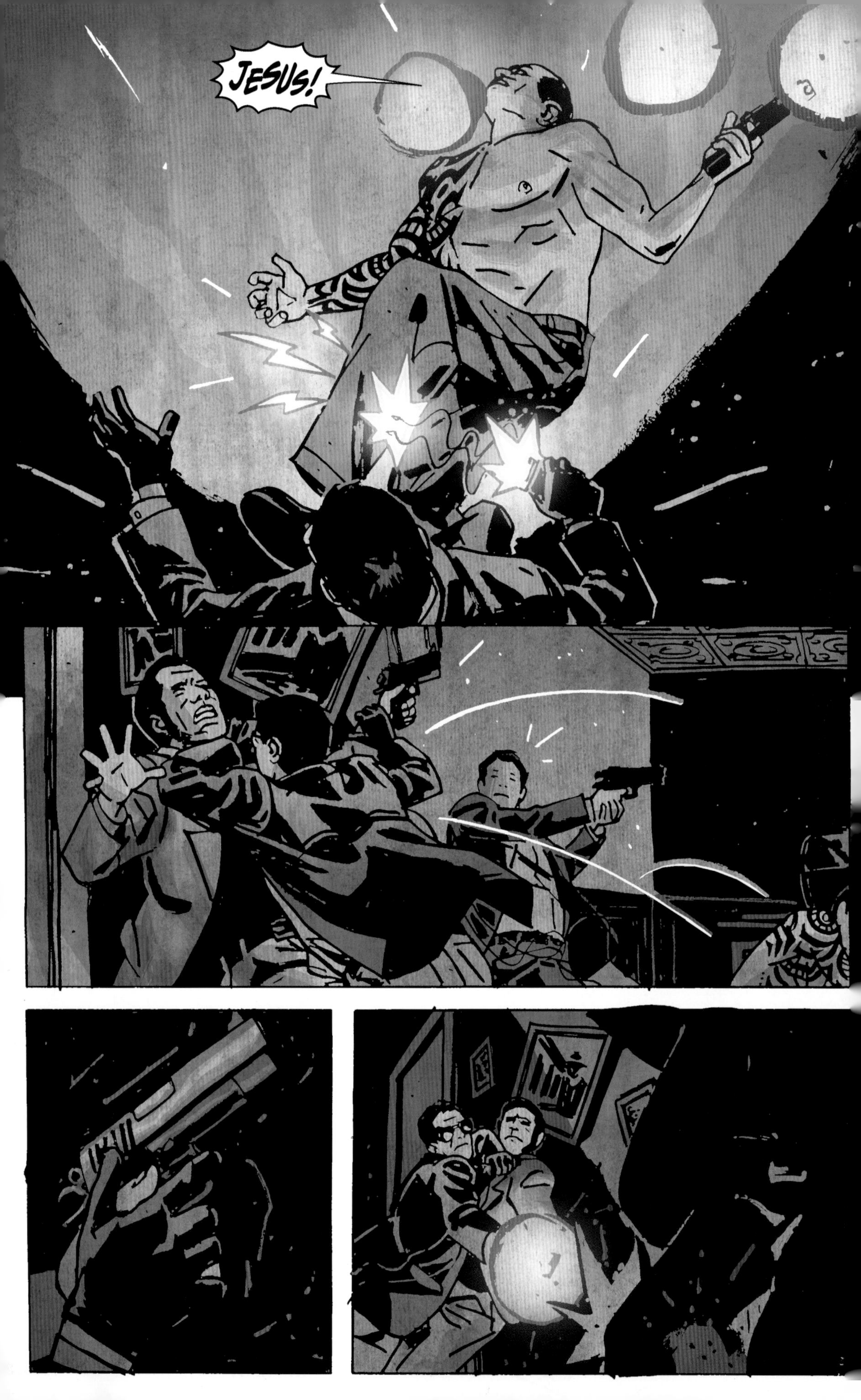
JESUS!

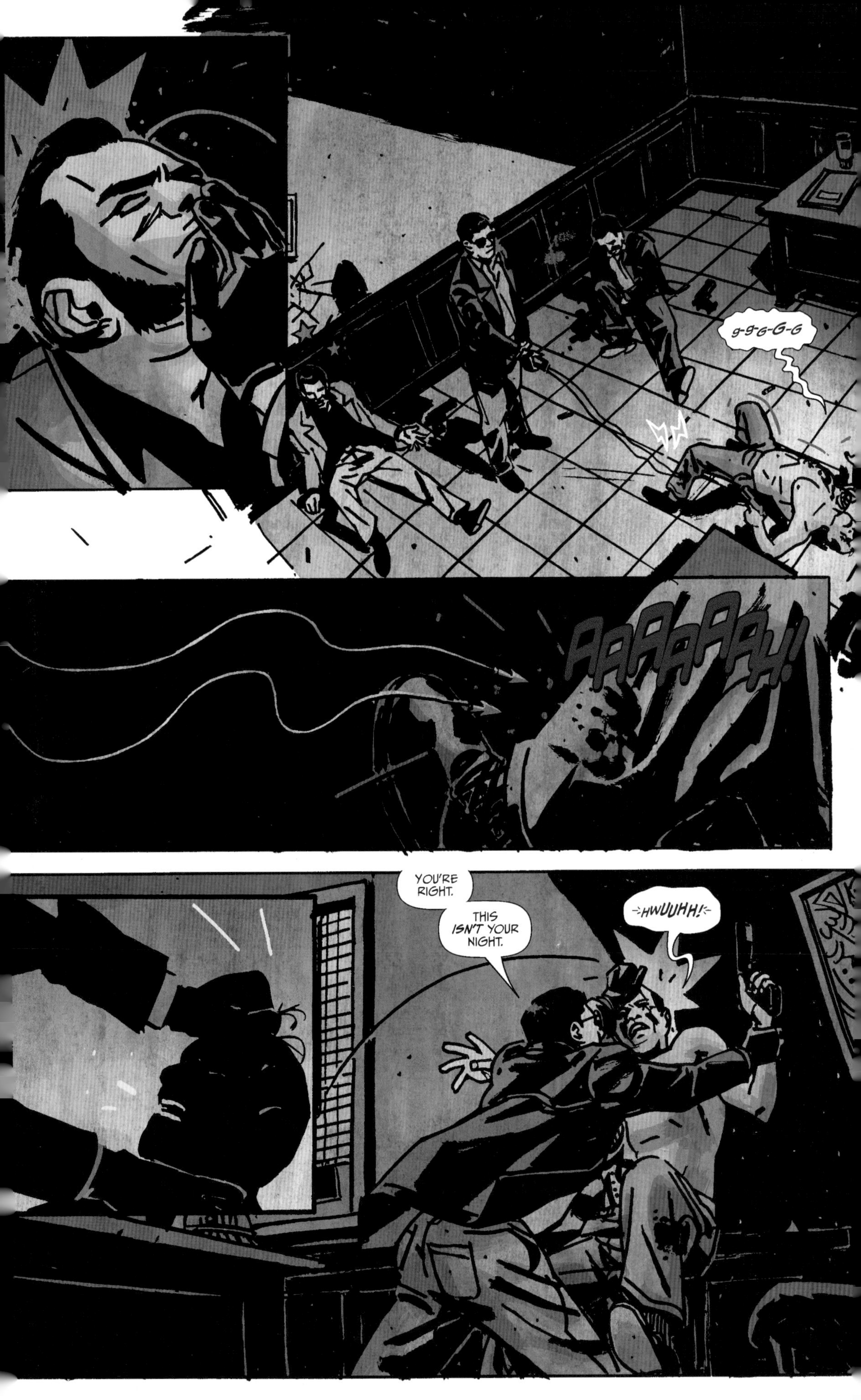
g-g-G-G-G
AAAAAAAH!
YOU'RE RIGHT.
THIS *ISN'T* YOUR NIGHT.
HWUUHH!

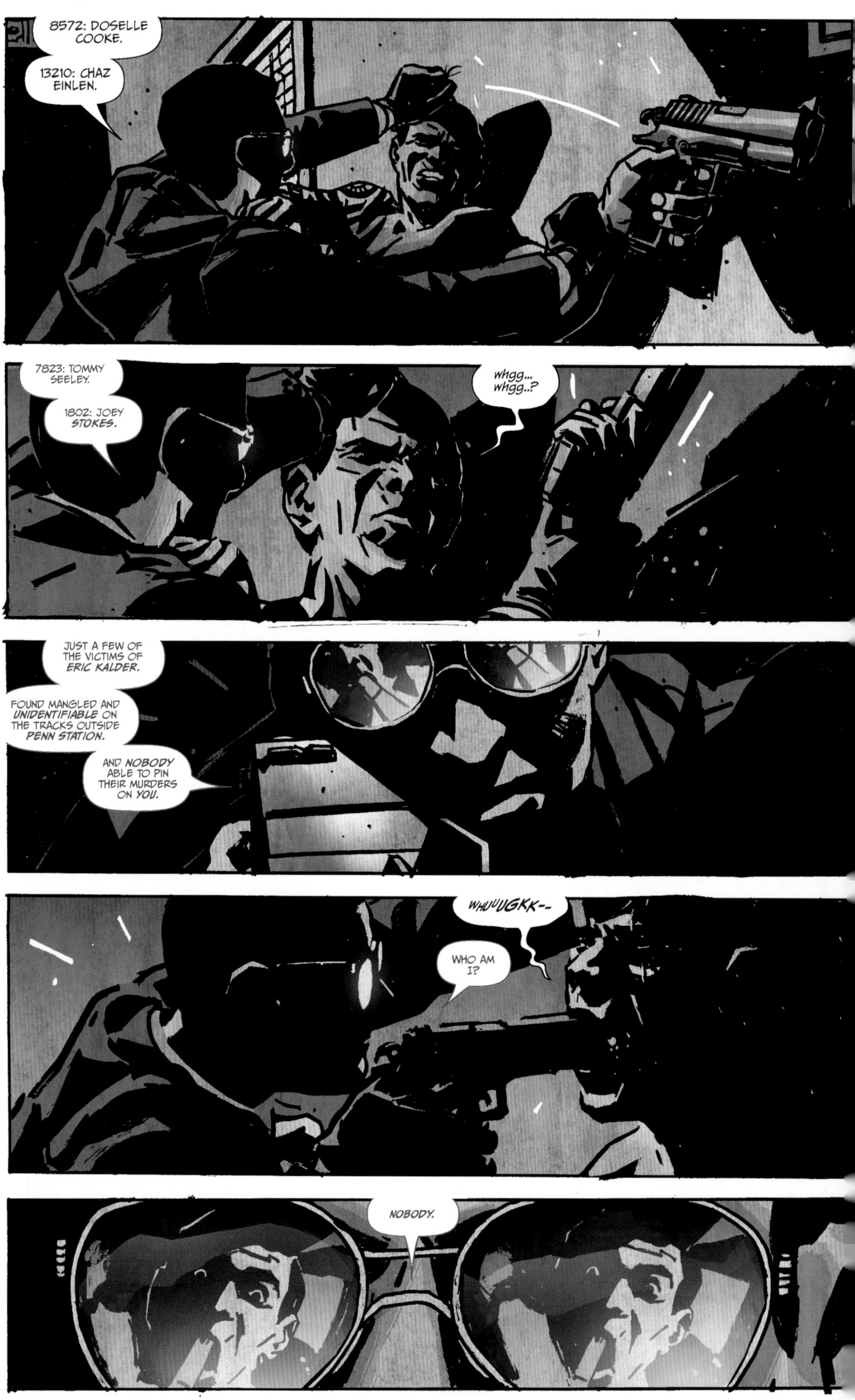
8572: DOSELLE COOKE.
13210: CHAZ EINLEN.
7823: TOMMY SEELEY.
1802: JOEY STOKES.
whgg... whgg..?
JUST A FEW OF THE VICTIMS OF ERIC KALDER.
FOUND MANGLED AND UNIDENTIFIABLE ON THE TRACKS OUTSIDE PENN STATION.
AND NOBODY ABLE TO PIN THEIR MURDERS ON YOU.
WHUUUGKK--
WHO AM I?
NOBODY.

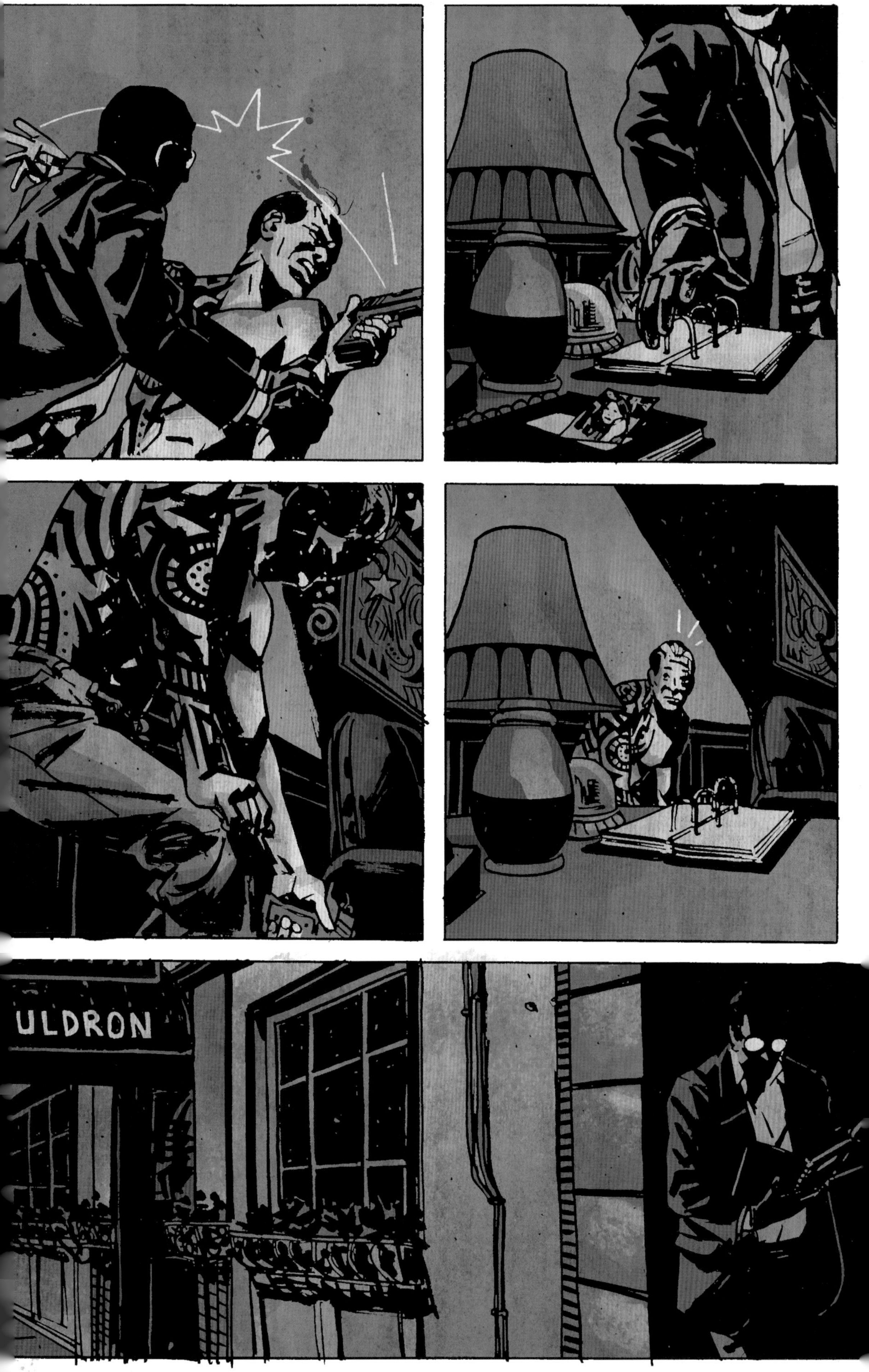
ULDRON

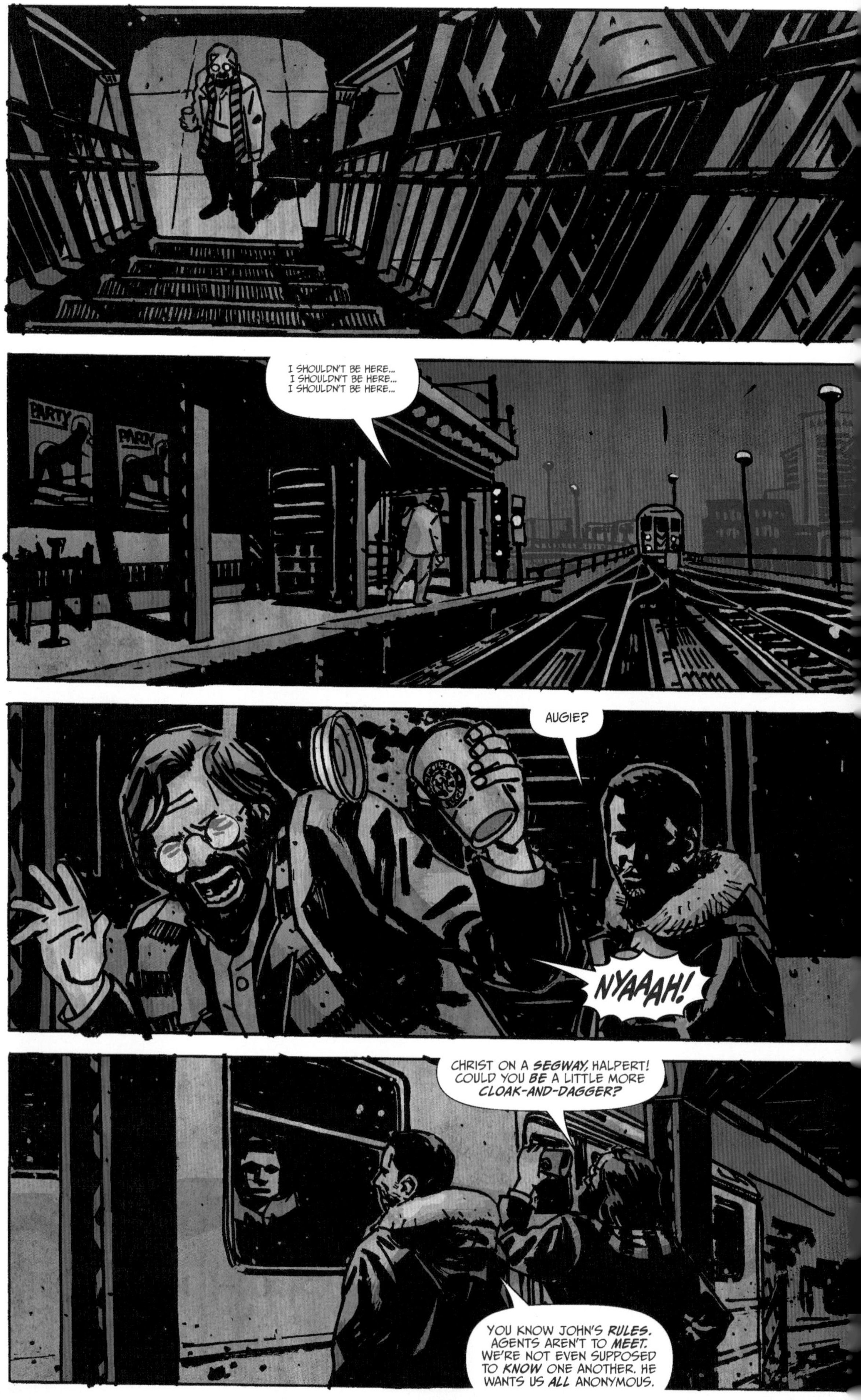

I SHOULDN'T BE HERE... I SHOULDN'T BE HERE... I SHOULDN'T BE HERE...
AUGIE?
NYAAAH!
CHRIST ON A SEGWAY, HALPERT! COULD YOU BE A LITTLE MORE CLOAK-AND-DAGGER?
YOU KNOW JOHN'S RULES. AGENTS AREN'T TO MEET. WE'RE NOT EVEN SUPPOSED TO KNOW ONE ANOTHER. HE WANTS US ALL ANONYMOUS.

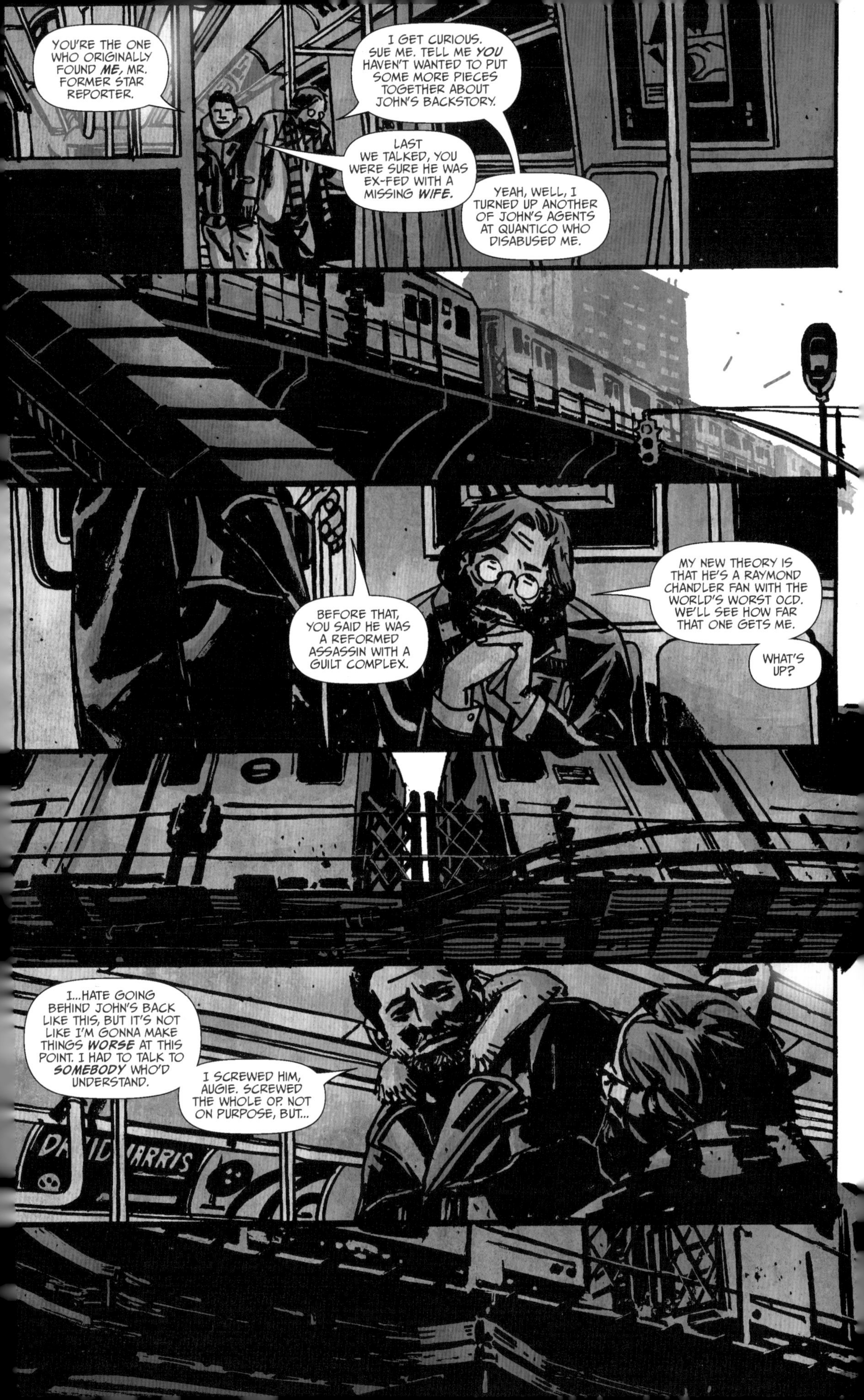
YOU'RE THE ONE WHO ORIGINALLY FOUND *ME*, MR. FORMER STAR REPORTER.
I GET CURIOUS. SUE ME. TELL ME *YOU* HAVEN'T WANTED TO PUT SOME MORE PIECES TOGETHER ABOUT JOHN'S BACKSTORY.
LAST WE TALKED, YOU WERE SURE HE WAS EX-FED WITH A MISSING *WIFE.*
YEAH, WELL, I TURNED UP ANOTHER OF JOHN'S AGENTS AT QUANTICO WHO DISABUSED ME.
BEFORE THAT, YOU SAID HE WAS A REFORMED ASSASSIN WITH A GUILT COMPLEX.
MY NEW THEORY IS THAT HE'S A RAYMOND CHANDLER FAN WITH THE WORLD'S WORST OCD. WE'LL SEE HOW FAR THAT ONE GETS ME.
WHAT'S UP?
I...HATE GOING BEHIND JOHN'S BACK LIKE THIS, BUT IT'S NOT LIKE I'M GONNA MAKE THINGS *WORSE* AT THIS POINT. I HAD TO TALK TO *SOMEBODY* WHO'D UNDERSTAND.
I SCREWED HIM, AUGIE. SCREWED THE WHOLE OP. NOT ON PURPOSE, BUT...

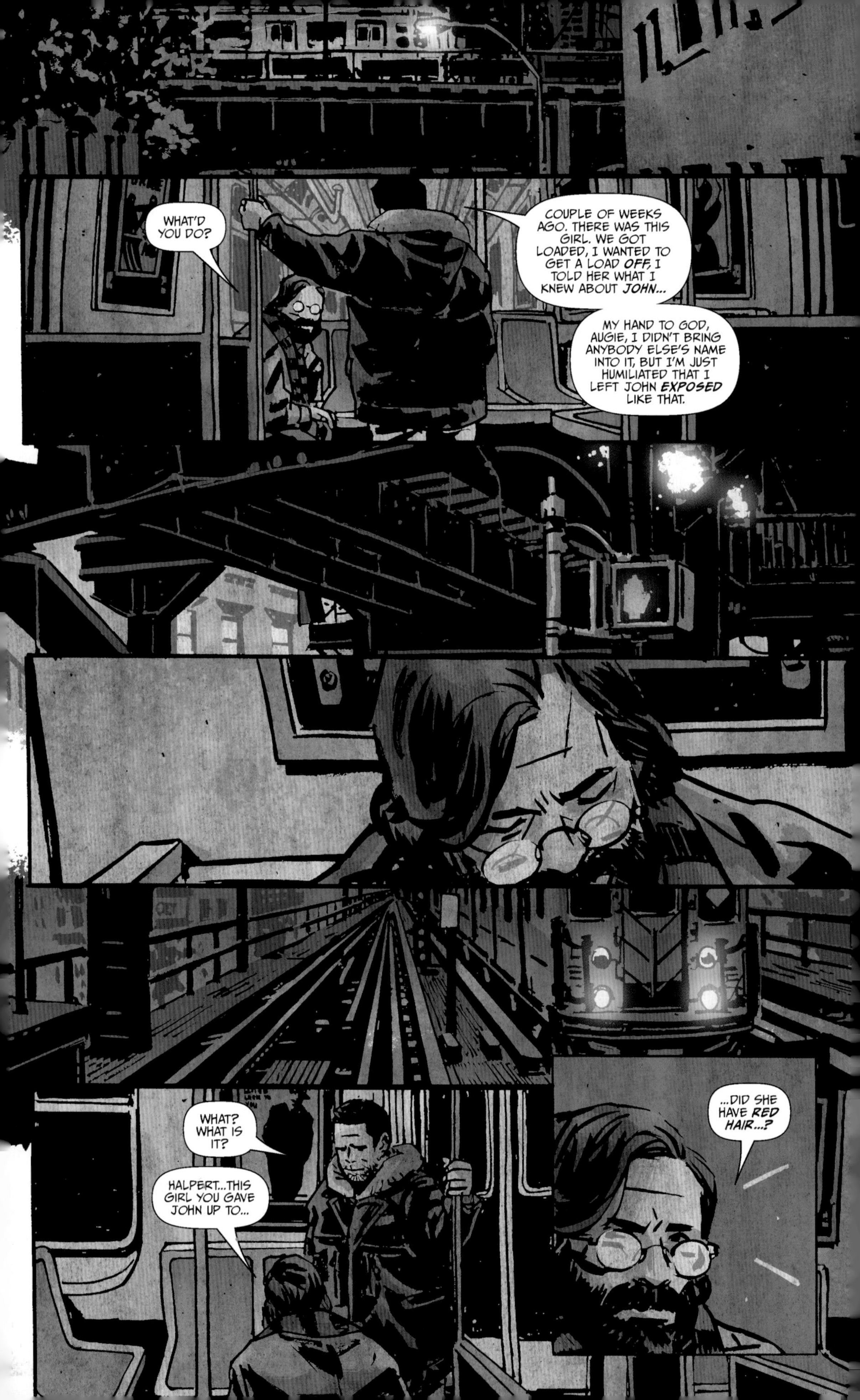
WHAT'D YOU DO?
COUPLE OF WEEKS AGO. THERE WAS THIS GIRL. WE GOT LOADED, I WANTED TO GET A LOAD OFF, I TOLD HER WHAT I KNEW ABOUT JOHN...
MY HAND TO GOD, AUGIE, I DIDN'T BRING ANYBODY ELSE'S NAME INTO IT, BUT I'M JUST HUMILIATED THAT I LEFT JOHN EXPOSED LIKE THAT.
WHAT? WHAT IS IT?
HALPERT...THIS GIRL YOU GAVE JOHN UP TO...
...DID SHE HAVE RED HAIR...?

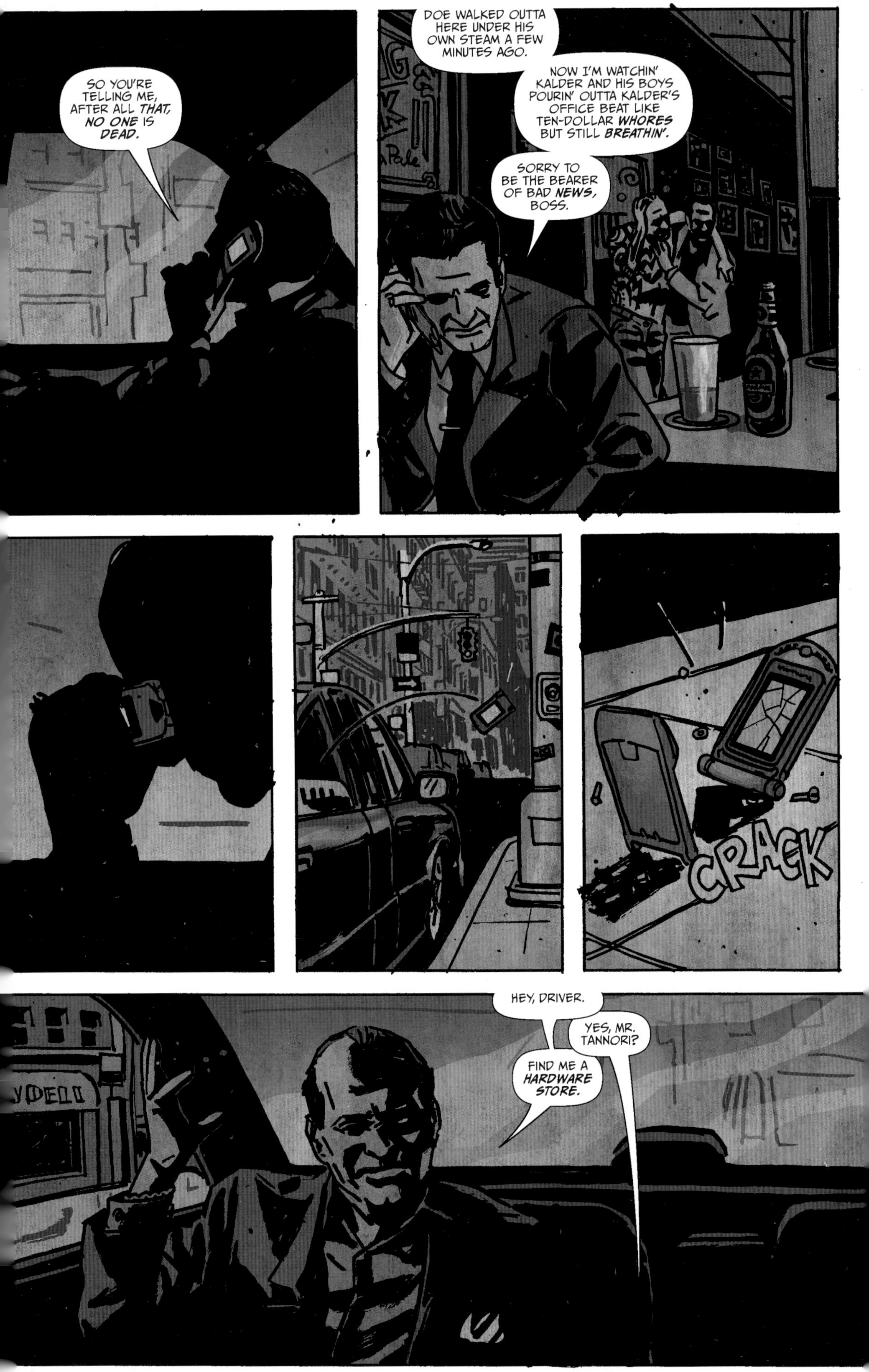
SO YOU'RE TELLING ME, AFTER ALL THAT, NO ONE IS DEAD.
DOE WALKED OUTTA HERE UNDER HIS OWN STEAM A FEW MINUTES AGO.
NOW I'M WATCHIN' KALDER AND HIS BOYS POURIN' OUTTA KALDER'S OFFICE BEAT LIKE TEN-DOLLAR WHORES BUT STILL BREATHIN'.
SORRY TO BE THE BEARER OF BAD NEWS, BOSS.
CRACK
HEY, DRIVER.
YES, MR. TANNORI?
FIND ME A HARDWARE STORE.

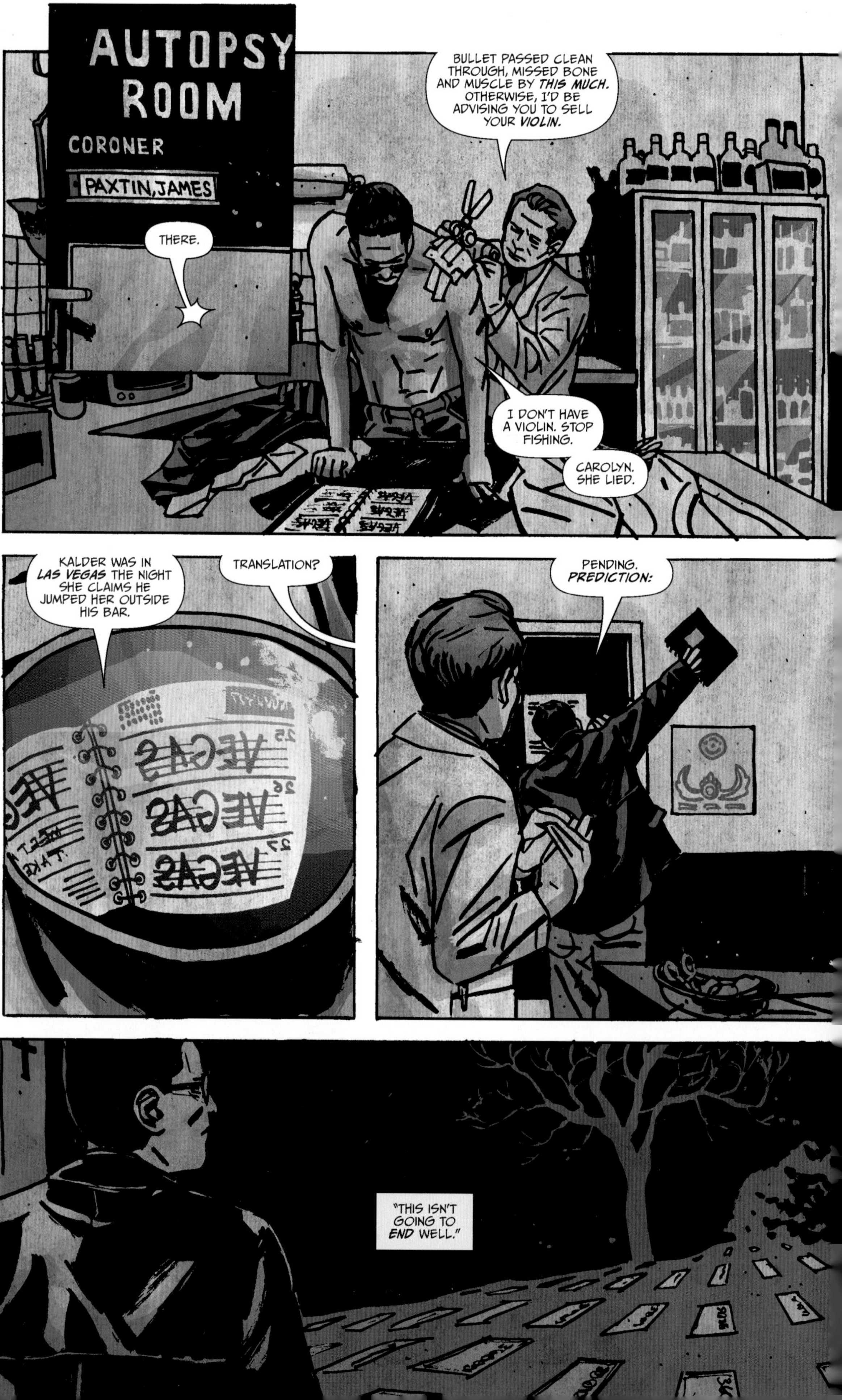
AUTOPSY ROOM
CORONER
PAXTIN, JAMES
BULLET PASSED CLEAN THROUGH, MISSED BONE AND MUSCLE BY ***THIS MUCH.*** OTHERWISE, I'D BE ADVISING YOU TO SELL YOUR ***VIOLIN.***
THERE.
I DON'T HAVE A VIOLIN. STOP FISHING.
CAROLYN. SHE LIED.
KALDER WAS IN ***LAS VEGAS*** THE NIGHT SHE CLAIMS HE JUMPED HER OUTSIDE HIS BAR.
TRANSLATION?
VEGAS
VEGAS
VEGAS
PENDING. ***PREDICTION:***
"THIS ISN'T GOING TO ***END*** WELL."

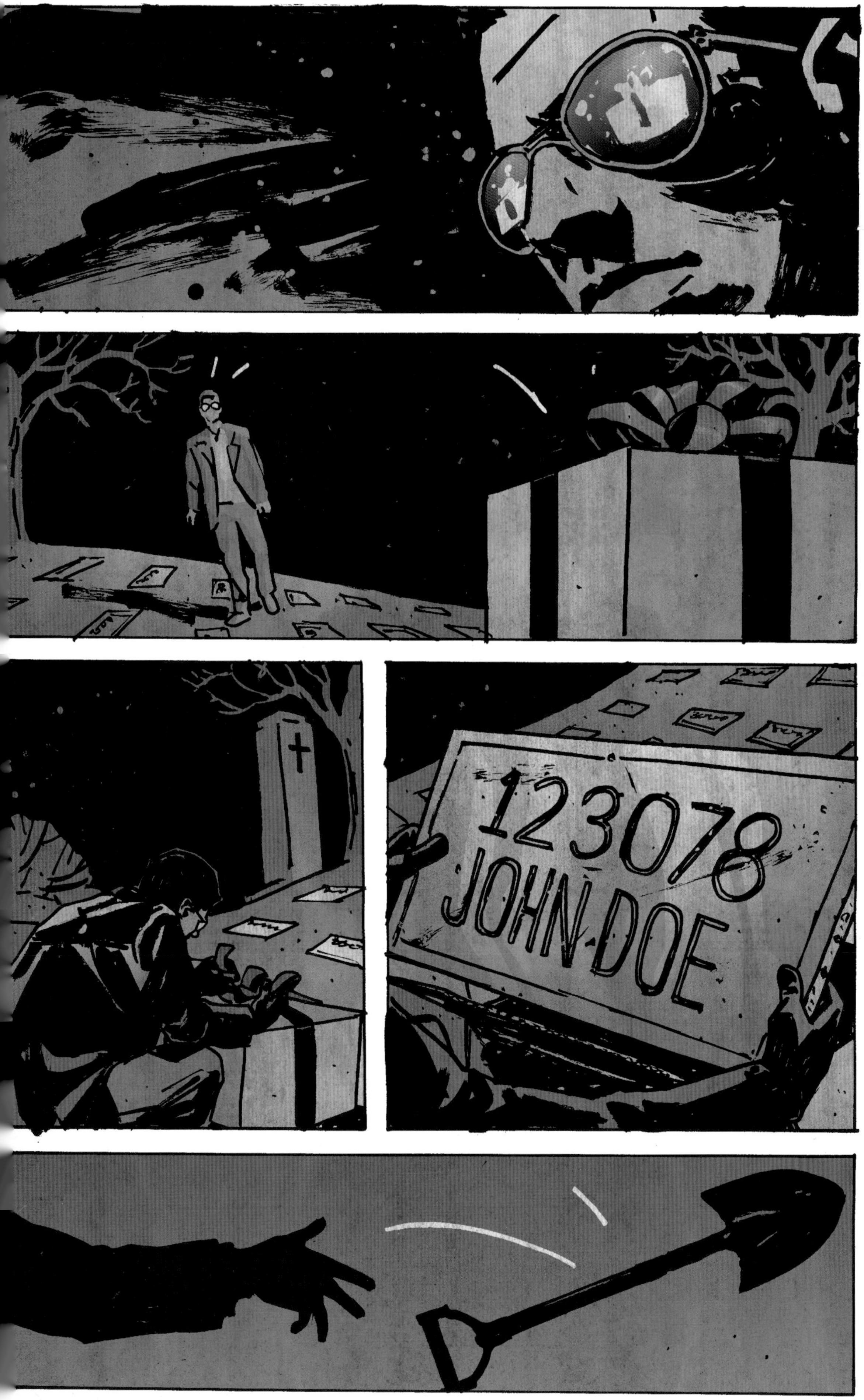
123078
JOHN DOE

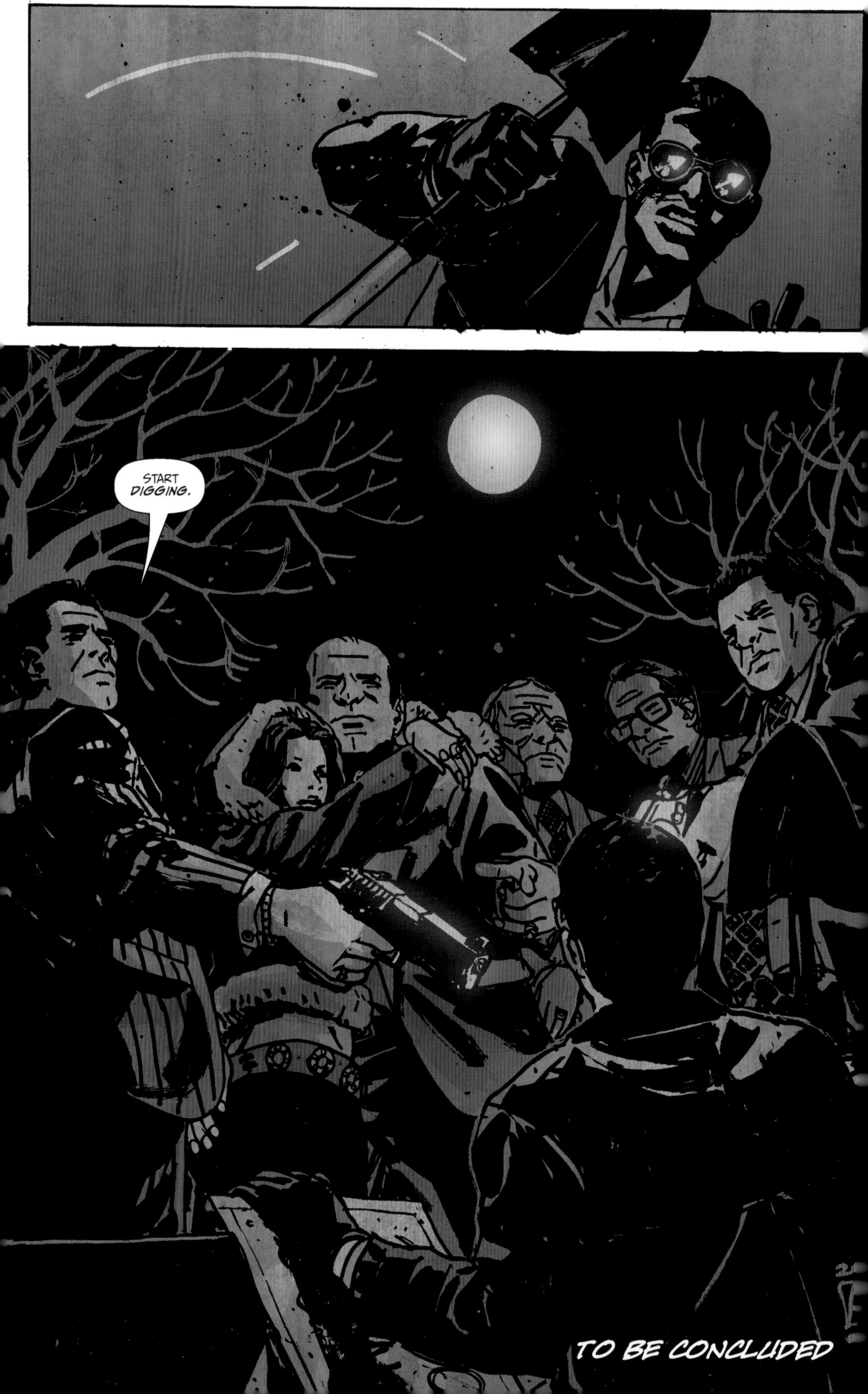
START DIGGING.
TO BE CONCLUDED

CHAPTER THREE

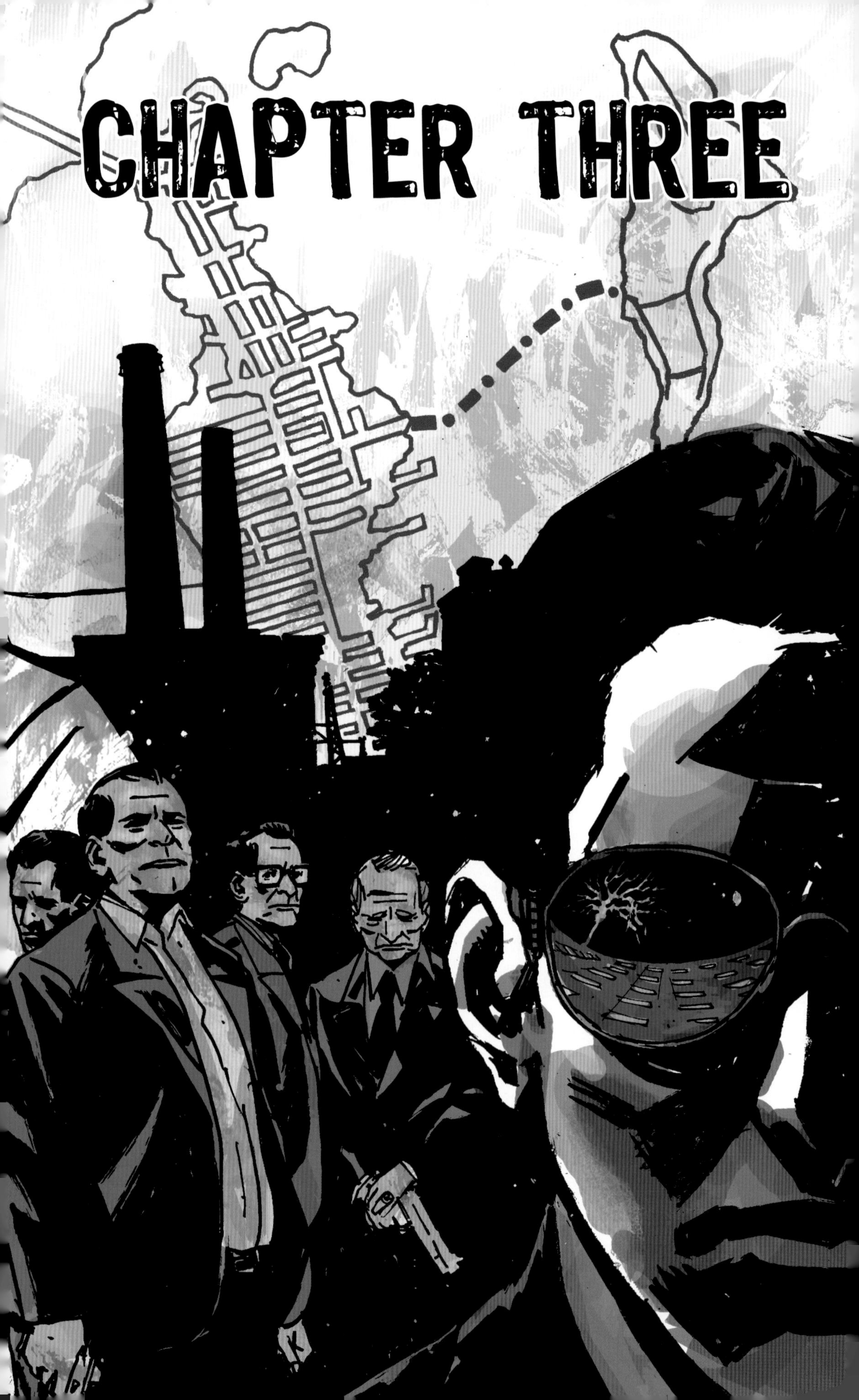

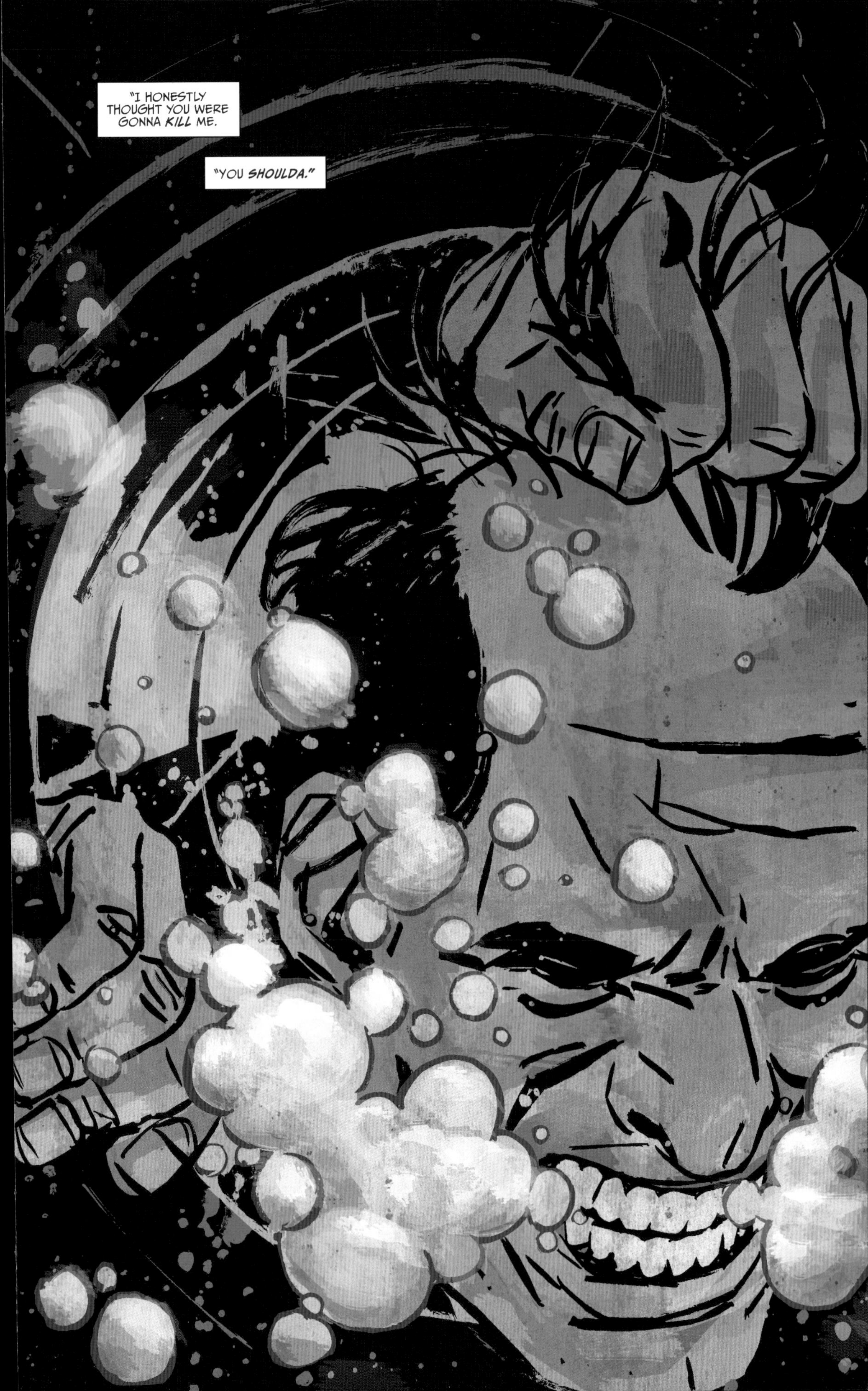
"I HONESTLY THOUGHT YOU WERE GONNA KILL ME.
"YOU SHOULDA."

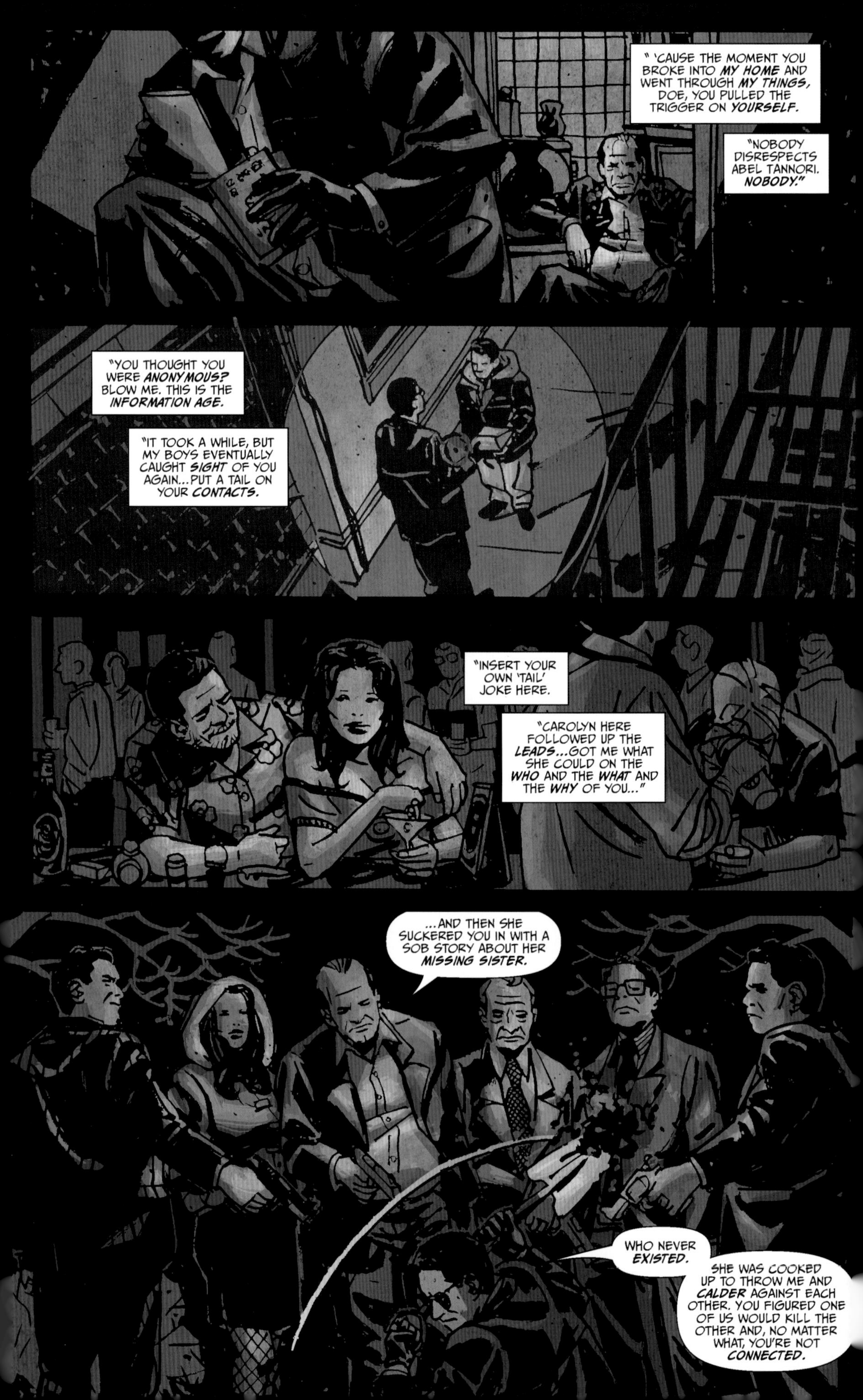

" 'CAUSE THE MOMENT YOU BROKE INTO MY HOME AND WENT THROUGH MY THINGS, DOE, YOU PULLED THE TRIGGER ON YOURSELF.
"NOBODY DISRESPECTS ABEL TANNORI. NOBODY."
"YOU THOUGHT YOU WERE ANONYMOUS? BLOW ME. THIS IS THE INFORMATION AGE.
"IT TOOK A WHILE, BUT MY BOYS EVENTUALLY CAUGHT SIGHT OF YOU AGAIN...PUT A TAIL ON YOUR CONTACTS.
"INSERT YOUR OWN 'TAIL' JOKE HERE.
"CAROLYN HERE FOLLOWED UP THE LEADS...GOT ME WHAT SHE COULD ON THE WHO AND THE WHAT AND THE WHY OF YOU..."
...AND THEN SHE SUCKERED YOU IN WITH A SOB STORY ABOUT HER MISSING SISTER.
WHO NEVER EXISTED.
SHE WAS COOKED UP TO THROW ME AND CALDER AGAINST EACH OTHER. YOU FIGURED ONE OF US WOULD KILL THE OTHER AND, NO MATTER WHAT, YOU'RE NOT CONNECTED.

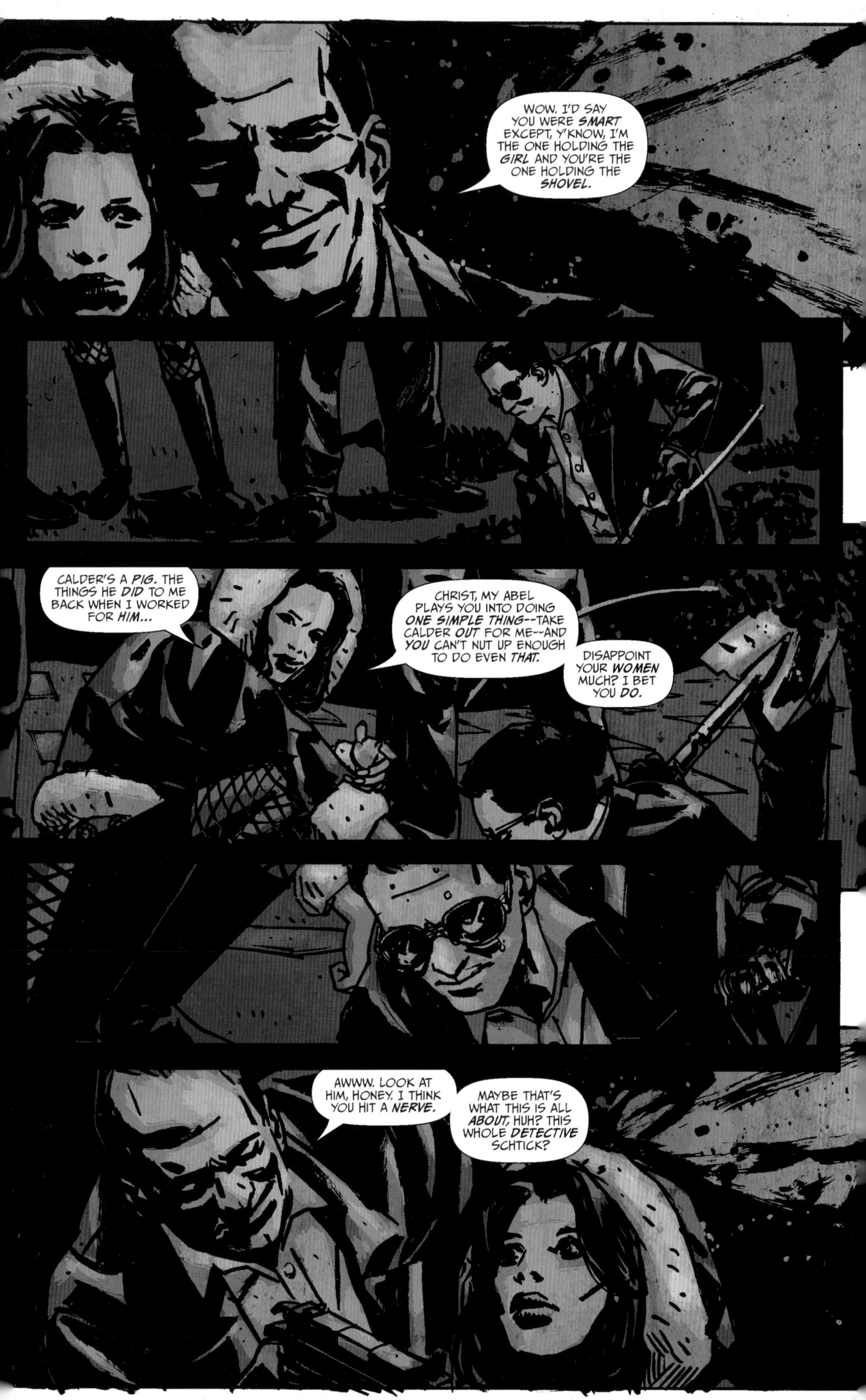
WOW. I'D SAY YOU WERE SMART EXCEPT, Y'KNOW, I'M THE ONE HOLDING THE GIRL AND YOU'RE THE ONE HOLDING THE SHOVEL.
CALDER'S A PIG. THE THINGS HE DID TO ME BACK WHEN I WORKED FOR HIM...
CHRIST, MY ABEL PLAYS YOU INTO DOING ONE SIMPLE THING--TAKE CALDER OUT FOR ME--AND YOU CAN'T NUT UP ENOUGH TO DO EVEN THAT.
DISAPPOINT YOUR WOMEN MUCH? I BET YOU DO.
AWWW. LOOK AT HIM, HONEY. I THINK YOU HIT A NERVE.
MAYBE THAT'S WHAT THIS IS ALL ABOUT, HUH? THIS WHOLE DETECTIVE SCHTICK?

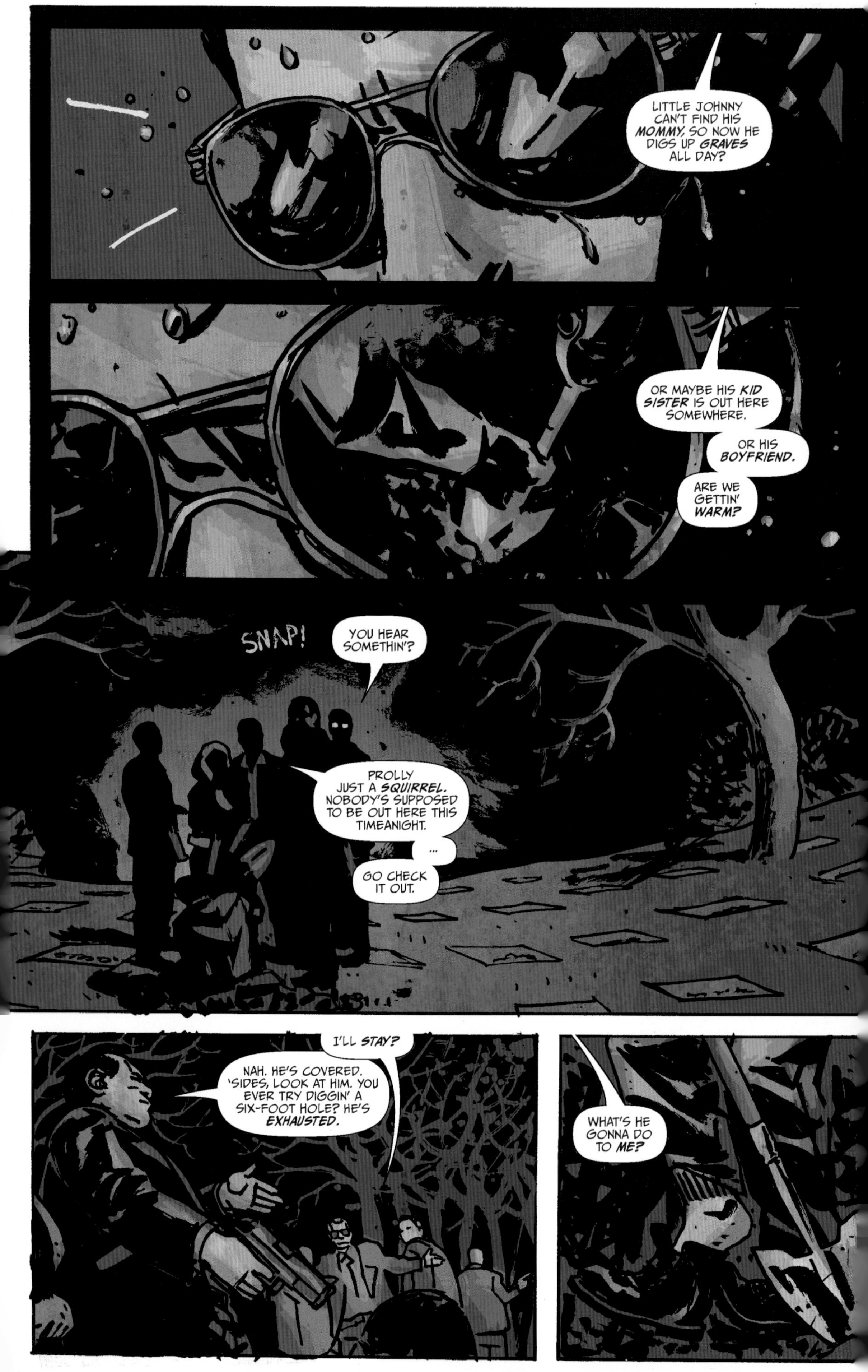
LITTLE JOHNNY CAN'T FIND HIS MOMMY, SO NOW HE DIGS UP GRAVES ALL DAY?
OR MAYBE HIS KID SISTER IS OUT HERE SOMEWHERE.
OR HIS BOYFRIEND.
ARE WE GETTIN' WARM?
SNAP!
YOU HEAR SOMETHIN'?
PROLLY JUST A SQUIRREL. NOBODY'S SUPPOSED TO BE OUT HERE THIS TIMEANIGHT.
...
GO CHECK IT OUT.
I'LL STAY?
NAH. HE'S COVERED. 'SIDES, LOOK AT HIM. YOU EVER TRY DIGGIN' A SIX-FOOT HOLE? HE'S EXHAUSTED.
WHAT'S HE GONNA DO TO ME?

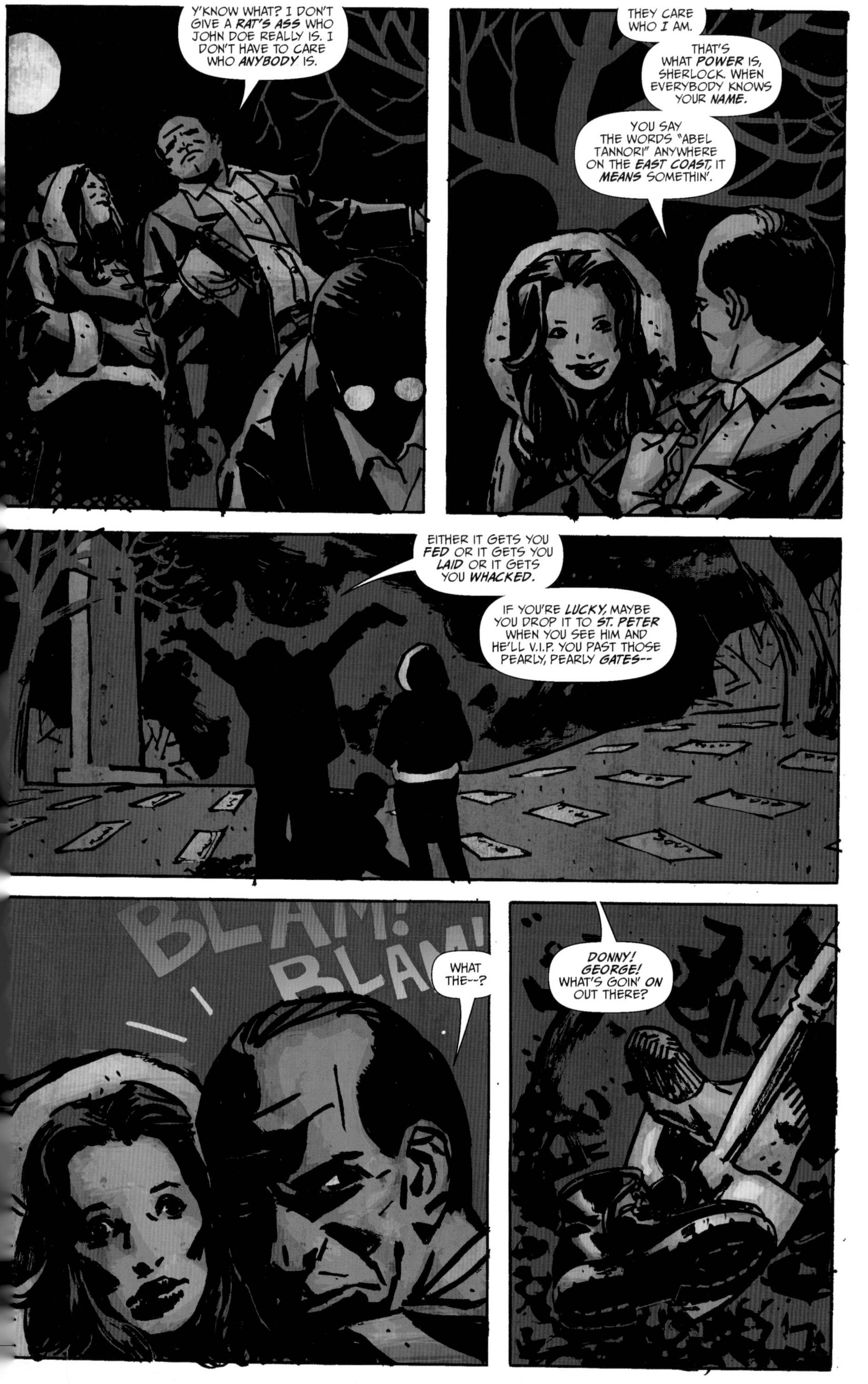
Y'KNOW WHAT? I DON'T GIVE A RAT'S ASS WHO JOHN DOE REALLY IS. I DON'T HAVE TO CARE WHO ANYBODY IS.
THEY CARE WHO I AM.
THAT'S WHAT POWER IS, SHERLOCK. WHEN EVERYBODY KNOWS YOUR NAME.
YOU SAY THE WORDS "ABEL TANNORI" ANYWHERE ON THE EAST COAST, IT MEANS SOMETHIN'.
EITHER IT GETS YOU FED OR IT GETS YOU LAID OR IT GETS YOU WHACKED.
IF YOU'RE LUCKY, MAYBE YOU DROP IT TO ST. PETER WHEN YOU SEE HIM AND HE'LL V.I.P. YOU PAST THOSE PEARLY, PEARLY GATES--
BLAM!
WHAT THE--?
DONNY! GEORGE! WHAT'S GOIN' ON OUT THERE?

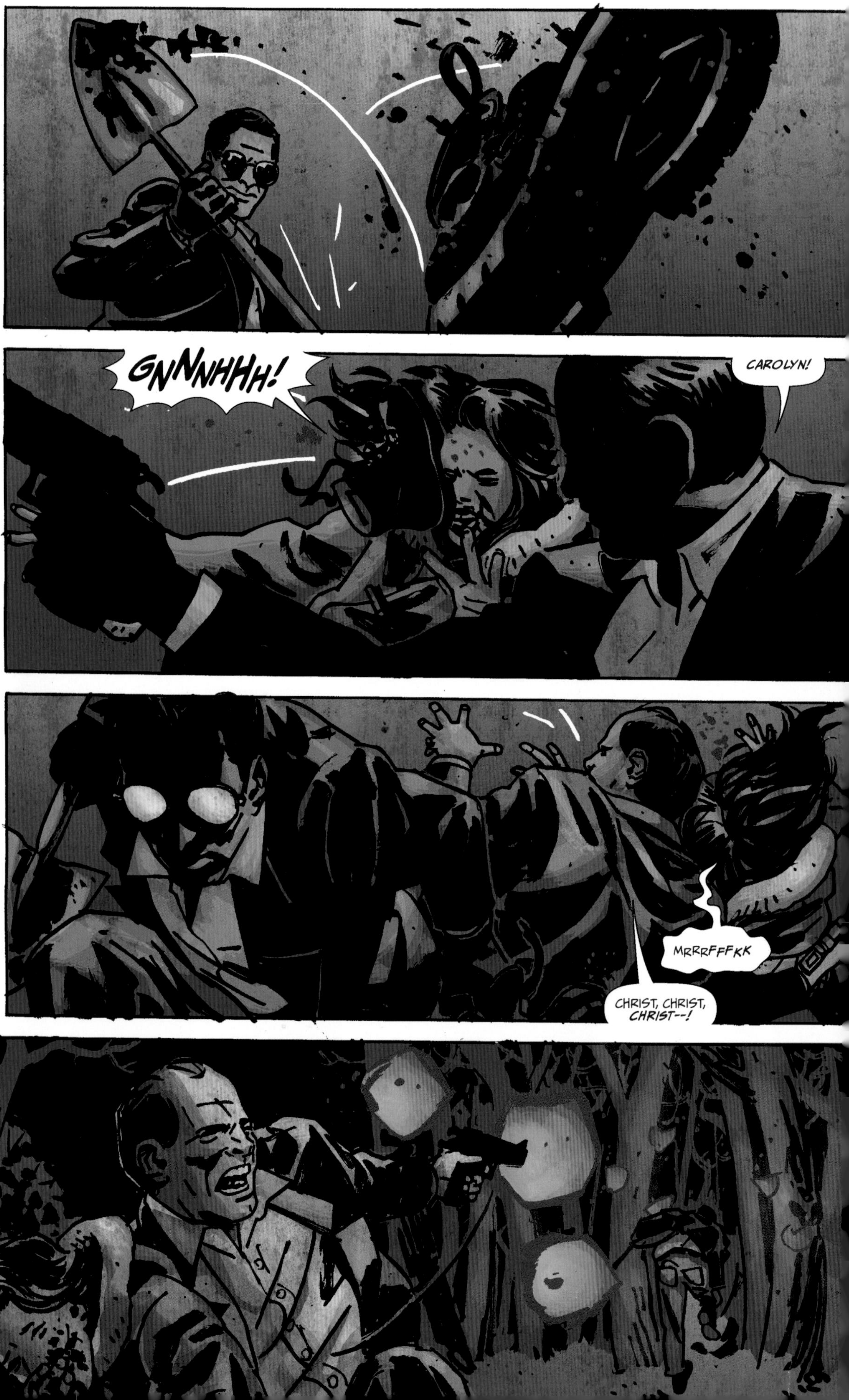
GNNNHHH!
CAROLYN!
MRRRFFFKK
CHRIST, CHRIST, CHRIST--!

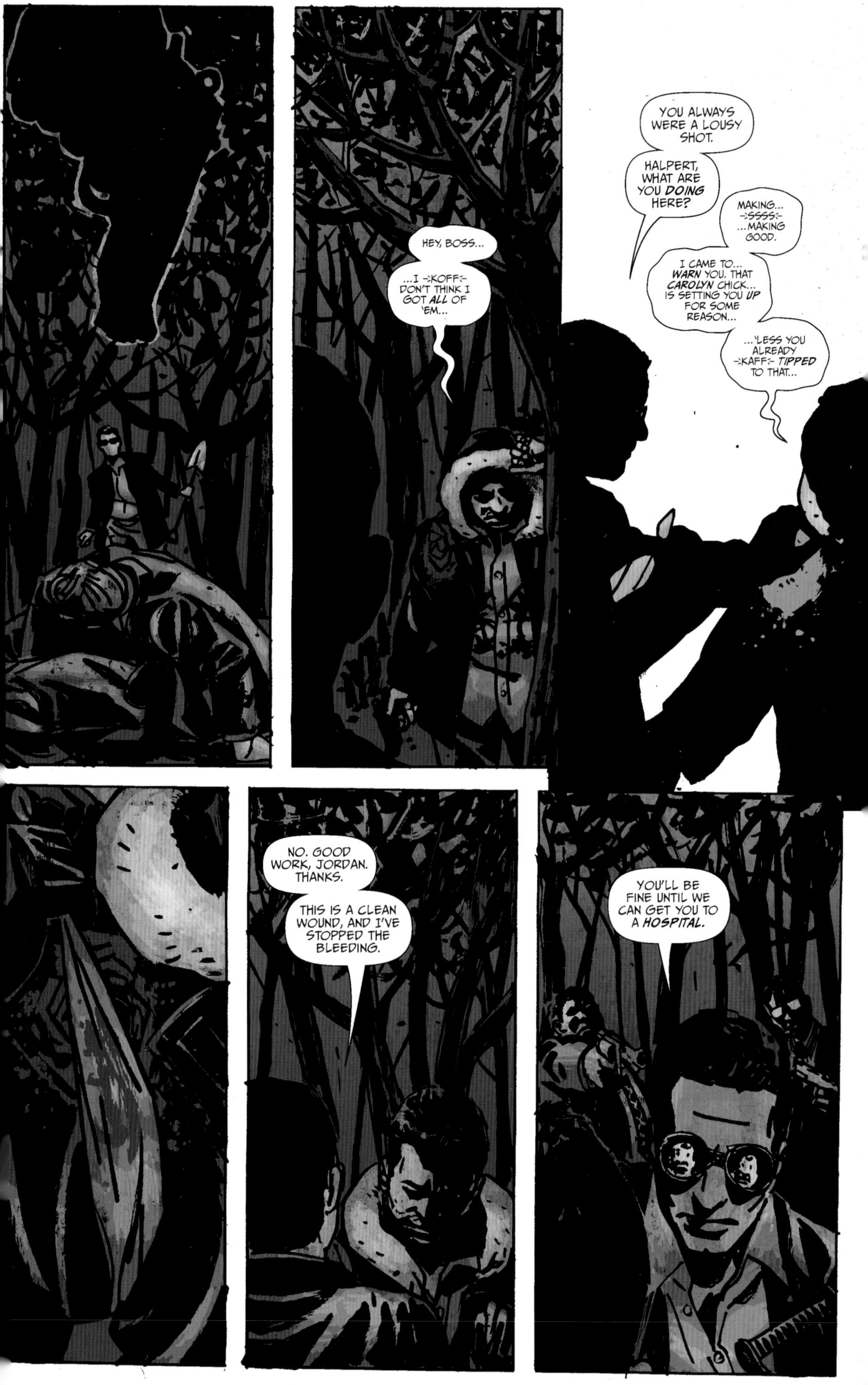

HEY, BOSS...
...I -KOFF- DON'T THINK I GOT ALL OF 'EM...
YOU ALWAYS WERE A LOUSY SHOT.
HALPERT, WHAT ARE YOU DOING HERE?
MAKING... -SSSS- ...MAKING GOOD.
I CAME TO... WARN YOU. THAT CAROLYN CHICK... IS SETTING YOU UP FOR SOME REASON...
...'LESS YOU ALREADY -KAFF- TIPPED TO THAT...
NO. GOOD WORK, JORDAN. THANKS.
THIS IS A CLEAN WOUND, AND I'VE STOPPED THE BLEEDING.
YOU'LL BE FINE UNTIL WE CAN GET YOU TO A HOSPITAL.

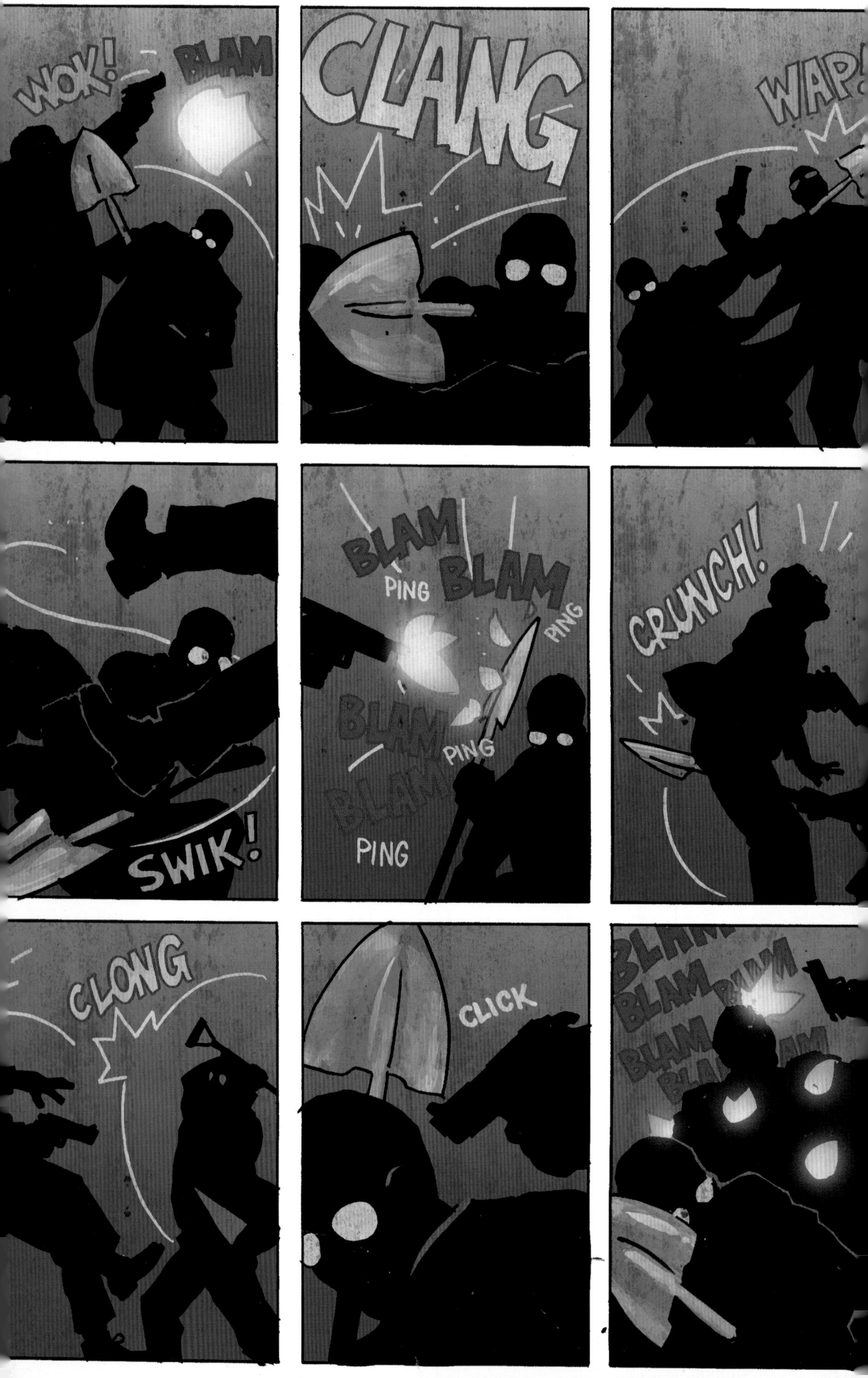
WOK!
BLAM
CLANG
WAP!
SWIK!
BLAM
PING
BLAM
PING
BLAM
PING
BLAM
PING
CRUNCH!
CLONG
CLICK
BLAM
BLAM

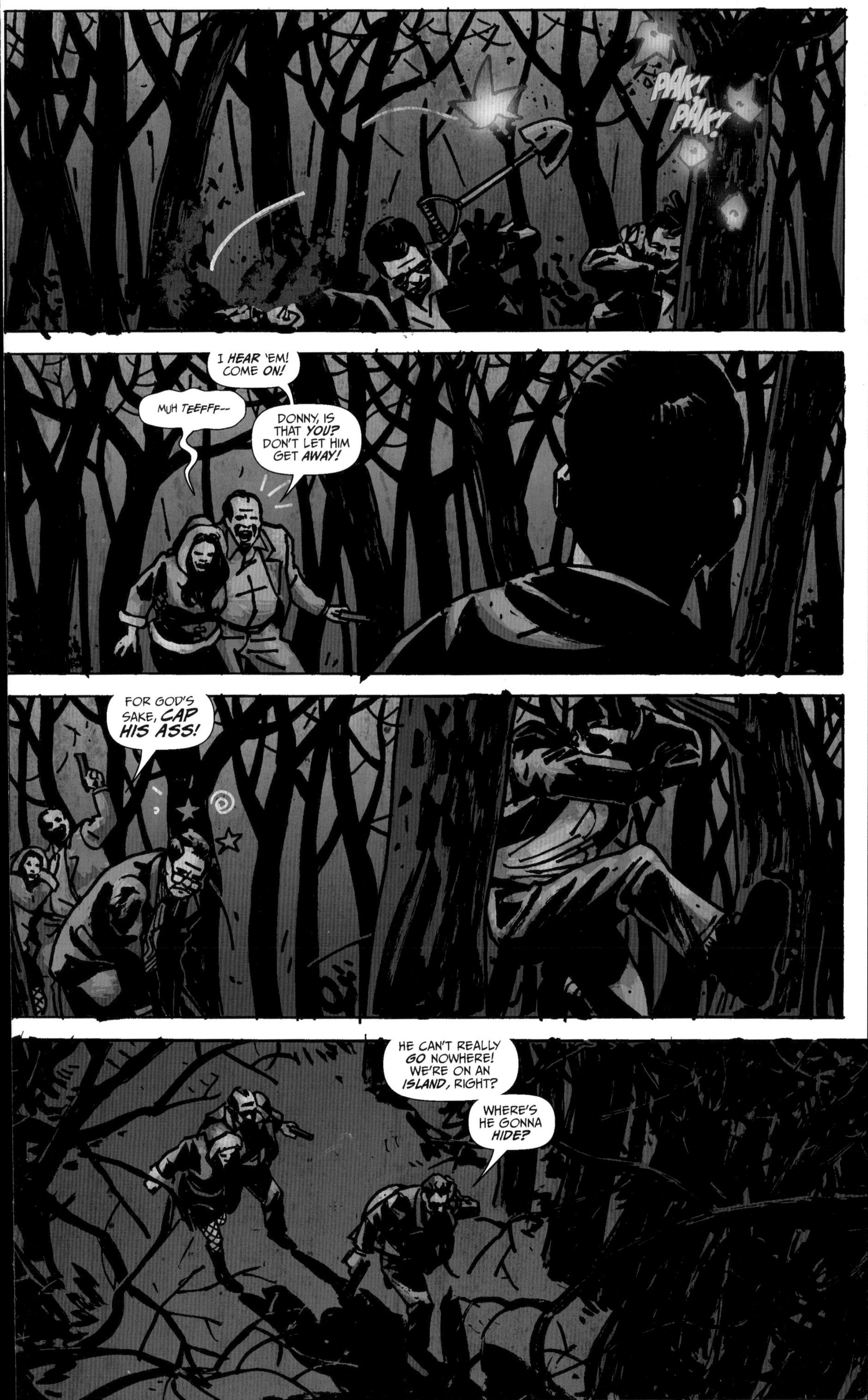
PAK! PAK!
I HEAR 'EM! COME ON!
MUH TEEFFF--
DONNY, IS THAT YOU? DON'T LET HIM GET AWAY!
FOR GOD'S SAKE, CAP HIS ASS!
HE CAN'T REALLY GO NOWHERE! WE'RE ON AN ISLAND, RIGHT?
WHERE'S HE GONNA HIDE?

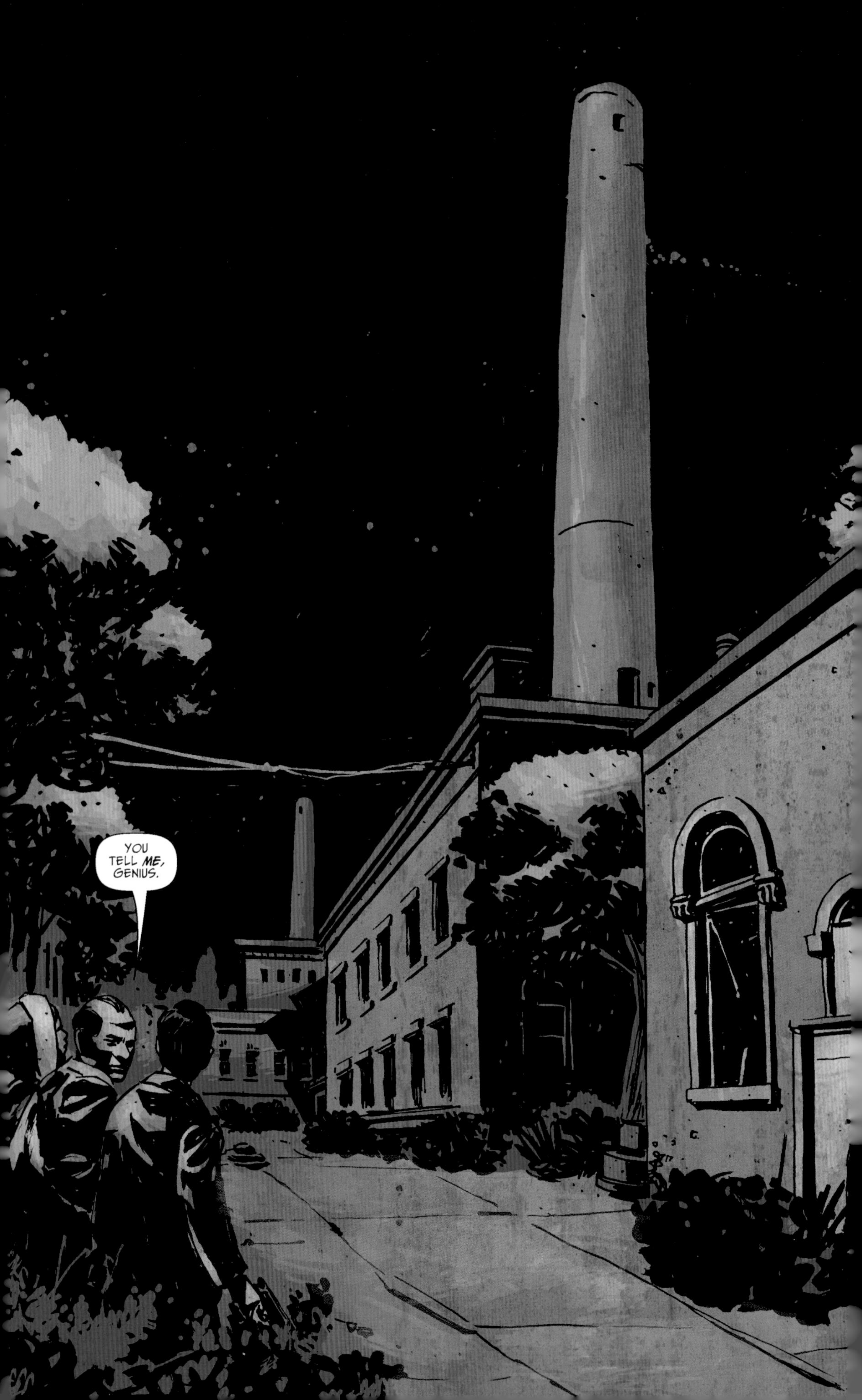
YOU TELL ME, GENIUS.

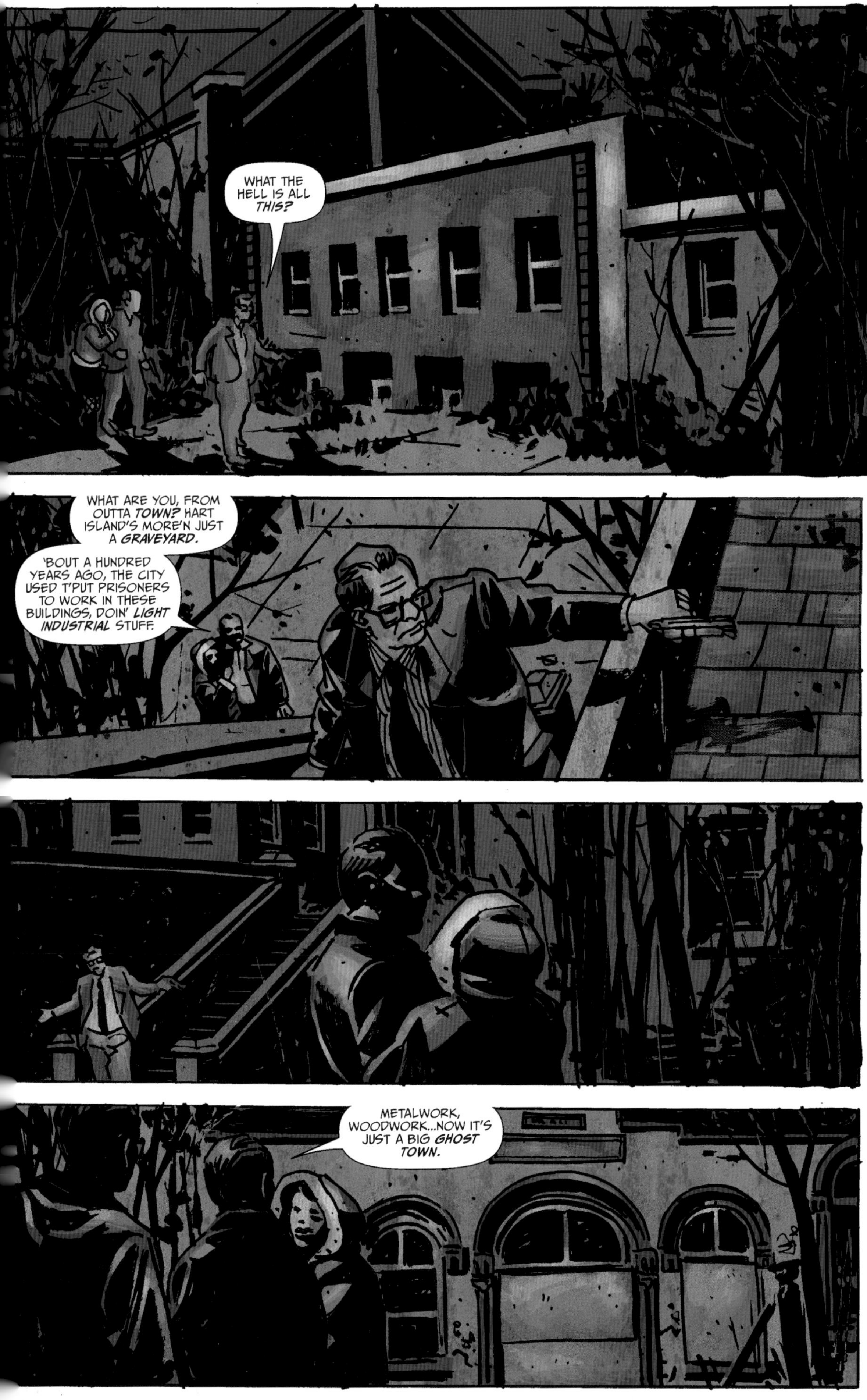
WHAT THE HELL IS ALL THIS?
WHAT ARE YOU, FROM OUTTA TOWN? HART ISLAND'S MORE'N JUST A GRAVEYARD.
'BOUT A HUNDRED YEARS AGO, THE CITY USED T'PUT PRISONERS TO WORK IN THESE BUILDINGS, DOIN' LIGHT INDUSTRIAL STUFF.
METALWORK, WOODWORK...NOW IT'S JUST A BIG GHOST TOWN.

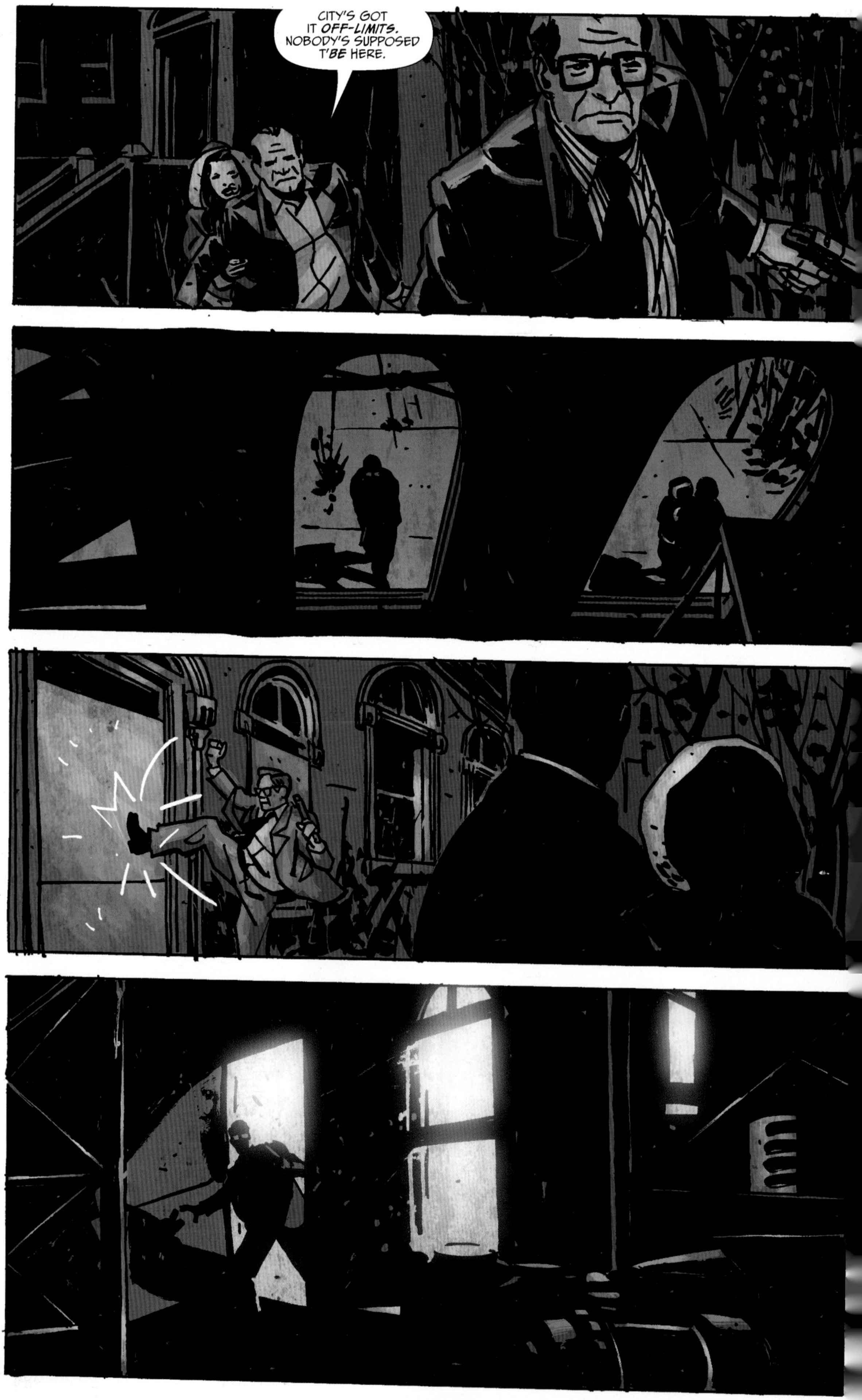
CITY'S GOT IT OFF-LIMITS. NOBODY'S SUPPOSED T'BE HERE.

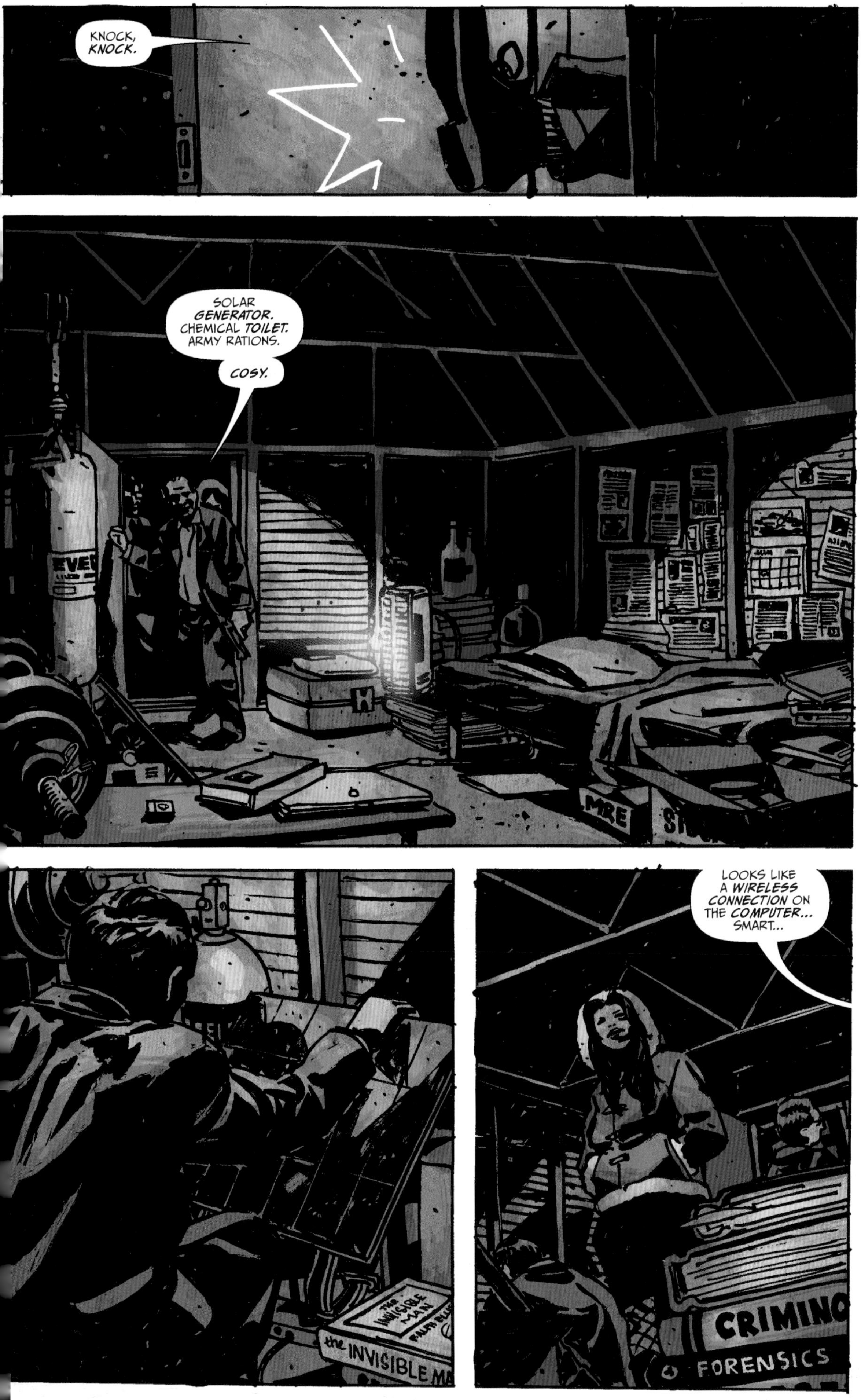
KNOCK, KNOCK.
SOLAR GENERATOR. CHEMICAL TOILET. ARMY RATIONS.
COSY.
MRE
LOOKS LIKE A WIRELESS CONNECTION ON THE COMPUTER... SMART...
CRIMINO
FORENSICS

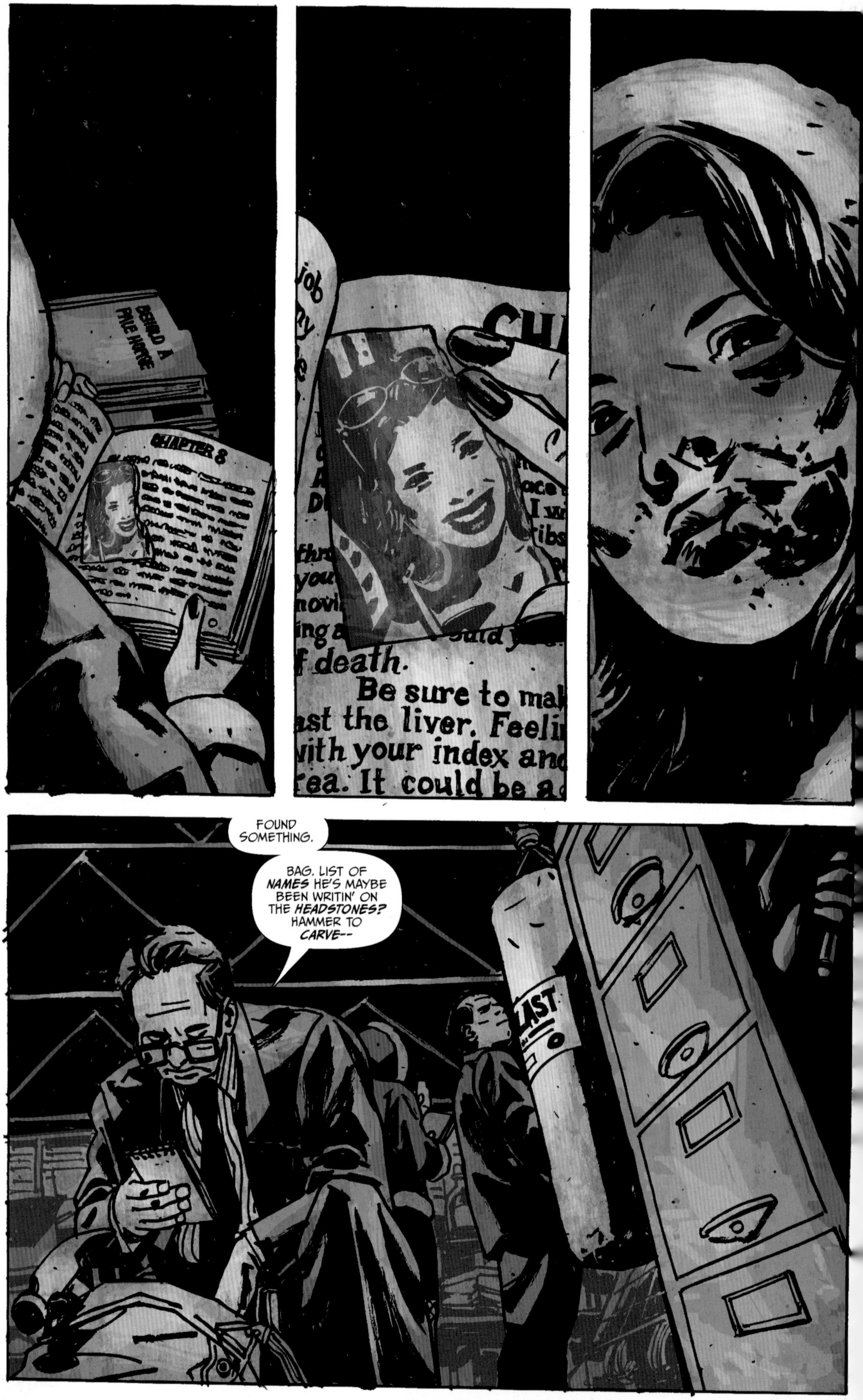
BEHOLD A PALE HORSE
CHAPTER 8
of death.
Be sure to mak
ast the liver. Feelir
with your index and
rea. It could be a
FOUND SOMETHING.
BAG. LIST OF *NAMES* HE'S MAYBE BEEN WRITIN' ON THE *HEADSTONES?* HAMMER TO *CARVE--*
LAST

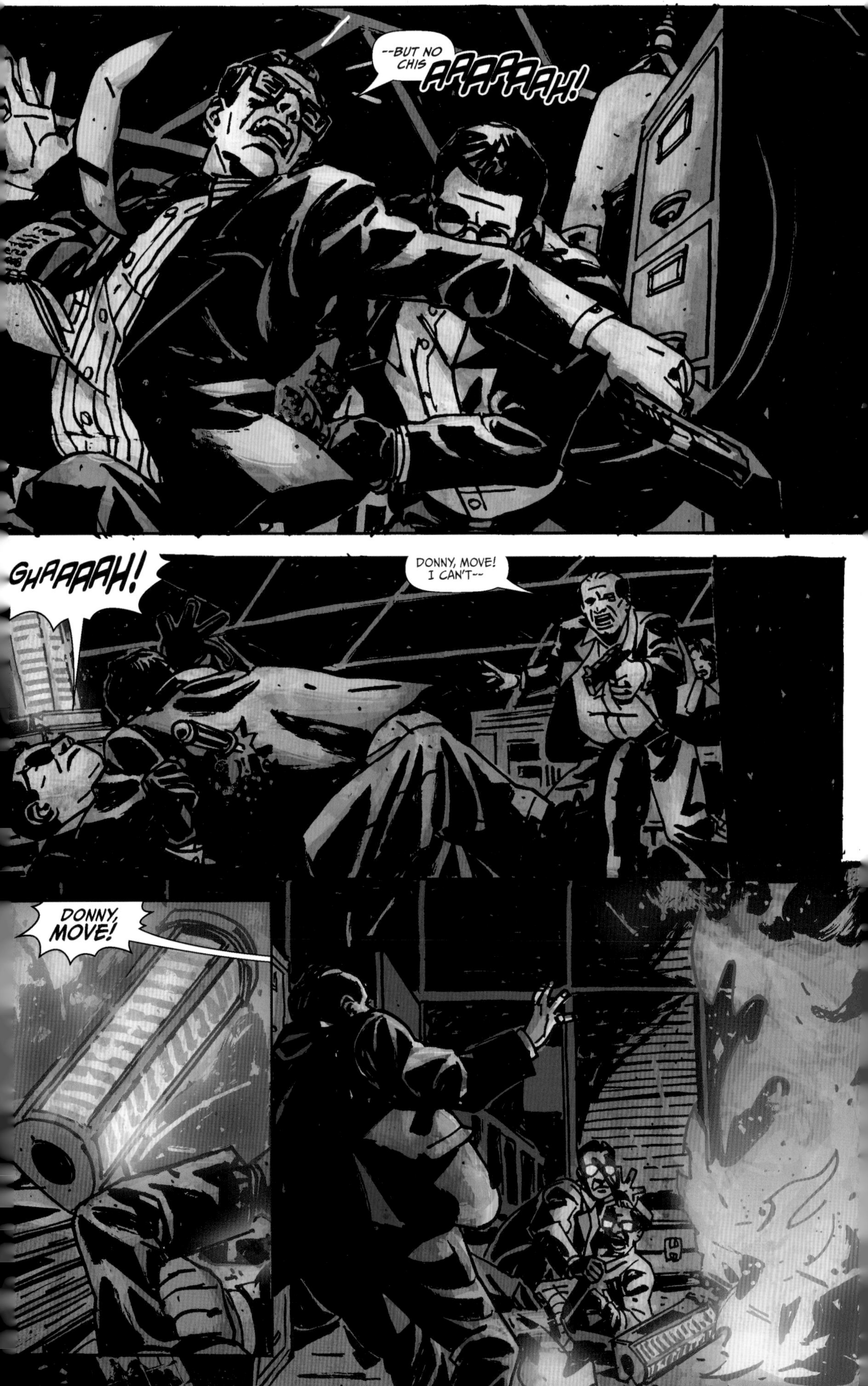
--BUT NO CHIS AAAAAAAH!
GHAAAAH!
DONNY, MOVE! I CAN'T--
DONNY, MOVE!

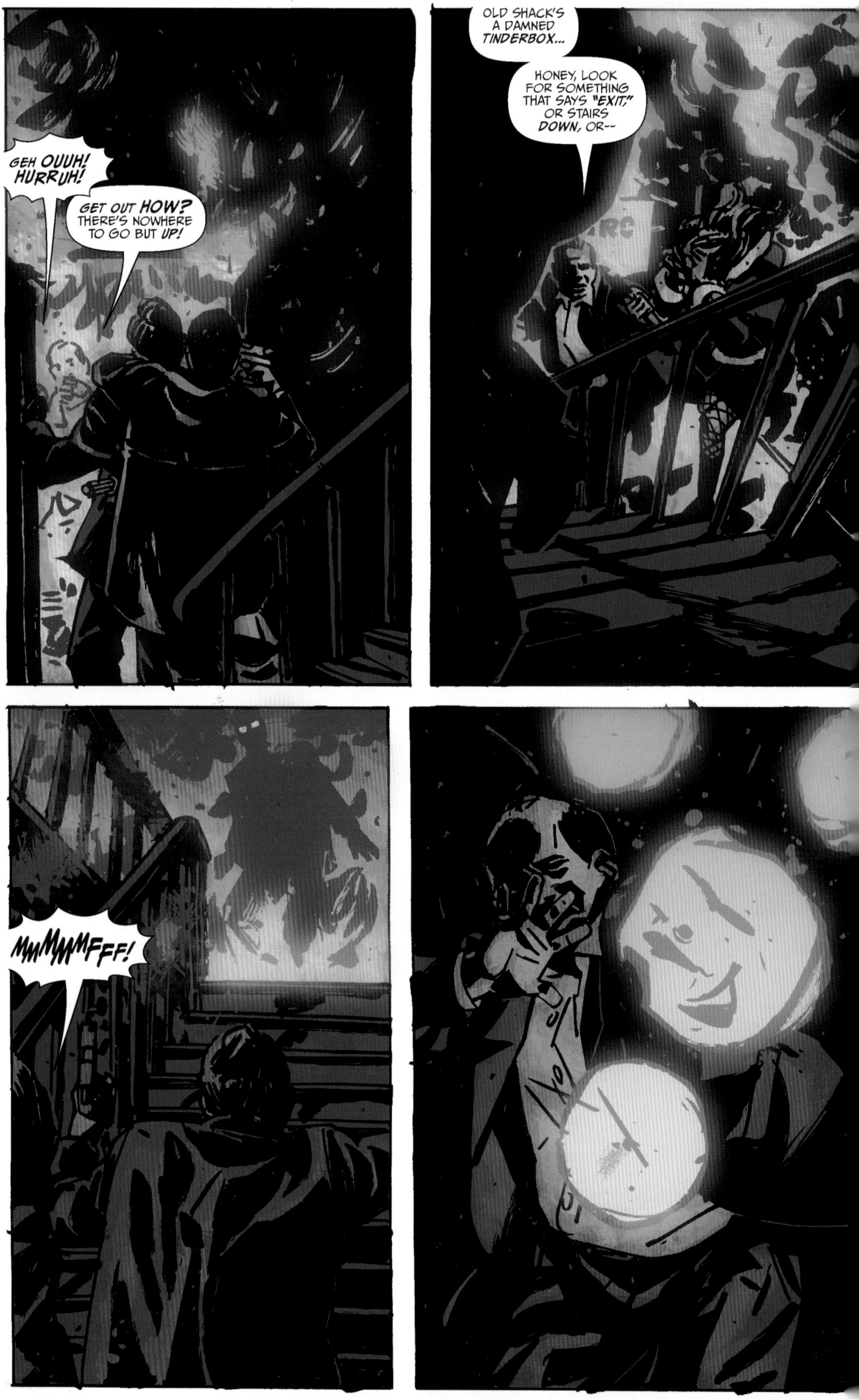
GEH OUUH! HURRUH!
GET OUT HOW? THERE'S NOWHERE TO GO BUT UP!
OLD SHACK'S A DAMNED TINDERBOX...
HONEY, LOOK FOR SOMETHING THAT SAYS "EXIT," OR STAIRS DOWN, OR--
MMMMMMFFF!

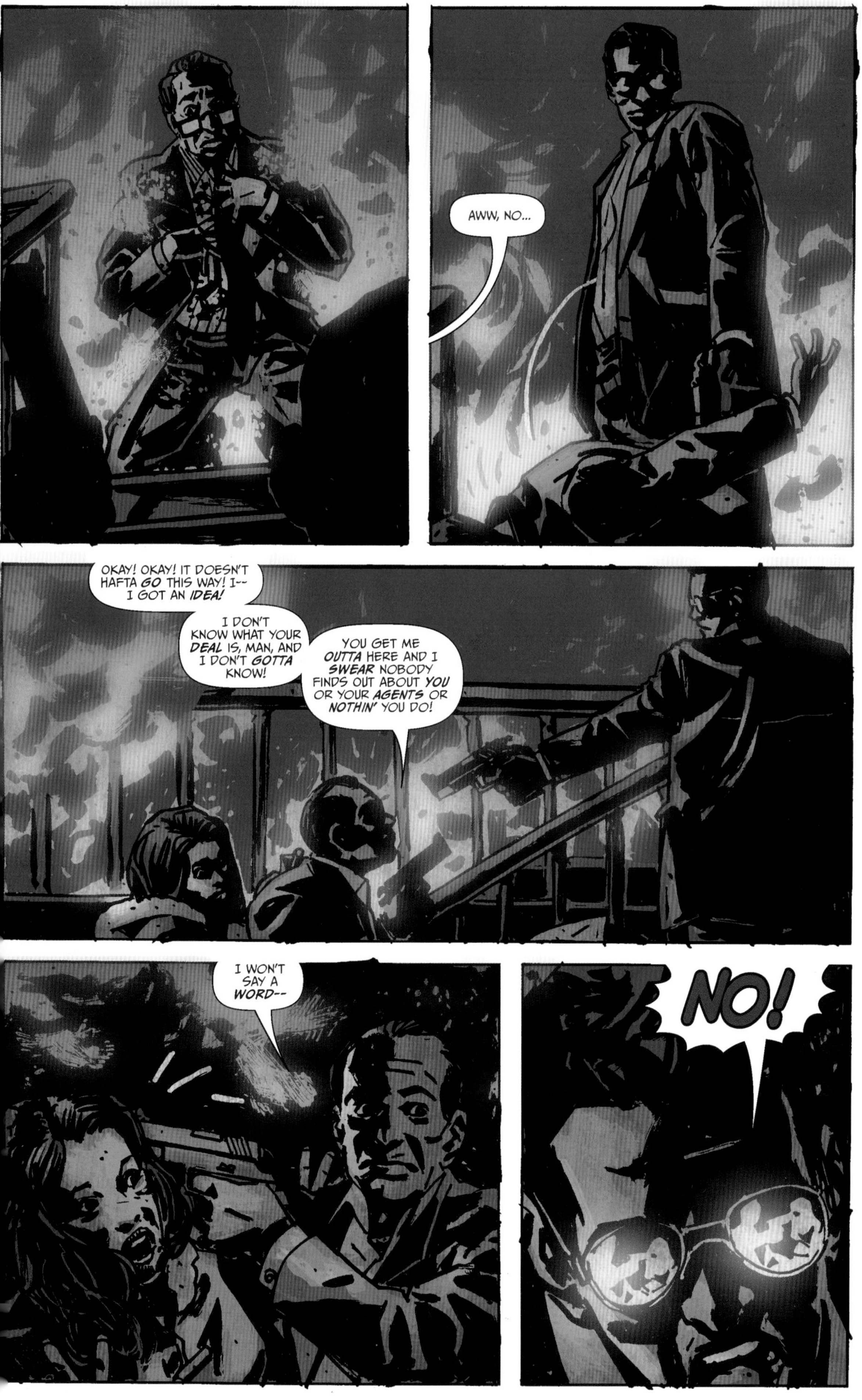
AWW, NO...
OKAY! OKAY! IT DOESN'T HAFTA GO THIS WAY! I-- I GOT AN IDEA!
I DON'T KNOW WHAT YOUR DEAL IS, MAN, AND I DON'T GOTTA KNOW!
YOU GET ME OUTTA HERE AND I SWEAR NOBODY FINDS OUT ABOUT YOU OR YOUR AGENTS OR NOTHIN' YOU DO!
I WON'T SAY A WORD--
NO!

--AND SHE WON'T, EITHER!

BLAM!

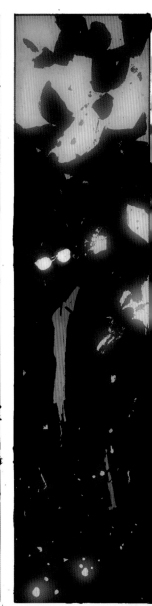

WAIT! ⤙KOFF!⤚ WAIT! WE HAVE A DEAL! WHERE'D YOU ⤙KOFF⤚

YOU SON OF A BITCH! YOU CAN'T ⤙KOFF⤚ ME!

I'M ⤙KOFF⤚ I'M A BIG MAN! I TOLD YOU, MY NAME MEANS SOMETHIN' IN THIS TOWN!

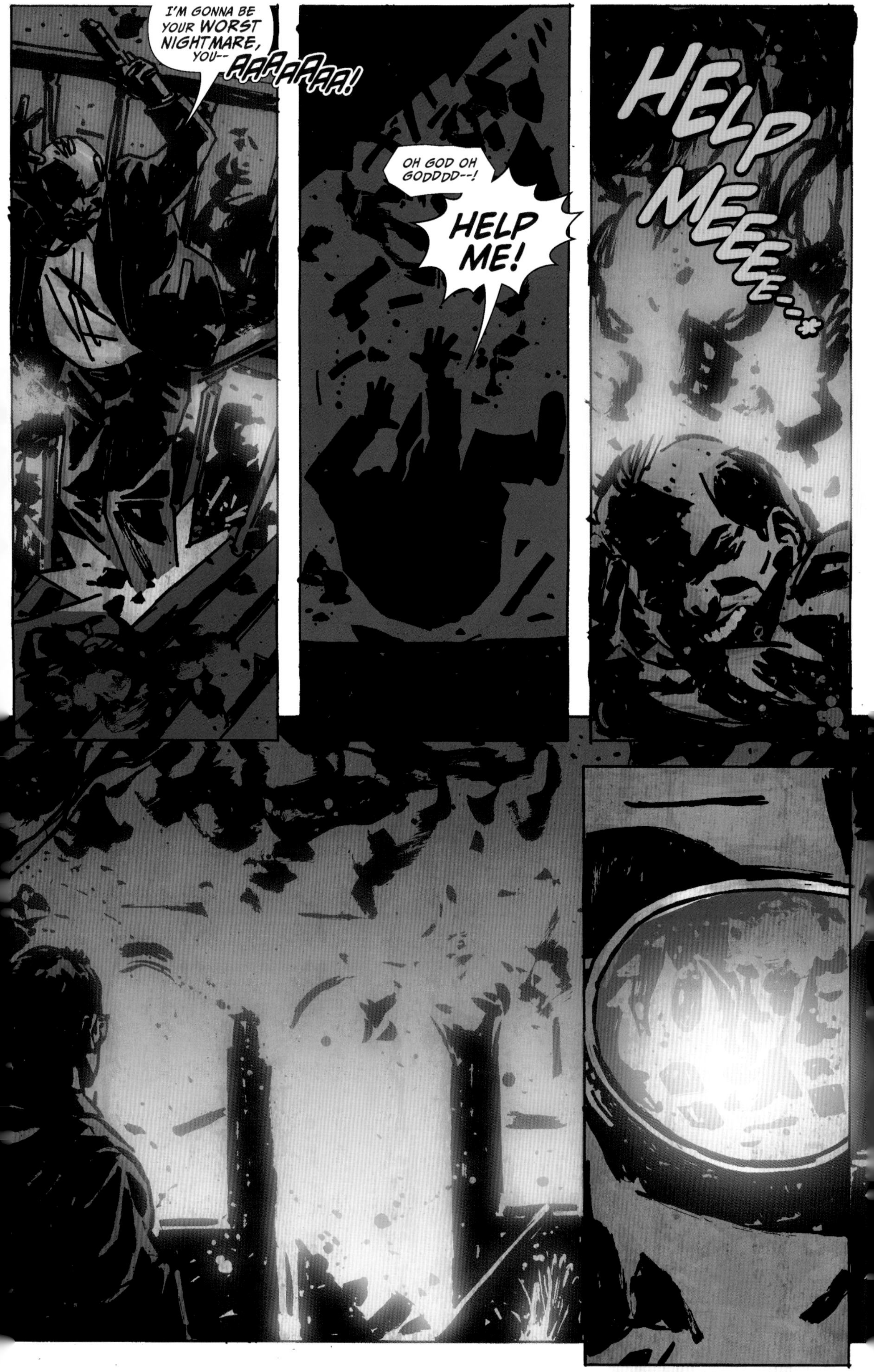
I'M GONNA BE YOUR WORST NIGHTMARE, YOU--
AAAAAAAA!
OH GOD OH GODDDD--!
HELP ME!
HELP MEEEE---*

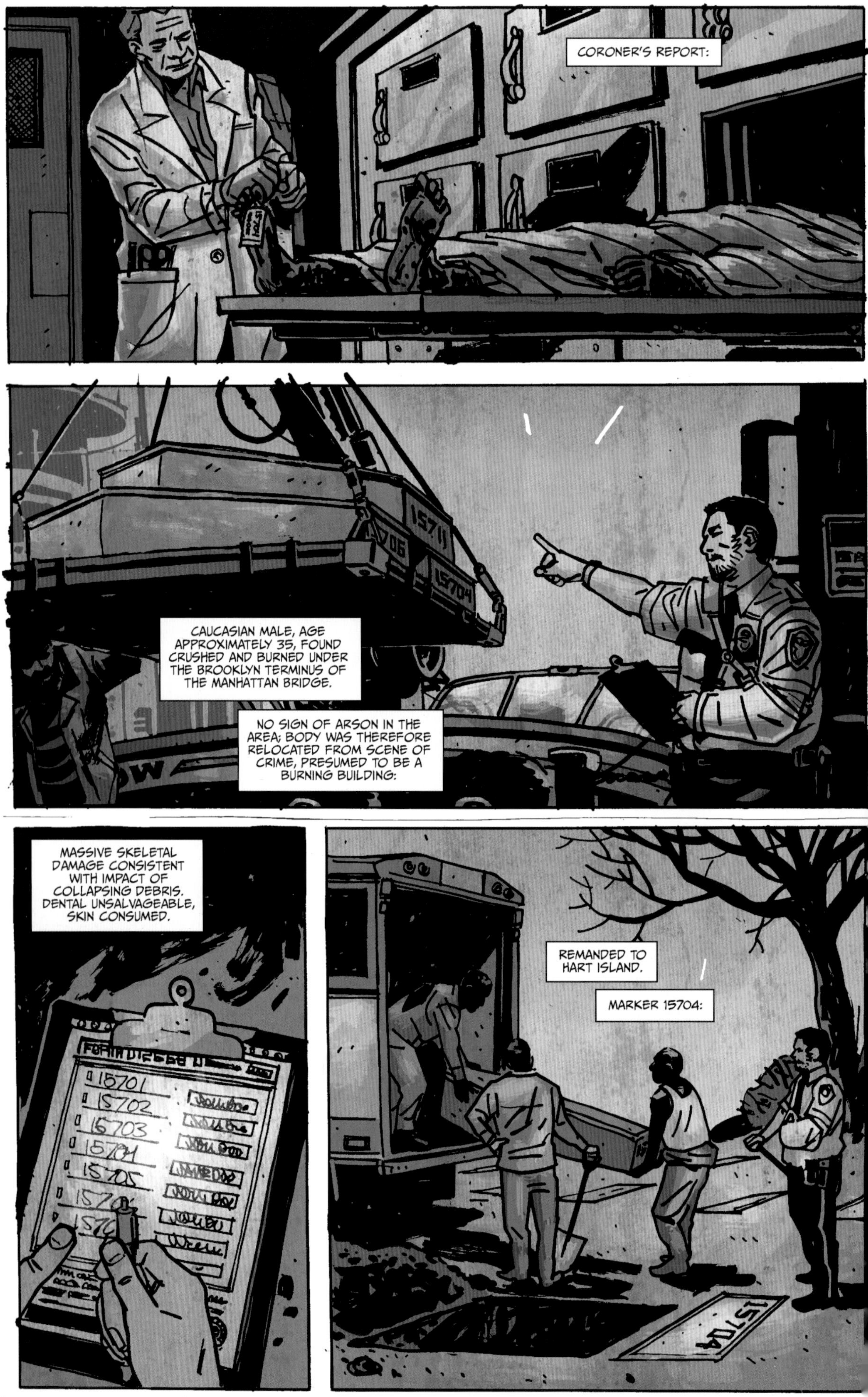
CORONER'S REPORT:
CAUCASIAN MALE, AGE APPROXIMATELY 35, FOUND CRUSHED AND BURNED UNDER THE BROOKLYN TERMINUS OF THE MANHATTAN BRIDGE.
NO SIGN OF ARSON IN THE AREA; BODY WAS THEREFORE RELOCATED FROM SCENE OF CRIME, PRESUMED TO BE A BURNING BUILDING:
MASSIVE SKELETAL DAMAGE CONSISTENT WITH IMPACT OF COLLAPSING DEBRIS. DENTAL UNSALVAGEABLE, SKIN CONSUMED.
REMANDED TO HART ISLAND.
MARKER 15704:

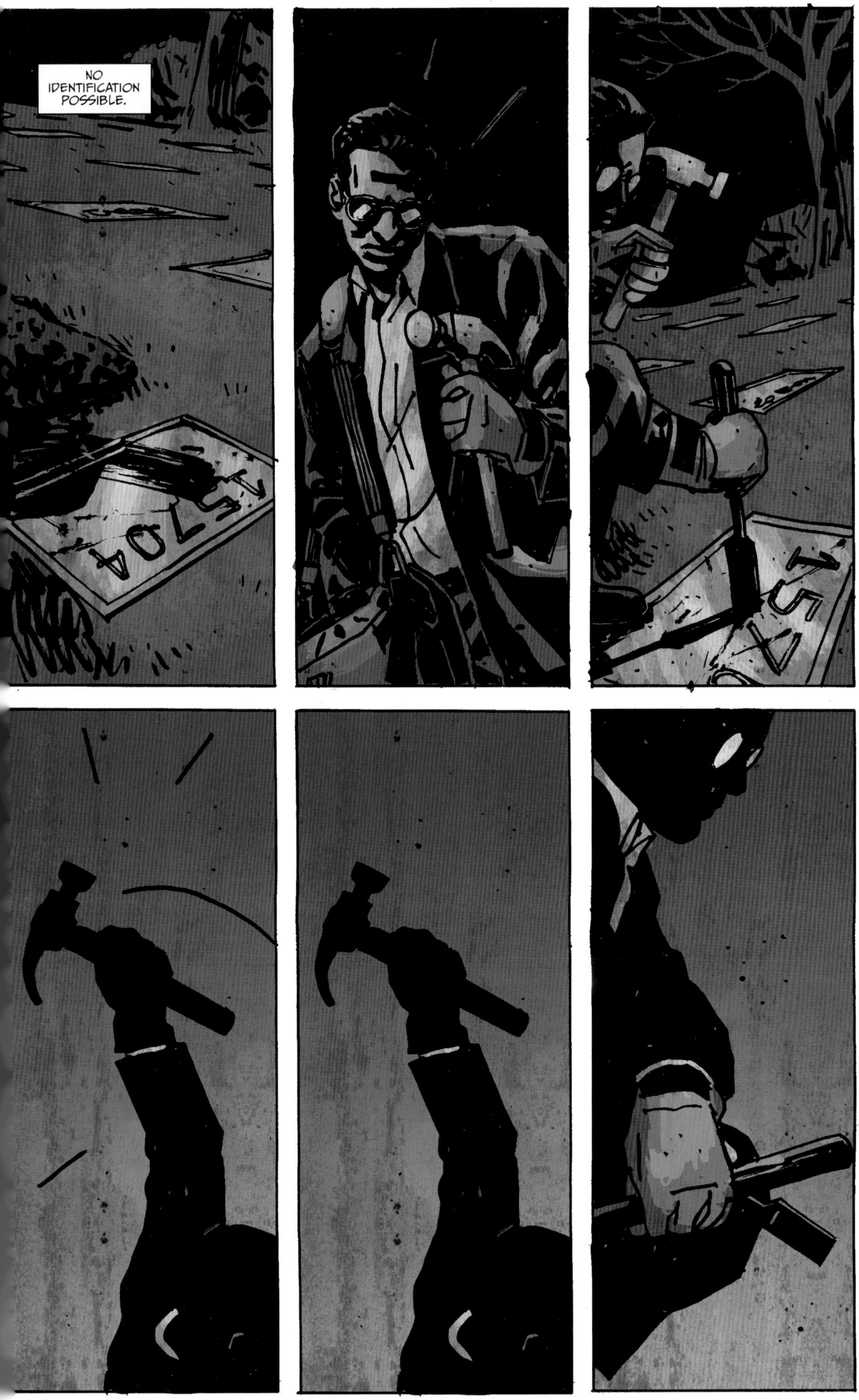
NO IDENTIFICATION POSSIBLE.
1570A
157A

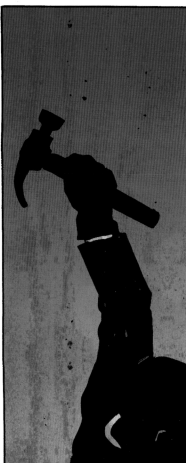

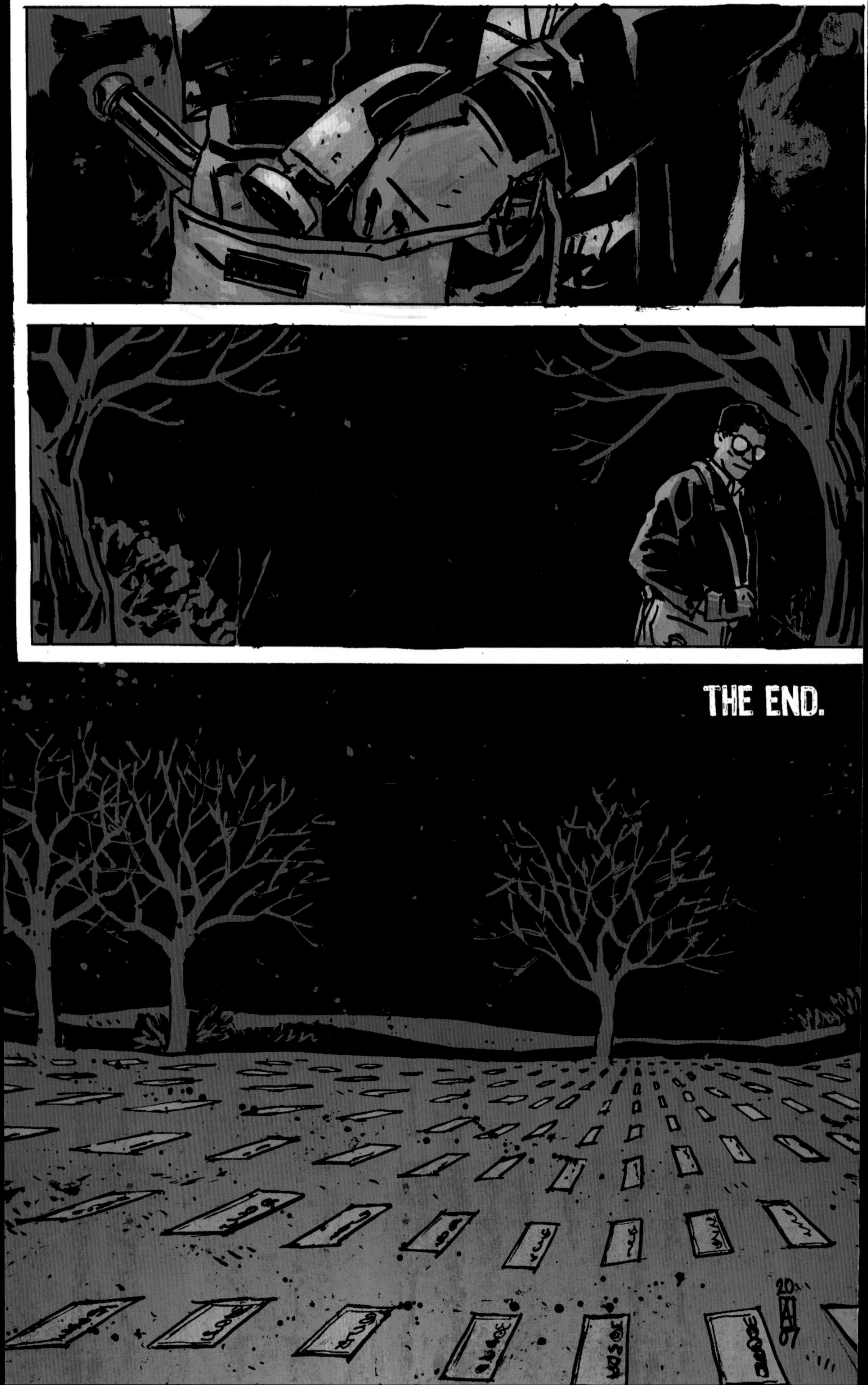
THE END.

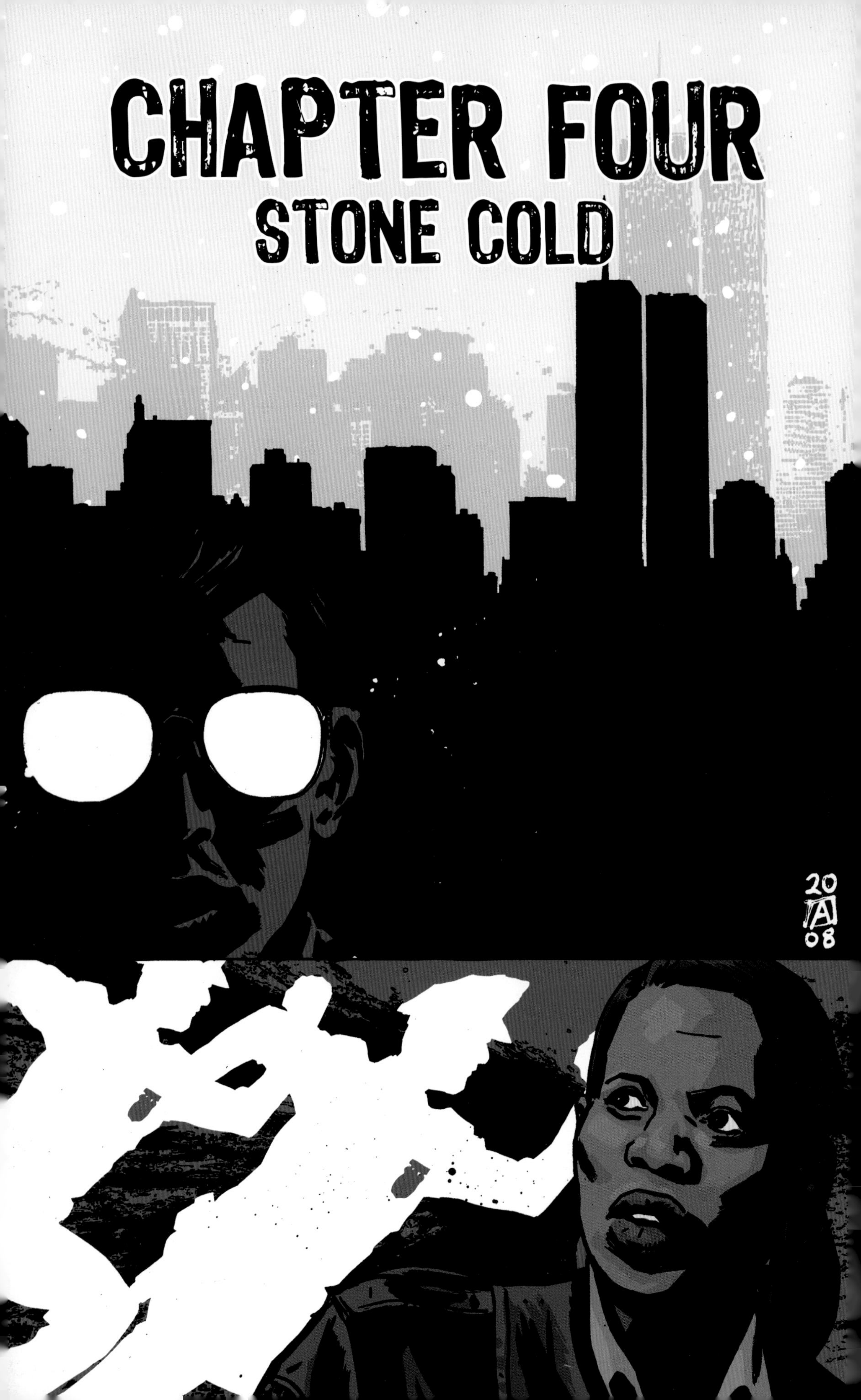
CHAPTER FOUR
STONE COLD
20 A 08

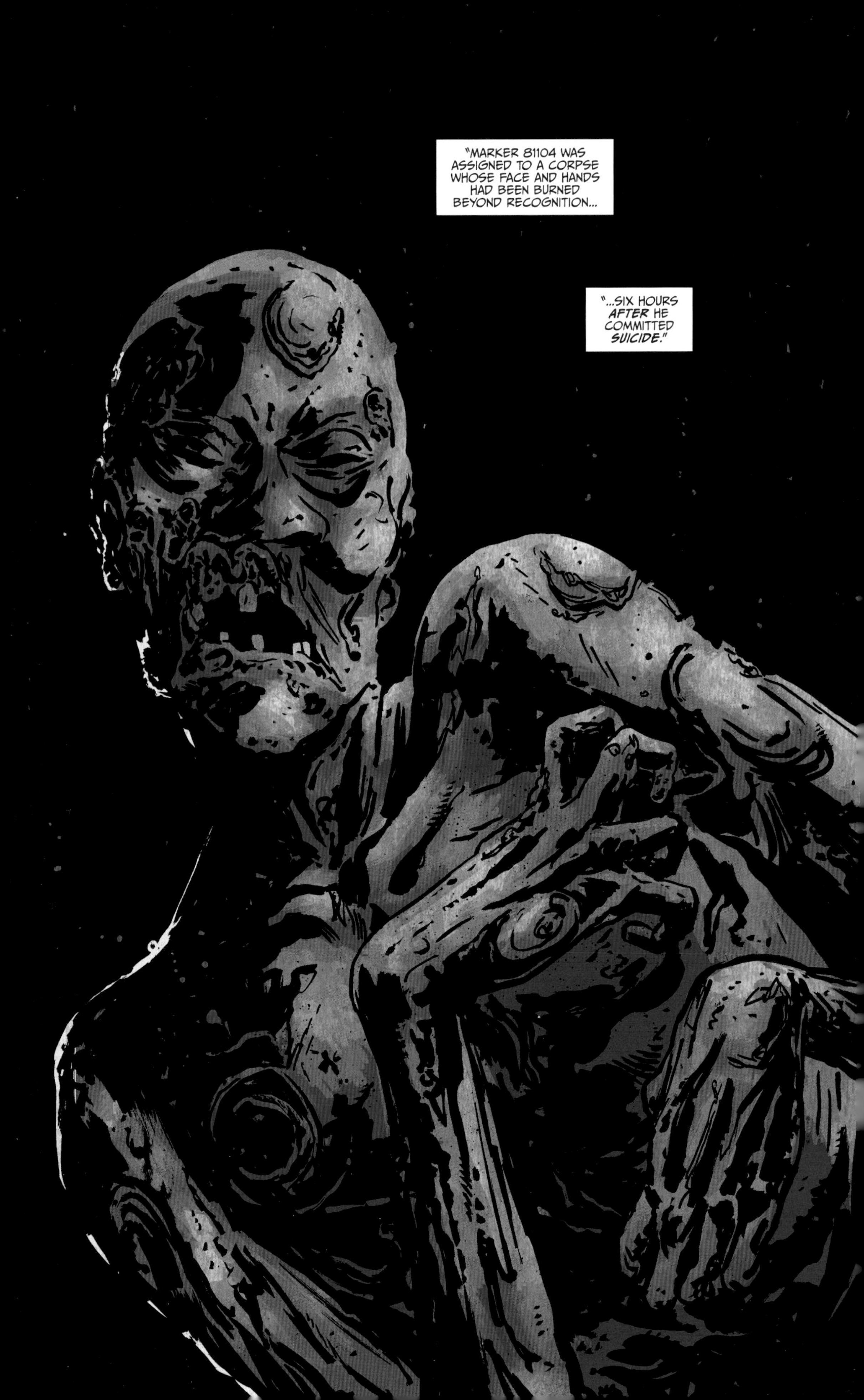
"MARKER 81104 WAS ASSIGNED TO A CORPSE WHOSE FACE AND HANDS HAD BEEN BURNED BEYOND RECOGNITION...
"...SIX HOURS *AFTER* HE COMMITTED *SUICIDE*."

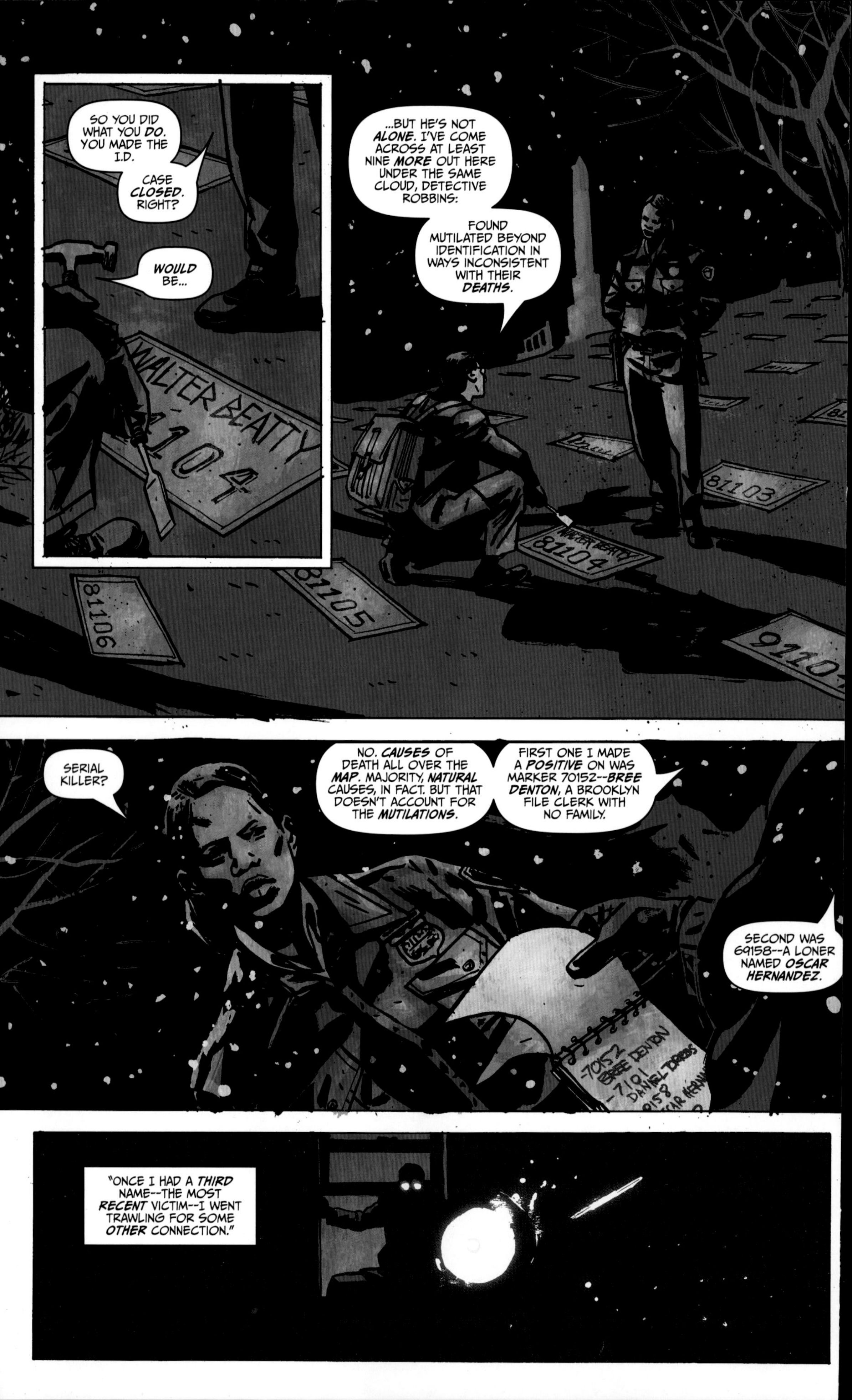

SO YOU DID WHAT YOU DO. YOU MADE THE I.D.
CASE CLOSED. RIGHT?
WOULD BE...
...BUT HE'S NOT ALONE. I'VE COME ACROSS AT LEAST NINE MORE OUT HERE UNDER THE SAME CLOUD, DETECTIVE ROBBINS:
FOUND MUTILATED BEYOND IDENTIFICATION IN WAYS INCONSISTENT WITH THEIR DEATHS.
WALTER BEATTY
81104
81103
81105
81106
SERIAL KILLER?
NO. CAUSES OF DEATH ALL OVER THE MAP. MAJORITY, NATURAL CAUSES, IN FACT. BUT THAT DOESN'T ACCOUNT FOR THE MUTILATIONS.
FIRST ONE I MADE A POSITIVE ON WAS MARKER 70152--BREE DENTON, A BROOKLYN FILE CLERK WITH NO FAMILY.
SECOND WAS 69158--A LONER NAMED OSCAR HERNANDEZ.
"ONCE I HAD A THIRD NAME--THE MOST RECENT VICTIM--I WENT TRAWLING FOR SOME OTHER CONNECTION."

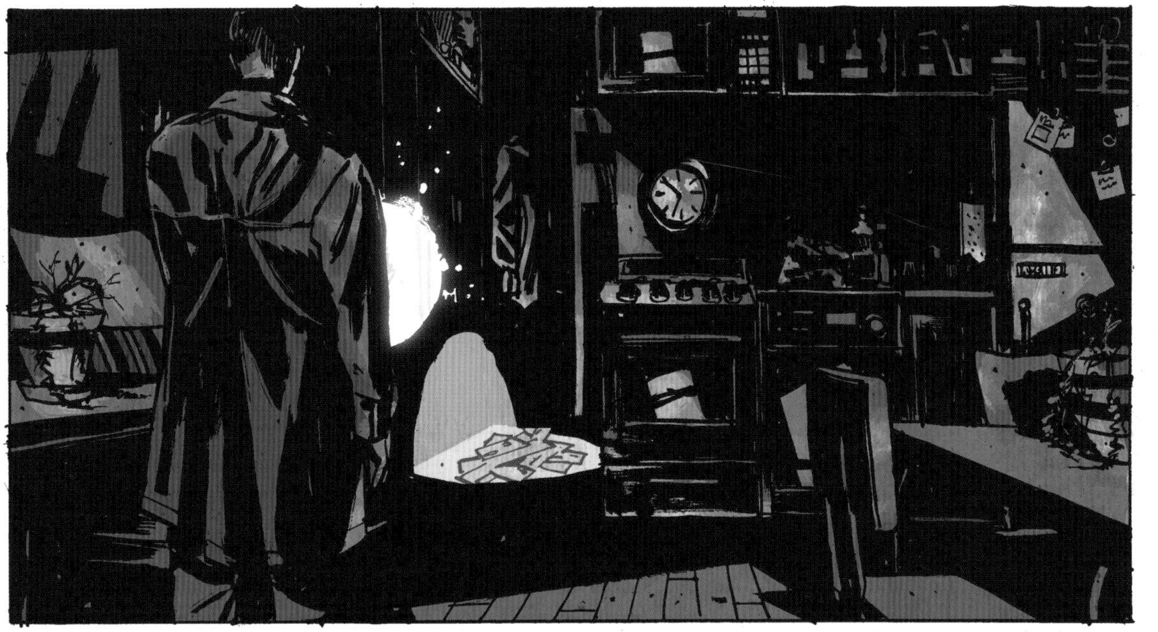

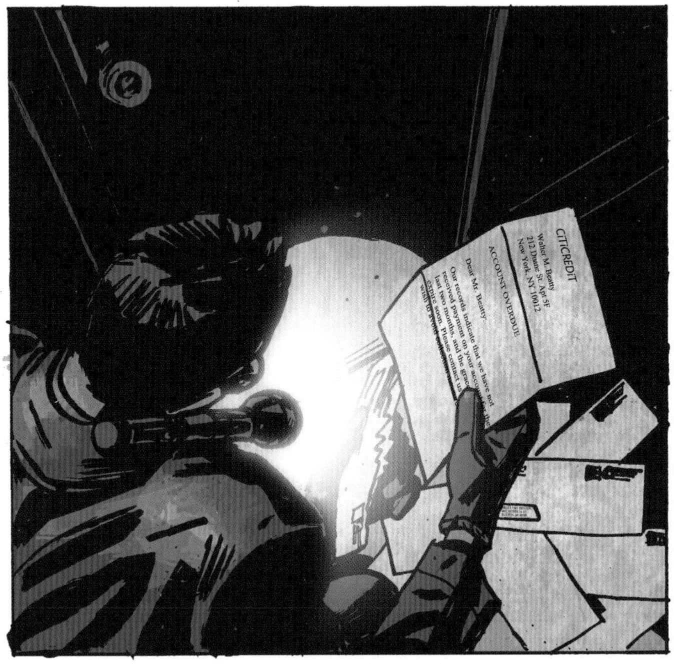
CiTiCREDiT
Walter M. Beatty
212 Duane St. Apt 5F
New York, NY 10012
ACCOUNT OVERDUE
Dear Mr. Beatty:

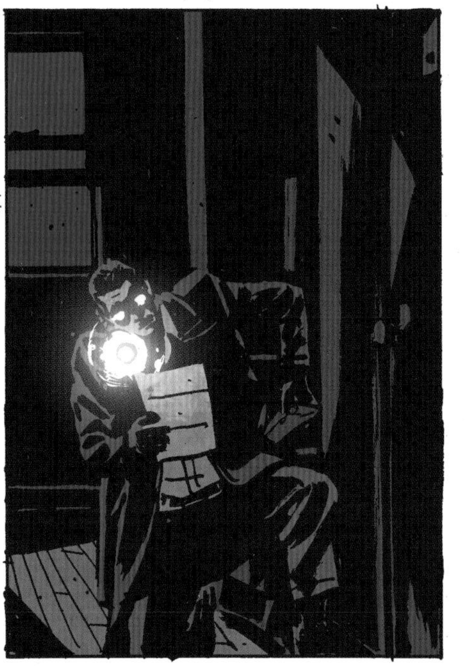

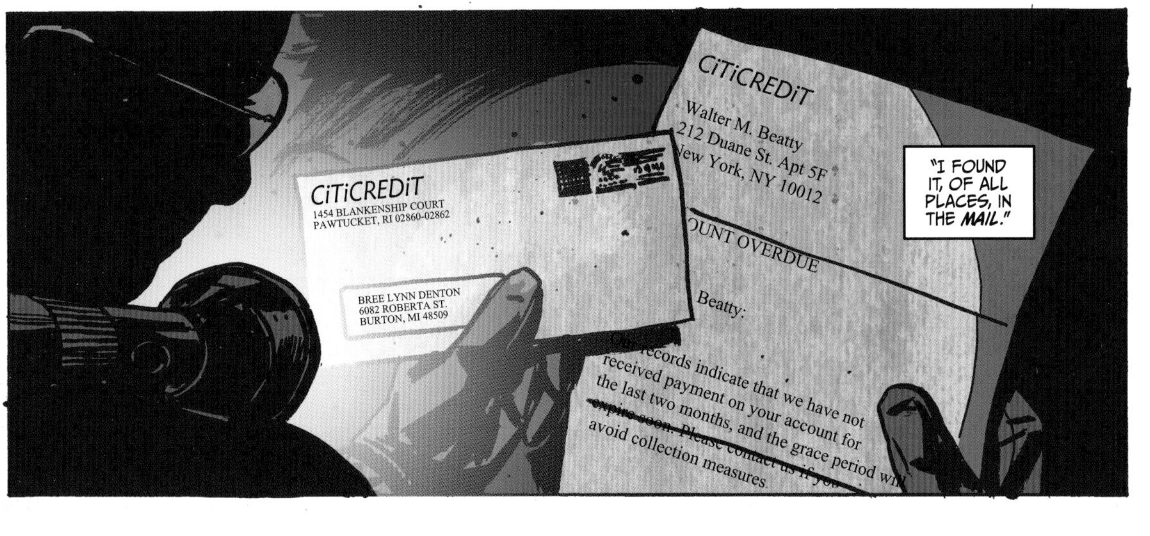
CiTiCREDiT
1454 BLANKENSHIP COURT
PAWTUCKET, RI 02860-02862
BREE LYNN DENTON
6082 ROBERTA ST.
BURTON, MI 48509
CiTiCREDiT
Walter M. Beatty
212 Duane St. Apt 5F
New York, NY 10012
OUNT OVERDUE
Beatty:
records indicate that we have not
received payment on your account for
the last two months, and the grace period wi
expire soon. Please contact us if yo
avoid collection measures.
"I FOUND IT, OF ALL PLACES, IN THE *MAIL*."

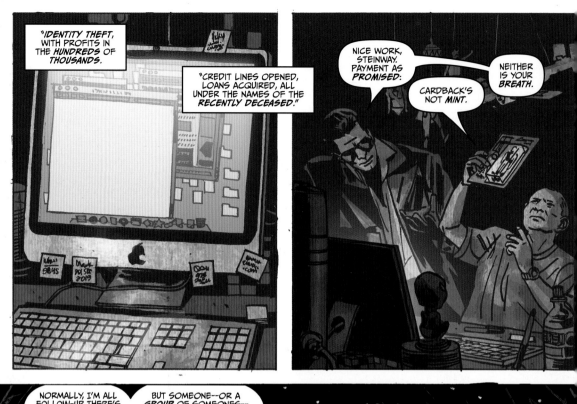

"IDENTITY THEFT, WITH PROFITS IN THE *HUNDREDS* OF *THOUSANDS.*"

"CREDIT LINES OPENED, LOANS ACQUIRED, ALL UNDER THE NAMES OF THE *RECENTLY DECEASED.*"

NICE WORK, STEINWAY. PAYMENT AS *PROMISED:*

CARDBACK'S NOT *MINT.*

NEITHER IS YOUR *BREATH.*

NORMALLY, I'M ALL FOLLOW-UP. THERE'S NOT MUCH I CAN DO IN THIS JOB IN THE WAY OF *PREVENTIVE MAINTENTANCE.*

BUT SOMEONE--OR A *GROUP* OF SOMEONES-- IS OUT THERE HARVESTING THE NAMES AND BACKGROUNDS OF NEW YORK'S *DEAD* AND SENDING *ME* WHAT'S LEFT.

AND WE'RE GOING TO *STOP* THAT.

I....

OH, GOD, THAT'S GRISLY. SURE. OKAY. OF COURSE.

WHO ELSE ARE YOU PULLING IN ON THIS?

JUST YOU. YOU'RE ENOUGH.

I APPRECIATE THE VOTE OF CONFIDENCE.

IT'S NOT ABOUT THAT.

THE MUTILATED BODIES HAVE BEEN SPREAD OUT OVER TIME--BUT NOT FAR OUT OVER *AREA.*

HARDLY ANY WERE FOUND NEAR A CRIME SCENE, BUT ALL OF THEM I'VE BEEN ABLE TO *NAME* LIVED IN TRIBECA OR THE FINANCIAL DISTRICT.

MY BEAT.

YEAH. AND I HAD TO ASK MYSELF WHY THE POLICE DIDN'T QUESTION THE *PATTERN.*

WHOEVER'S *DOING* THIS MAY NOT BE DOING THE ACTUAL *KILLING*-- BUT HE, OR THEY, CAN SUSS OUT PRETTY *QUICKLY* WHICH CORPSES ARE *PRIME TARGETS* TO TURN *ANONYMOUS.*

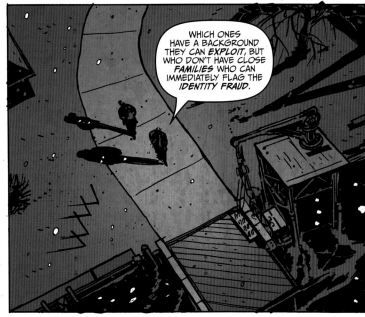

WHICH ONES HAVE A BACKGROUND THEY CAN *EXPLOIT,* BUT WHO DON'T HAVE CLOSE *FAMILIES* WHO CAN IMMEDIATELY FLAG THE *IDENTITY FRAUD.*

THAT NARROWS IT DOWN *SOME,* I SUPPOSE.

LET'S GO *FURTHER.* TO DO HIS *WORK,* WHOEVER'S FINDING THE BODIES HAS TO BE *FIRST* ON SCENE.

I DON'T UNDERSTAND. HOW ARE THEY COMING IN AHEAD OF THE *COPS?*

...

THEY'RE *NOT,* DETECTIVE.

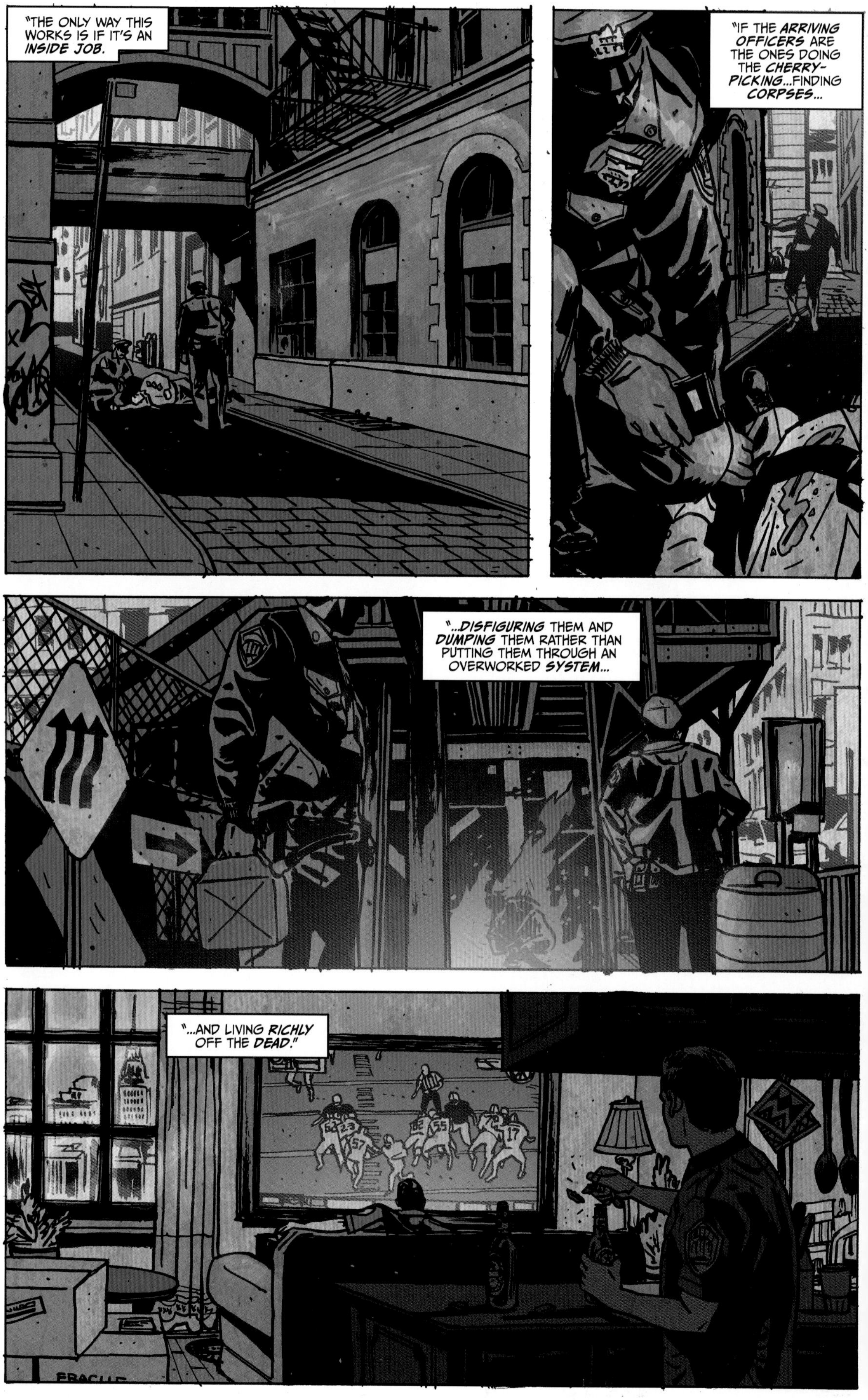
"THE ONLY WAY THIS WORKS IS IF IT'S AN INSIDE JOB.
"IF THE ARRIVING OFFICERS ARE THE ONES DOING THE CHERRY-PICKING...FINDING CORPSES...
"...DISFIGURING THEM AND DUMPING THEM RATHER THAN PUTTING THEM THROUGH AN OVERWORKED SYSTEM...
"...AND LIVING RICHLY OFF THE DEAD."

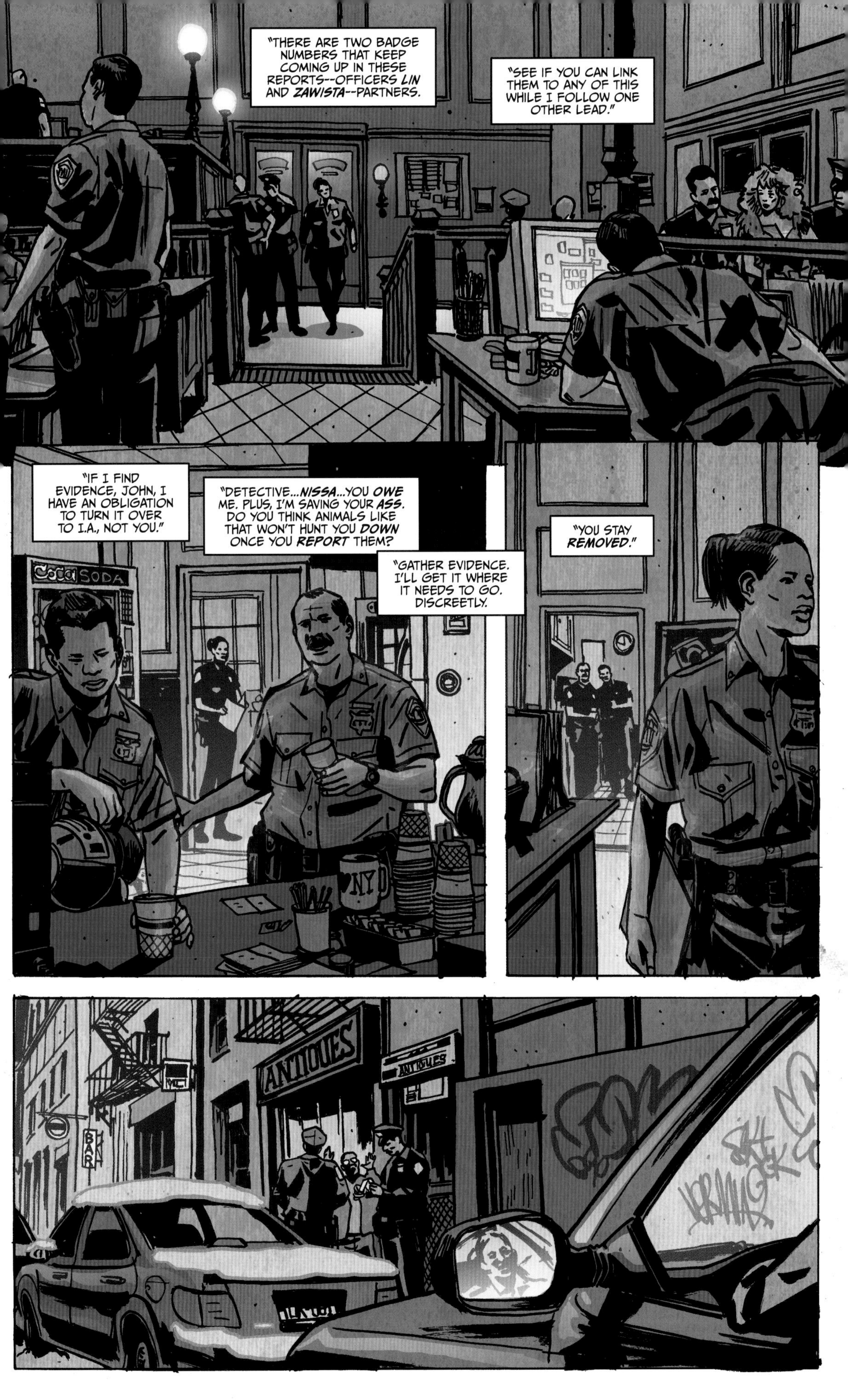
"THERE ARE TWO BADGE NUMBERS THAT KEEP COMING UP IN THESE REPORTS--OFFICERS LIN AND ZAWISTA--PARTNERS.
"SEE IF YOU CAN LINK THEM TO ANY OF THIS WHILE I FOLLOW ONE OTHER LEAD."
"IF I FIND EVIDENCE, JOHN, I HAVE AN OBLIGATION TO TURN IT OVER TO I.A., NOT YOU."
"DETECTIVE...NISSA...YOU OWE ME. PLUS, I'M SAVING YOUR ASS. DO YOU THINK ANIMALS LIKE THAT WON'T HUNT YOU DOWN ONCE YOU REPORT THEM?
"GATHER EVIDENCE. I'LL GET IT WHERE IT NEEDS TO GO. DISCREETLY.
"YOU STAY REMOVED."
SODA
ANTIQUES
ANTIQUES
BAR

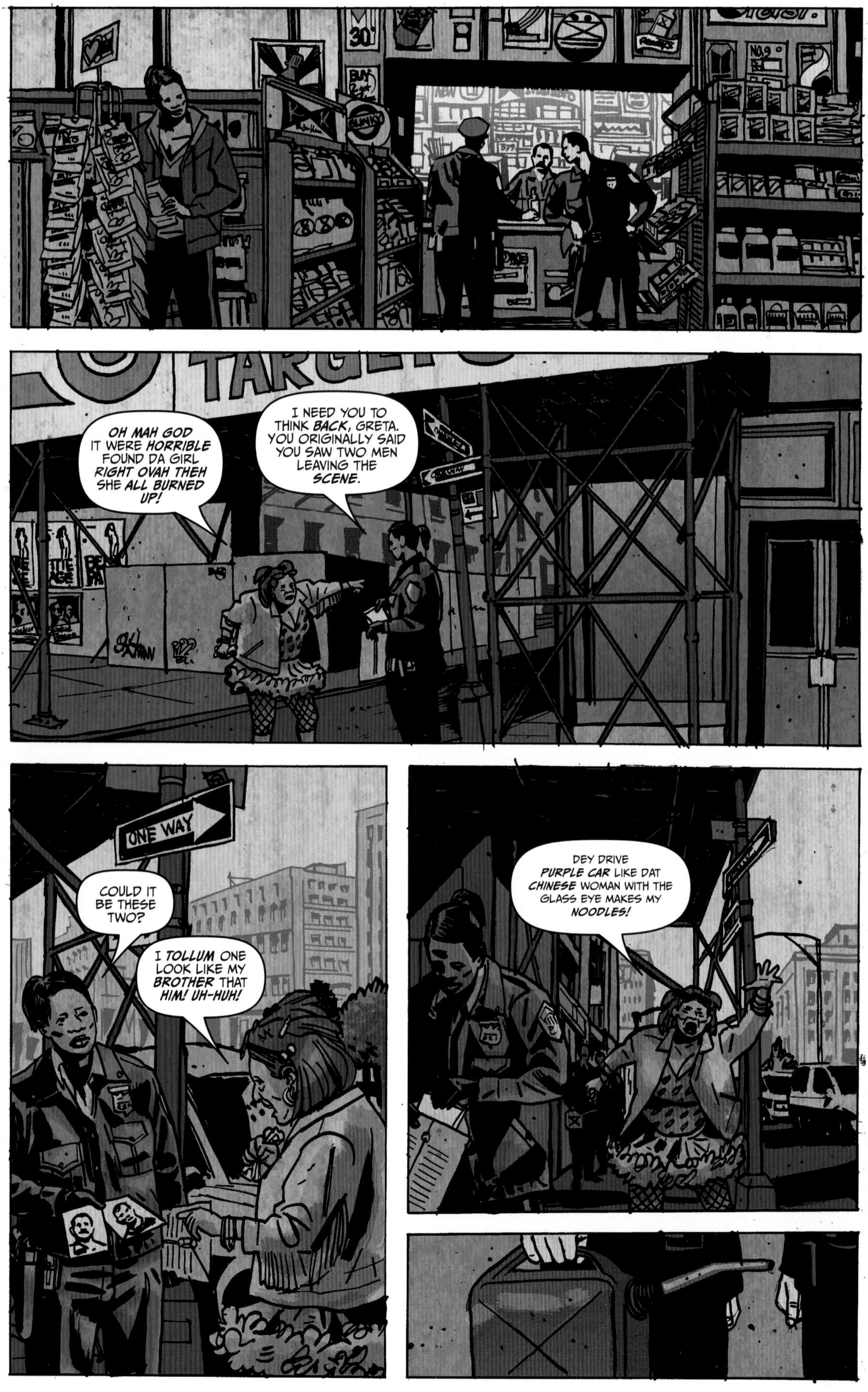
OH MAH GOD IT WERE HORRIBLE FOUND DA GIRL RIGHT OVAH THEH SHE ALL BURNED UP!
I NEED YOU TO THINK BACK, GRETA. YOU ORIGINALLY SAID YOU SAW TWO MEN LEAVING THE SCENE.
ONE WAY
COULD IT BE THESE TWO?
I TOLLUM ONE LOOK LIKE MY BROTHER THAT HIM! UH-HUH!
DEY DRIVE PURPLE CAR LIKE DAT CHINESE WOMAN WITH THE GLASS EYE MAKES MY NOODLES!

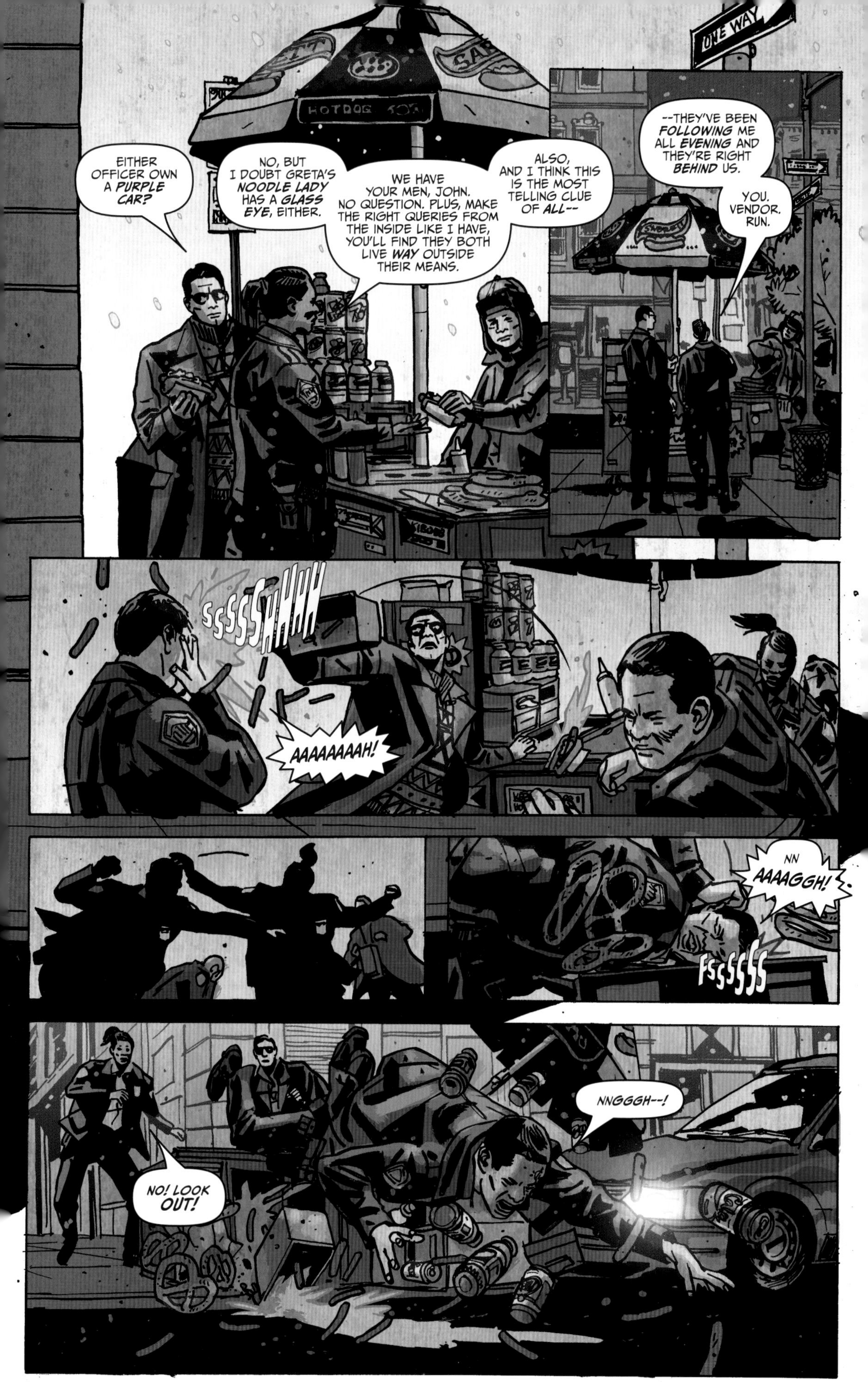
EITHER OFFICER OWN A PURPLE CAR?
NO, BUT I DOUBT GRETA'S NOODLE LADY HAS A GLASS EYE, EITHER.
WE HAVE YOUR MEN, JOHN. NO QUESTION. PLUS, MAKE THE RIGHT QUERIES FROM THE INSIDE LIKE I HAVE, YOU'LL FIND THEY BOTH LIVE WAY OUTSIDE THEIR MEANS.
ALSO, AND I THINK THIS IS THE MOST TELLING CLUE OF ALL--
--THEY'VE BEEN FOLLOWING ME ALL EVENING AND THEY'RE RIGHT BEHIND US.
YOU. VENDOR. RUN.
SSSSSHHHHH
AAAAAAAAH!
NN AAAAAGGH!
FSSSSSS
NNGGGH--!
NO! LOOK OUT!

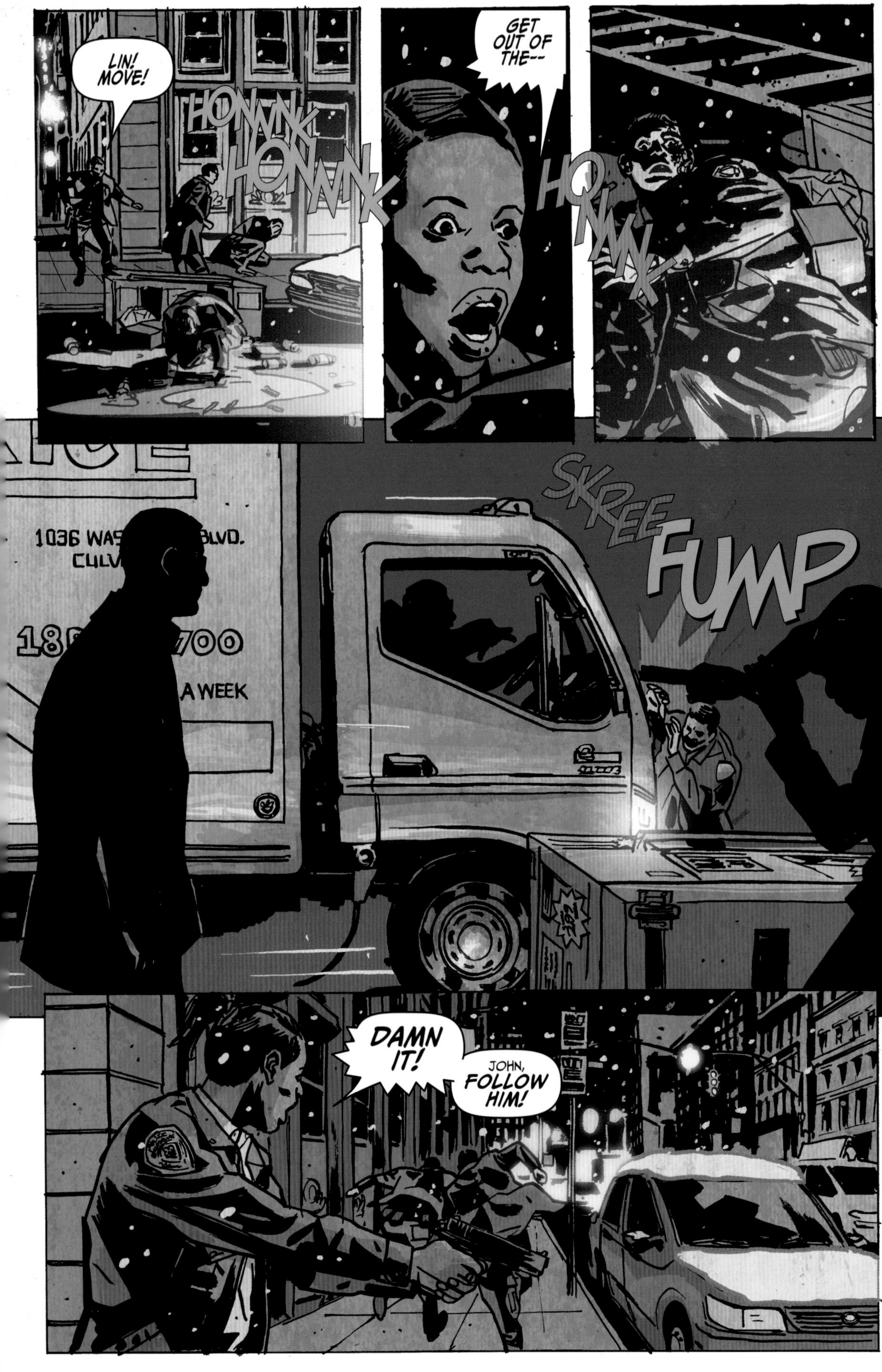
LIN! MOVE!
HONNNK
HONNNK
GET OUT OF THE--
HONNNK
SKREE
FUMP
1036 WAS BLVD.
CULV
18 700
A WEEK
DAMN IT!
JOHN, FOLLOW HIM!

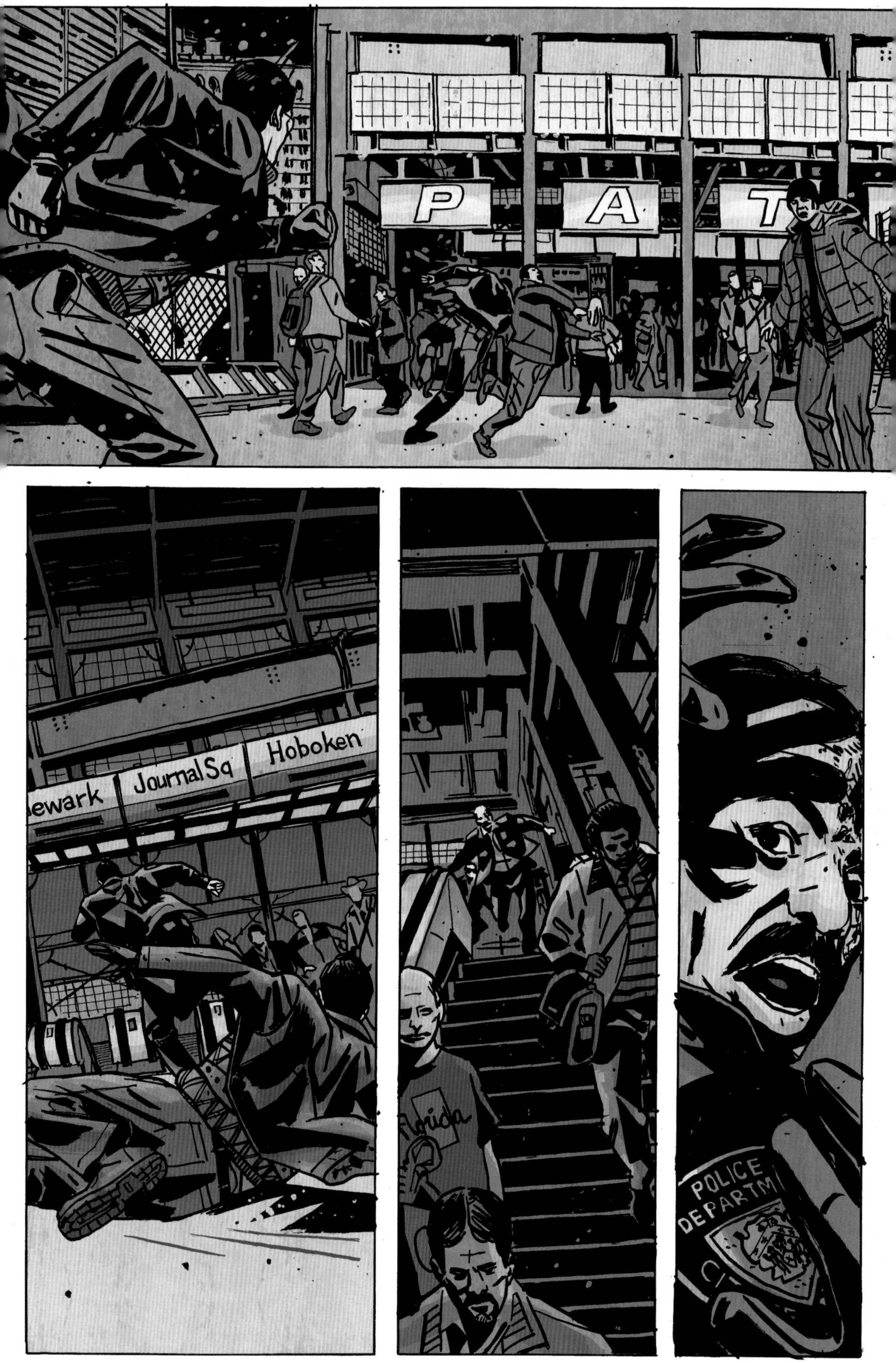
P A T
ewark
Journal Sq
Hoboken
Florida
POLICE
DEPARTM

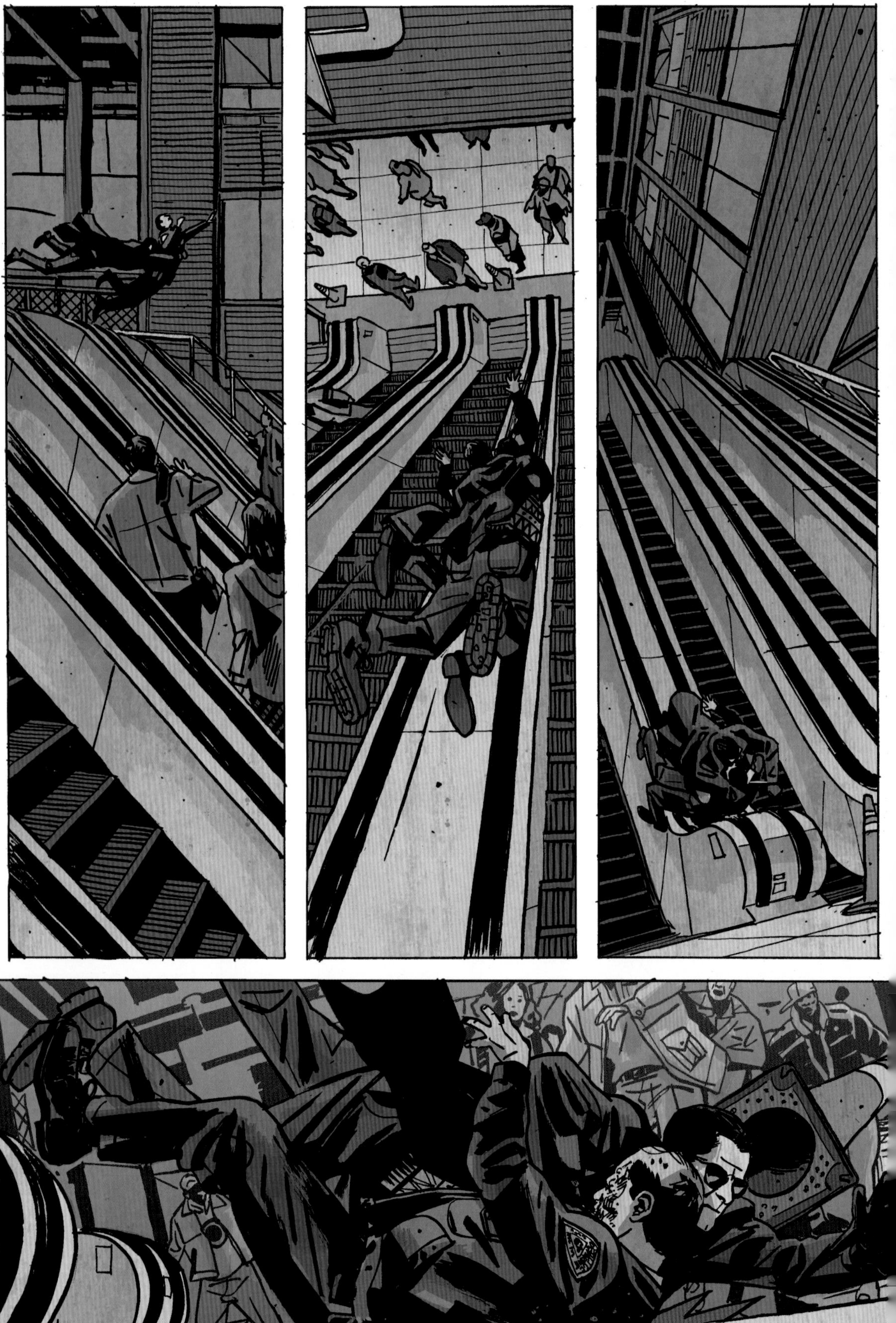

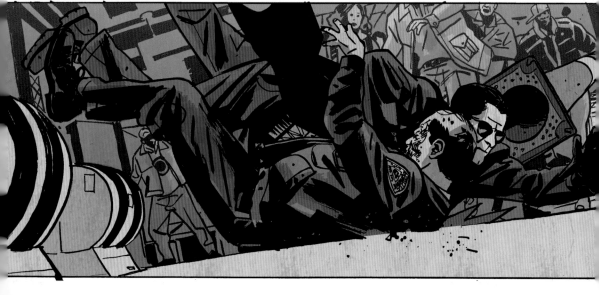

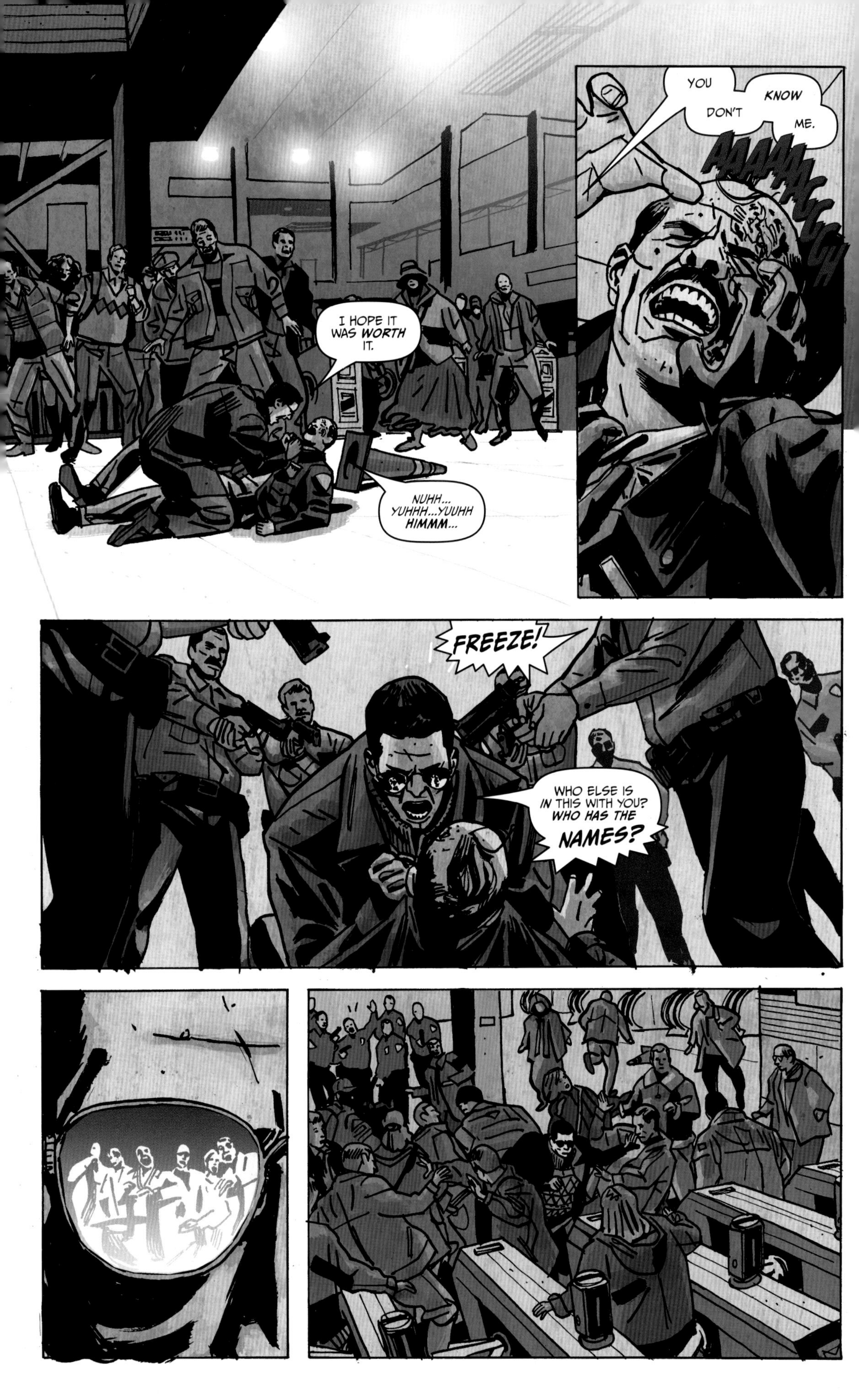
I HOPE IT WAS WORTH IT.
NUHH... YUHHH...YUUHH HIMMM...
YOU DON'T KNOW ME.
AAAAAAGGGH
FREEZE!
WHO ELSE IS IN THIS WITH YOU? WHO HAS THE NAMES?

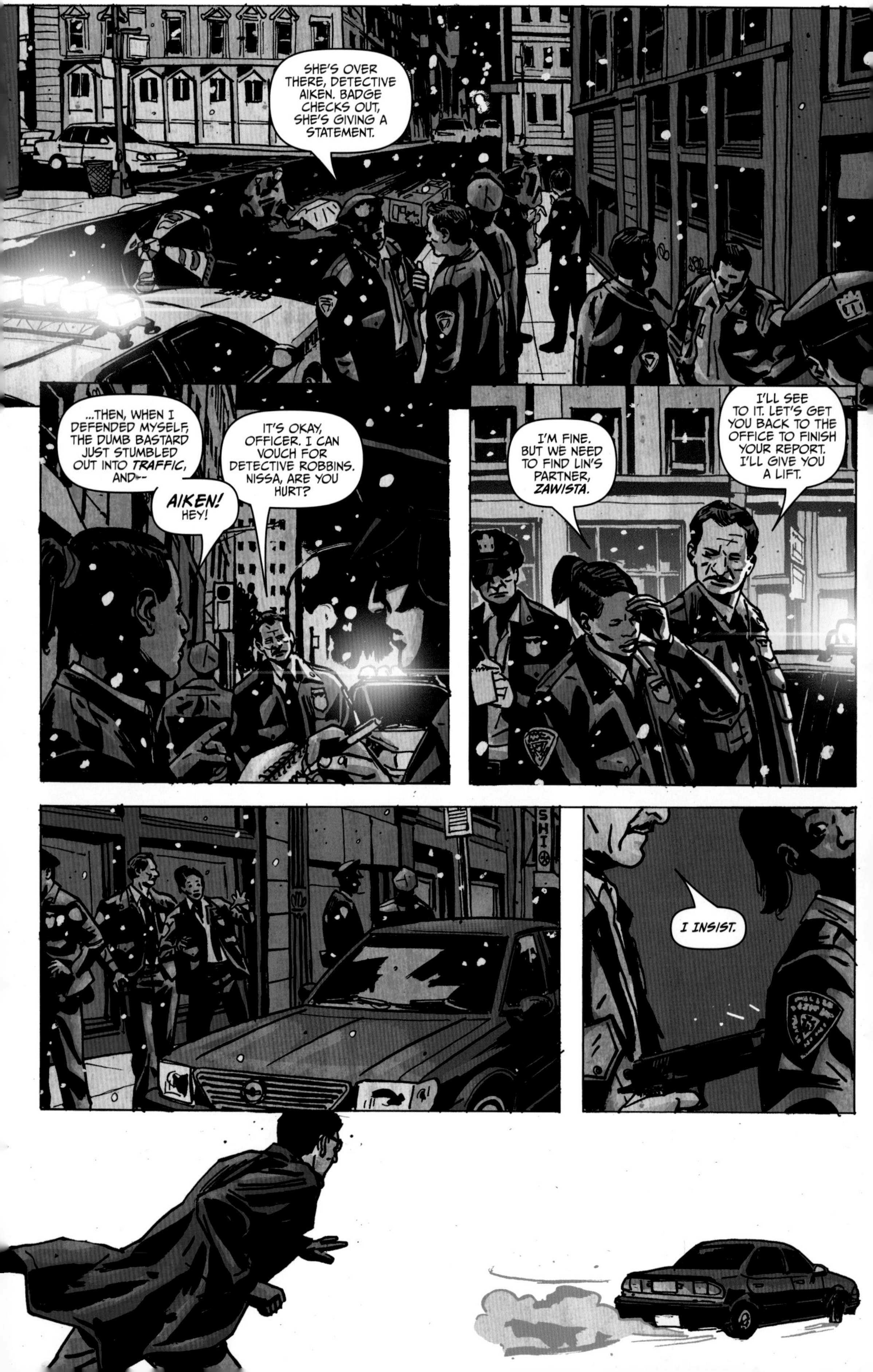
SHE'S OVER THERE, DETECTIVE AIKEN. BADGE CHECKS OUT, SHE'S GIVING A STATEMENT.
...THEN, WHEN I DEFENDED MYSELF, THE DUMB BASTARD JUST STUMBLED OUT INTO TRAFFIC, AND--
AIKEN! HEY!
IT'S OKAY, OFFICER. I CAN VOUCH FOR DETECTIVE ROBBINS. NISSA, ARE YOU HURT?
I'M FINE. BUT WE NEED TO FIND LIN'S PARTNER, ZAWISTA.
I'LL SEE TO IT. LET'S GET YOU BACK TO THE OFFICE TO FINISH YOUR REPORT. I'LL GIVE YOU A LIFT.
I INSIST.

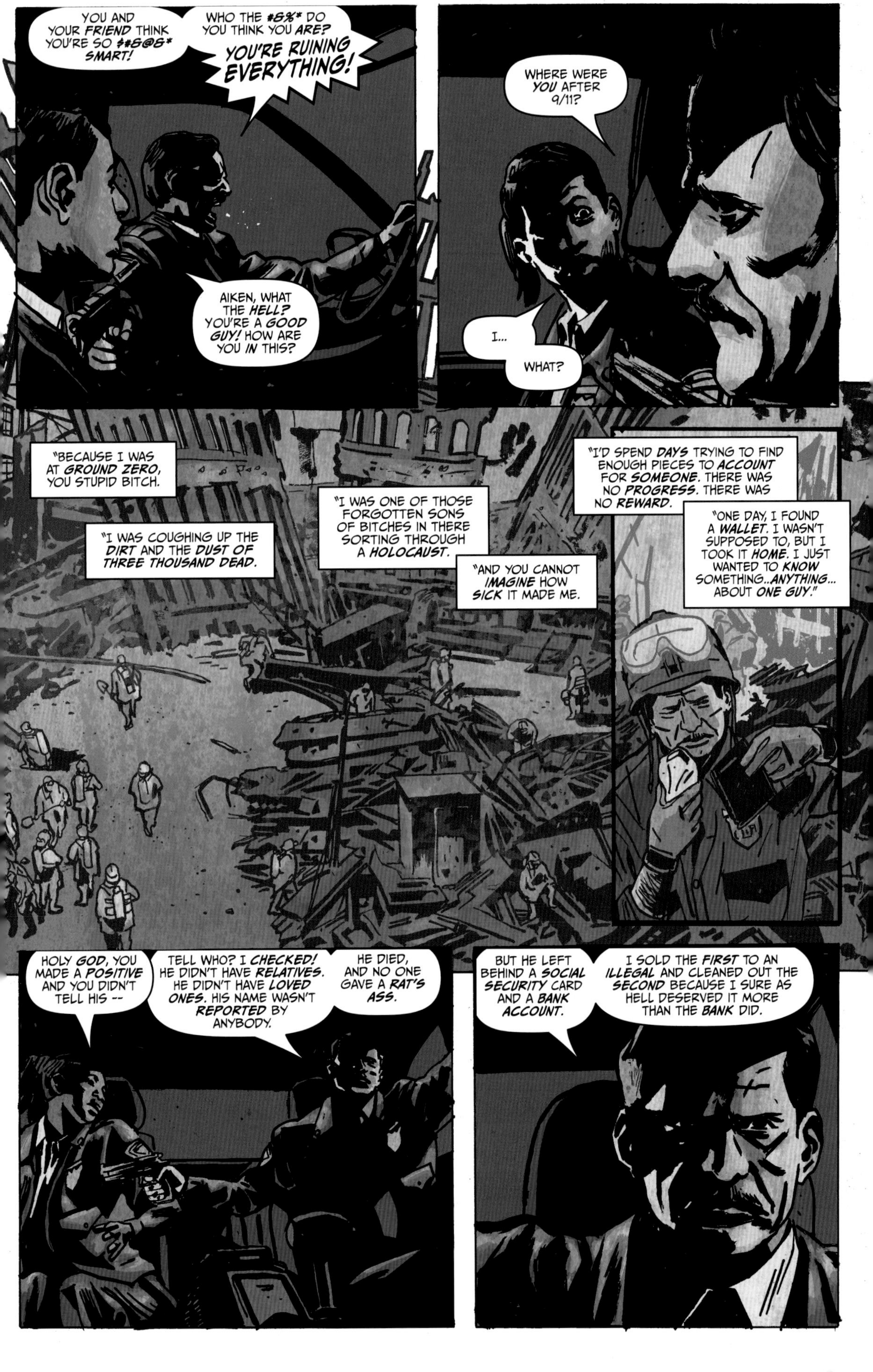

YOU AND YOUR FRIEND THINK YOU'RE SO $#&@&* SMART!
WHO THE #&%* DO YOU THINK YOU ARE? YOU'RE RUINING EVERYTHING!
AIKEN, WHAT THE HELL? YOU'RE A GOOD GUY! HOW ARE YOU IN THIS?
WHERE WERE YOU AFTER 9/11?
I...
WHAT?
"BECAUSE I WAS AT GROUND ZERO, YOU STUPID BITCH.
"I WAS COUGHING UP THE DIRT AND THE DUST OF THREE THOUSAND DEAD.
"I WAS ONE OF THOSE FORGOTTEN SONS OF BITCHES IN THERE SORTING THROUGH A HOLOCAUST.
"AND YOU CANNOT IMAGINE HOW SICK IT MADE ME.
"I'D SPEND DAYS TRYING TO FIND ENOUGH PIECES TO ACCOUNT FOR SOMEONE. THERE WAS NO PROGRESS. THERE WAS NO REWARD.
"ONE DAY, I FOUND A WALLET. I WASN'T SUPPOSED TO, BUT I TOOK IT HOME. I JUST WANTED TO KNOW SOMETHING...ANYTHING... ABOUT ONE GUY."
HOLY GOD, YOU MADE A POSITIVE AND YOU DIDN'T TELL HIS --
TELL WHO? I CHECKED! HE DIDN'T HAVE RELATIVES. HE DIDN'T HAVE LOVED ONES. HIS NAME WASN'T REPORTED BY ANYBODY.
HE DIED, AND NO ONE GAVE A RAT'S ASS.
BUT HE LEFT BEHIND A SOCIAL SECURITY CARD AND A BANK ACCOUNT.
I SOLD THE FIRST TO AN ILLEGAL AND CLEANED OUT THE SECOND BECAUSE I SURE AS HELL DESERVED IT MORE THAN THE BANK DID.

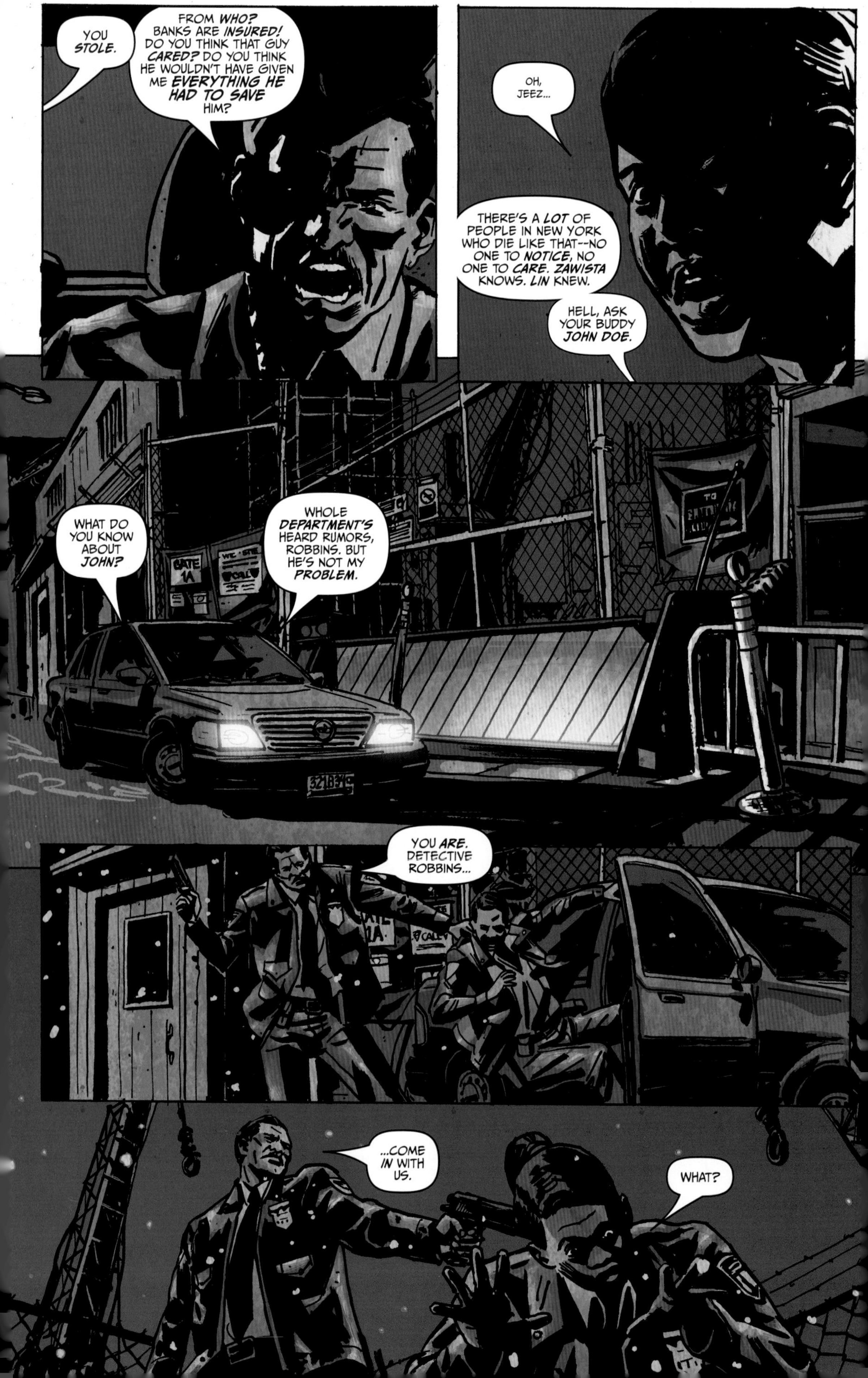

YOU STOLE.
FROM WHO? BANKS ARE INSURED! DO YOU THINK THAT GUY CARED? DO YOU THINK HE WOULDN'T HAVE GIVEN ME EVERYTHING HE HAD TO SAVE HIM?
OH, JEEZ...
THERE'S A LOT OF PEOPLE IN NEW YORK WHO DIE LIKE THAT--NO ONE TO NOTICE, NO ONE TO CARE. ZAWISTA KNOWS. LIN KNEW.
HELL, ASK YOUR BUDDY JOHN DOE.
WHAT DO YOU KNOW ABOUT JOHN?
WHOLE DEPARTMENT'S HEARD RUMORS, ROBBINS. BUT HE'S NOT MY PROBLEM.
GATE 1A
YOU ARE. DETECTIVE ROBBINS...
...COME IN WITH US.
WHAT?

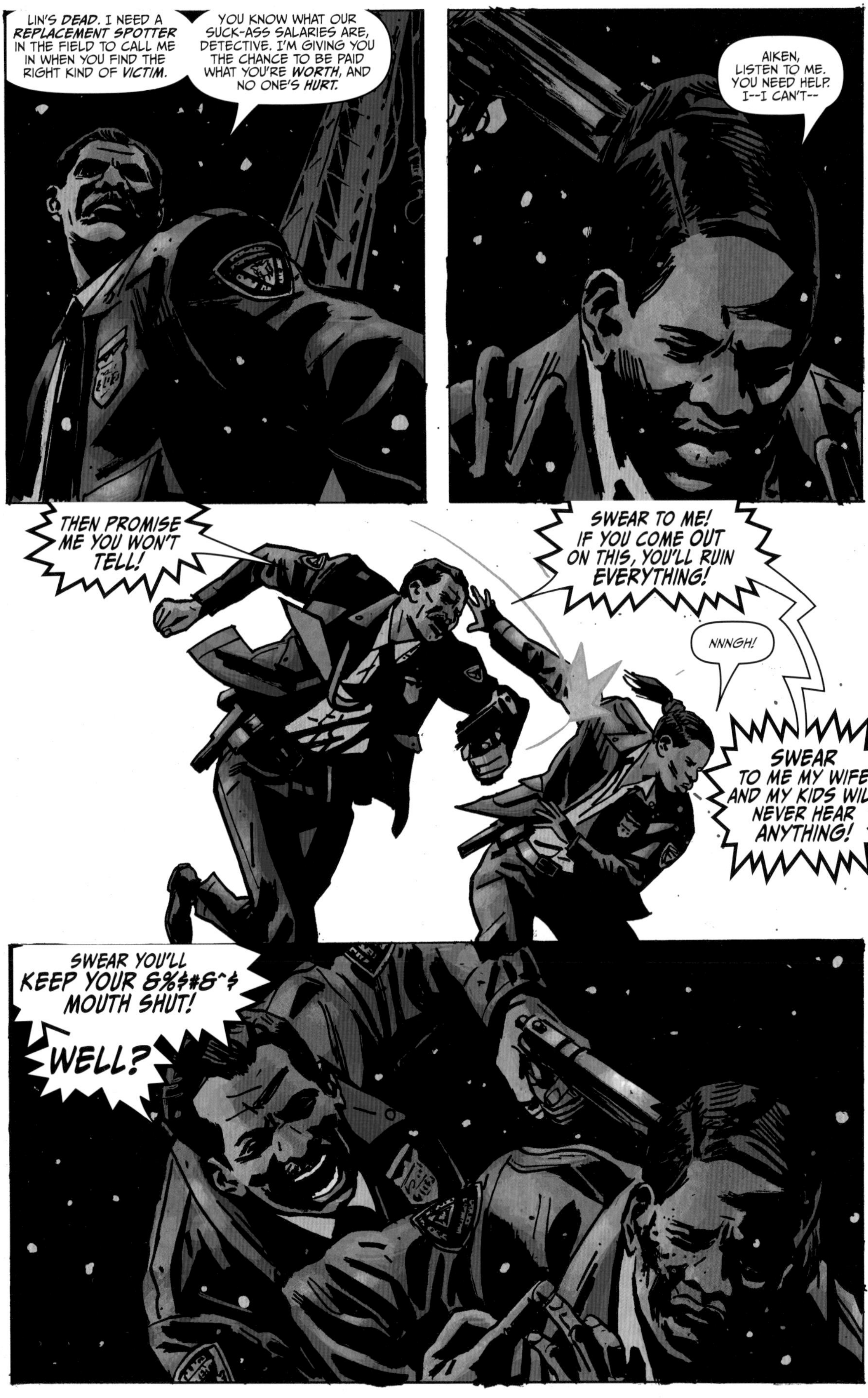
LIN'S DEAD. I NEED A REPLACEMENT SPOTTER IN THE FIELD TO CALL ME IN WHEN YOU FIND THE RIGHT KIND OF VICTIM.
YOU KNOW WHAT OUR SUCK-ASS SALARIES ARE, DETECTIVE. I'M GIVING YOU THE CHANCE TO BE PAID WHAT YOU'RE WORTH, AND NO ONE'S HURT.
AIKEN, LISTEN TO ME. YOU NEED HELP. I--I CAN'T--
THEN PROMISE ME YOU WON'T TELL!
SWEAR TO ME! IF YOU COME OUT ON THIS, YOU'LL RUIN EVERYTHING!
NNNGH!
SWEAR TO ME MY WIFE AND MY KIDS WILL NEVER HEAR ANYTHING!
SWEAR YOU'LL KEEP YOUR &%$#&^$ MOUTH SHUT!
WELL?

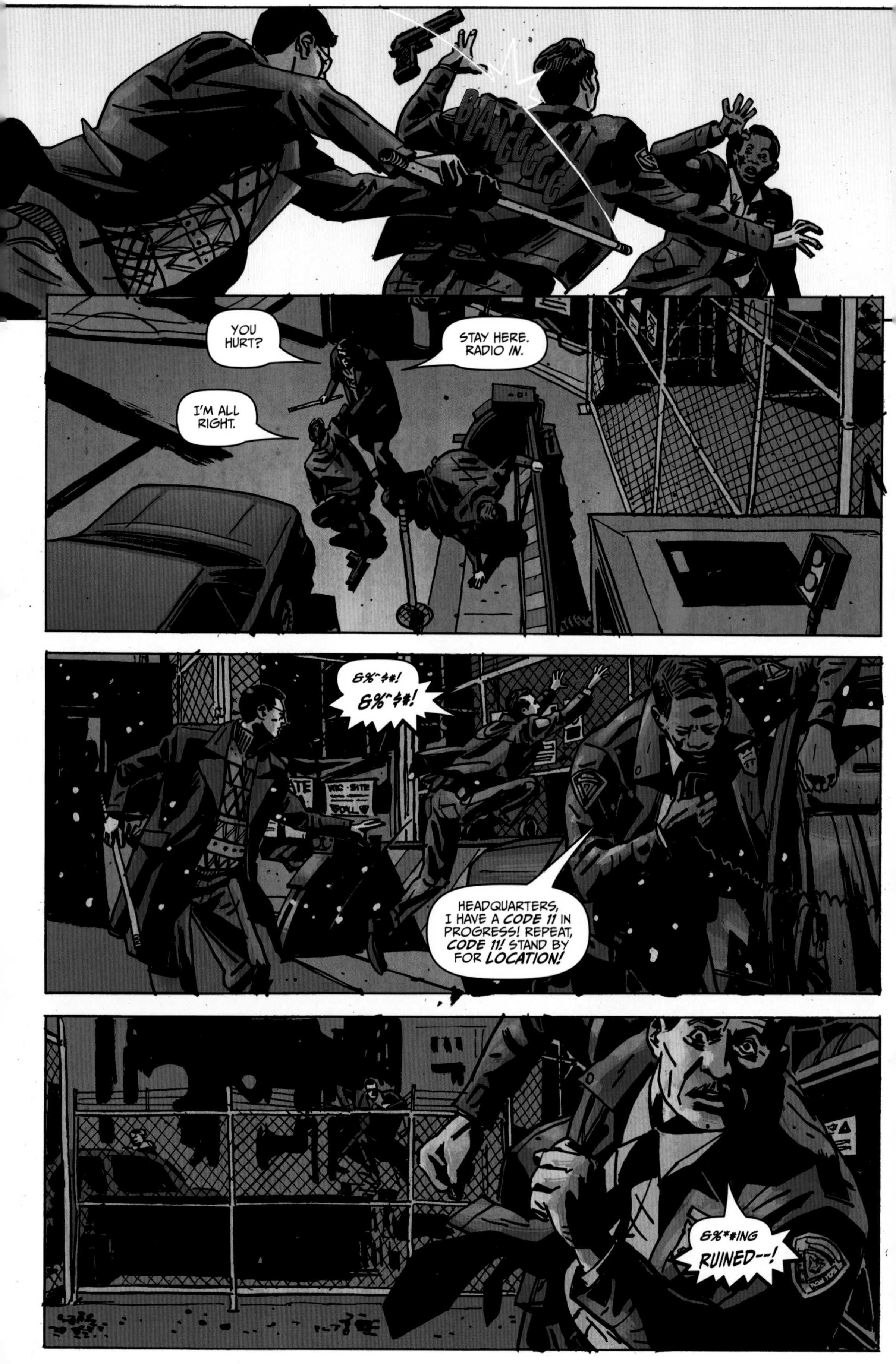
BLANGGGG
YOU HURT?
STAY HERE. RADIO IN.
I'M ALL RIGHT.
&%^$#!
&%^$#!
HEADQUARTERS, I HAVE A CODE 11 IN PROGRESS! REPEAT, CODE 11! STAND BY FOR LOCATION!
&%*#ING RUINED--!

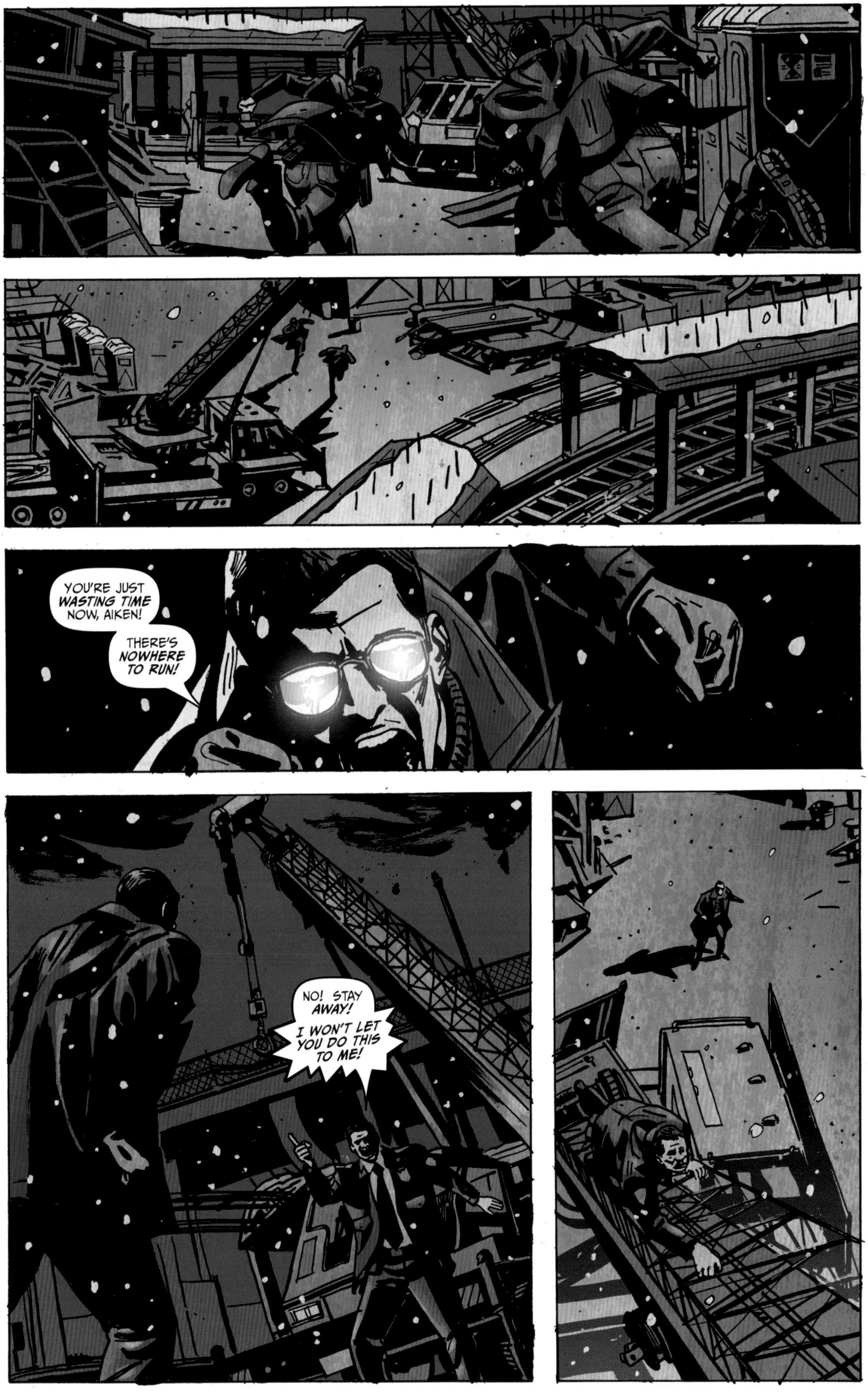
YOU'RE JUST WASTING TIME NOW, AIKEN!
THERE'S NOWHERE TO RUN!
NO! STAY AWAY!
I WON'T LET YOU DO THIS TO ME!

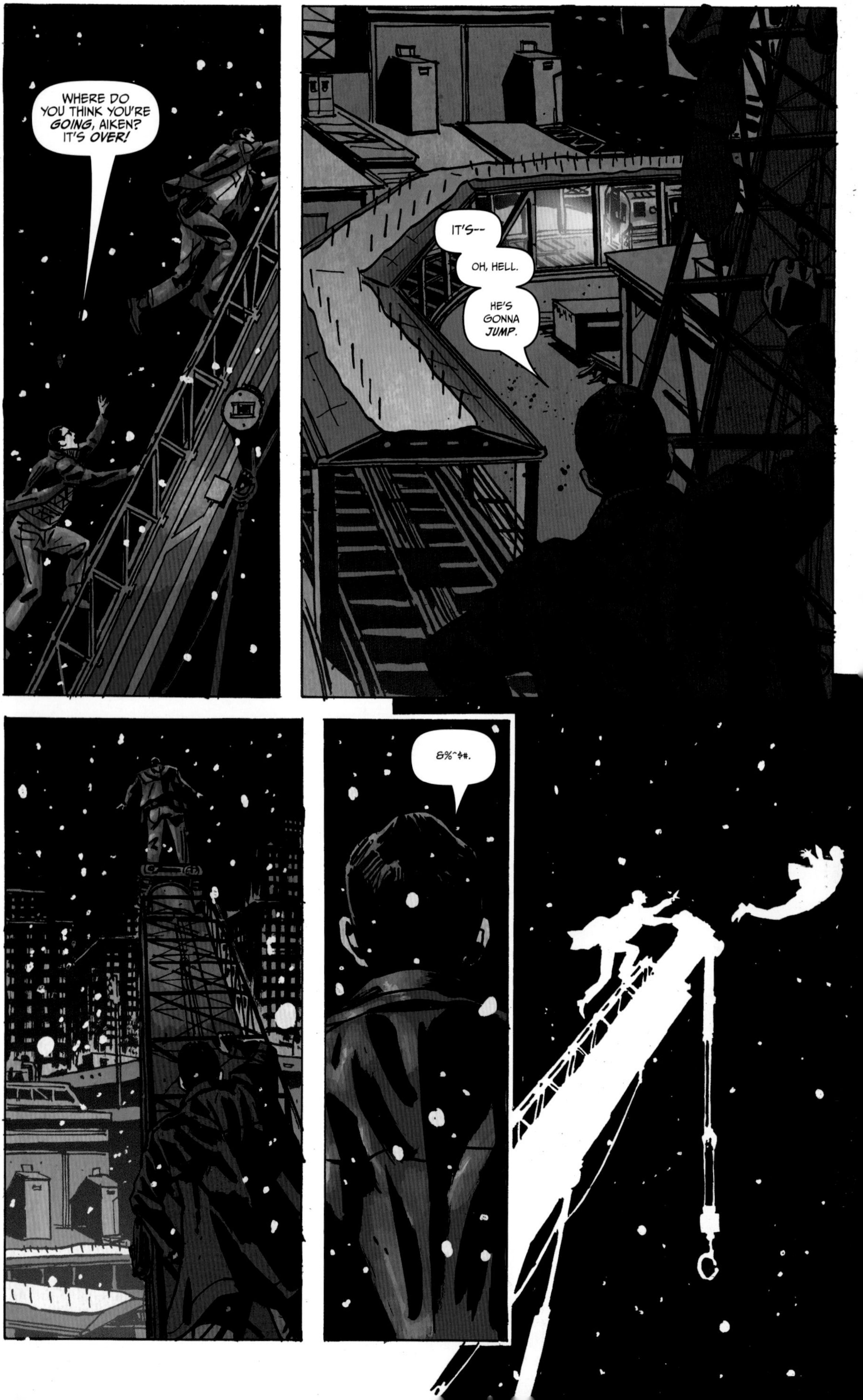
WHERE DO YOU THINK YOU'RE GOING, AIKEN? IT'S OVER!
IT'S--
OH, HELL.
HE'S GONNA JUMP.
&%^$#.

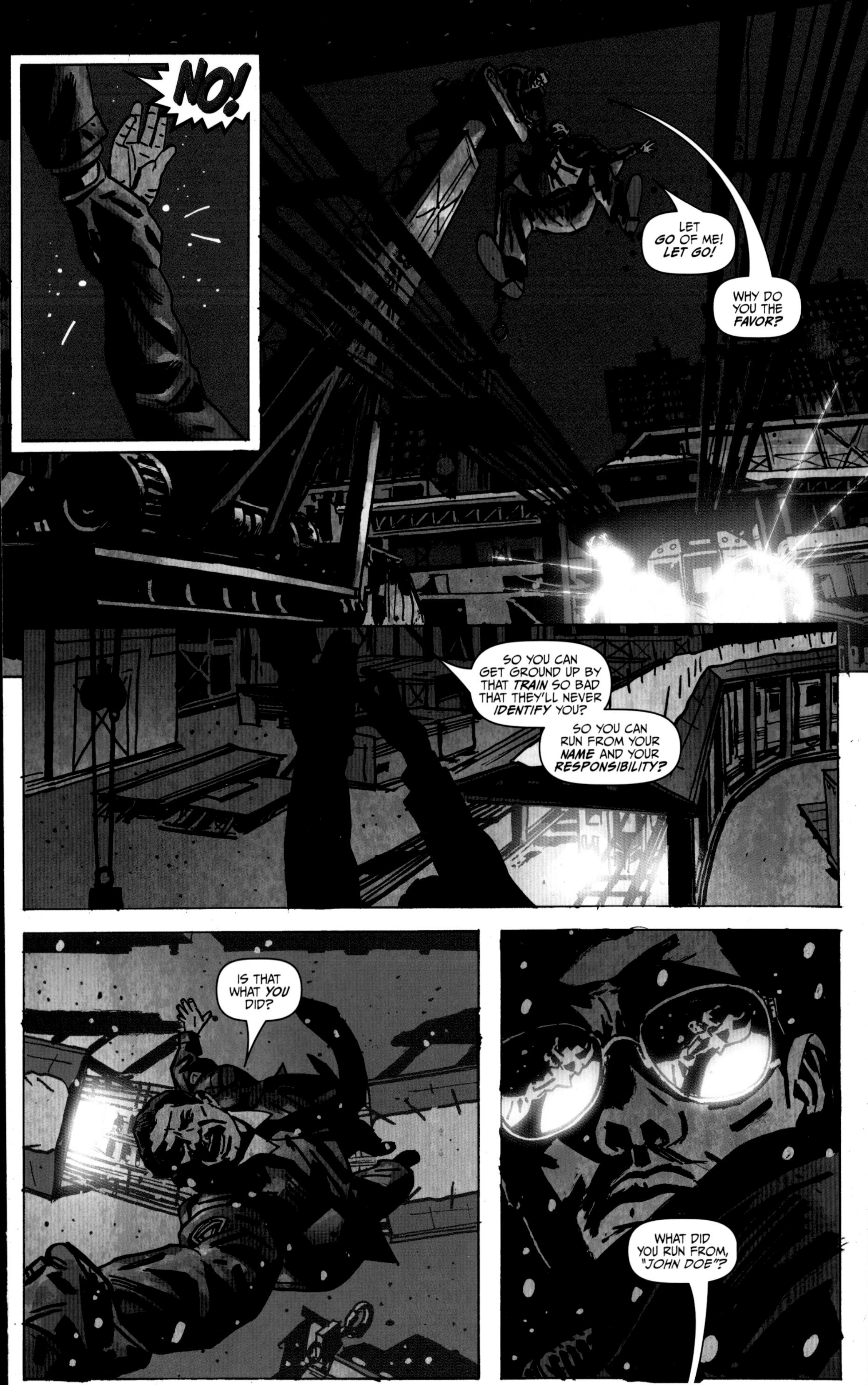
NO!
LET GO OF ME! LET GO!
WHY DO YOU THE FAVOR?
SO YOU CAN GET GROUND UP BY THAT TRAIN SO BAD THAT THEY'LL NEVER IDENTIFY YOU?
SO YOU CAN RUN FROM YOUR NAME AND YOUR RESPONSIBILITY?
IS THAT WHAT YOU DID?
WHAT DID YOU RUN FROM, "JOHN DOE"?

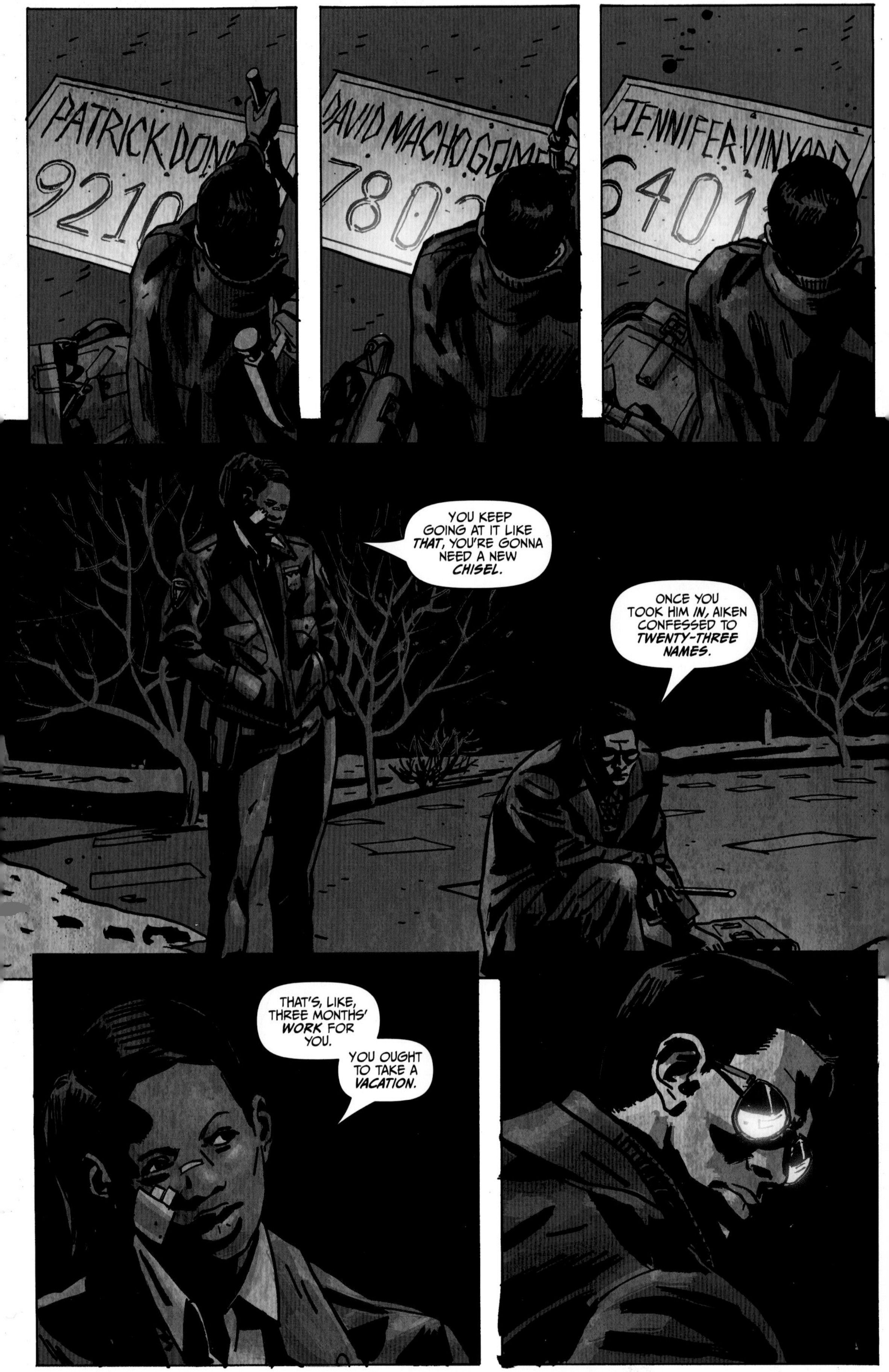
PATRICK DON
9210
DAVID MACHO GOME
780
JENNIFER VINYARD
6401
YOU KEEP GOING AT IT LIKE *THAT*, YOU'RE GONNA NEED A NEW ***CHISEL***.
ONCE YOU TOOK HIM *IN*, AIKEN CONFESSED TO ***TWENTY-THREE NAMES***.
THAT'S, LIKE, THREE MONTHS' ***WORK*** FOR YOU.
YOU OUGHT TO TAKE A ***VACATION***.

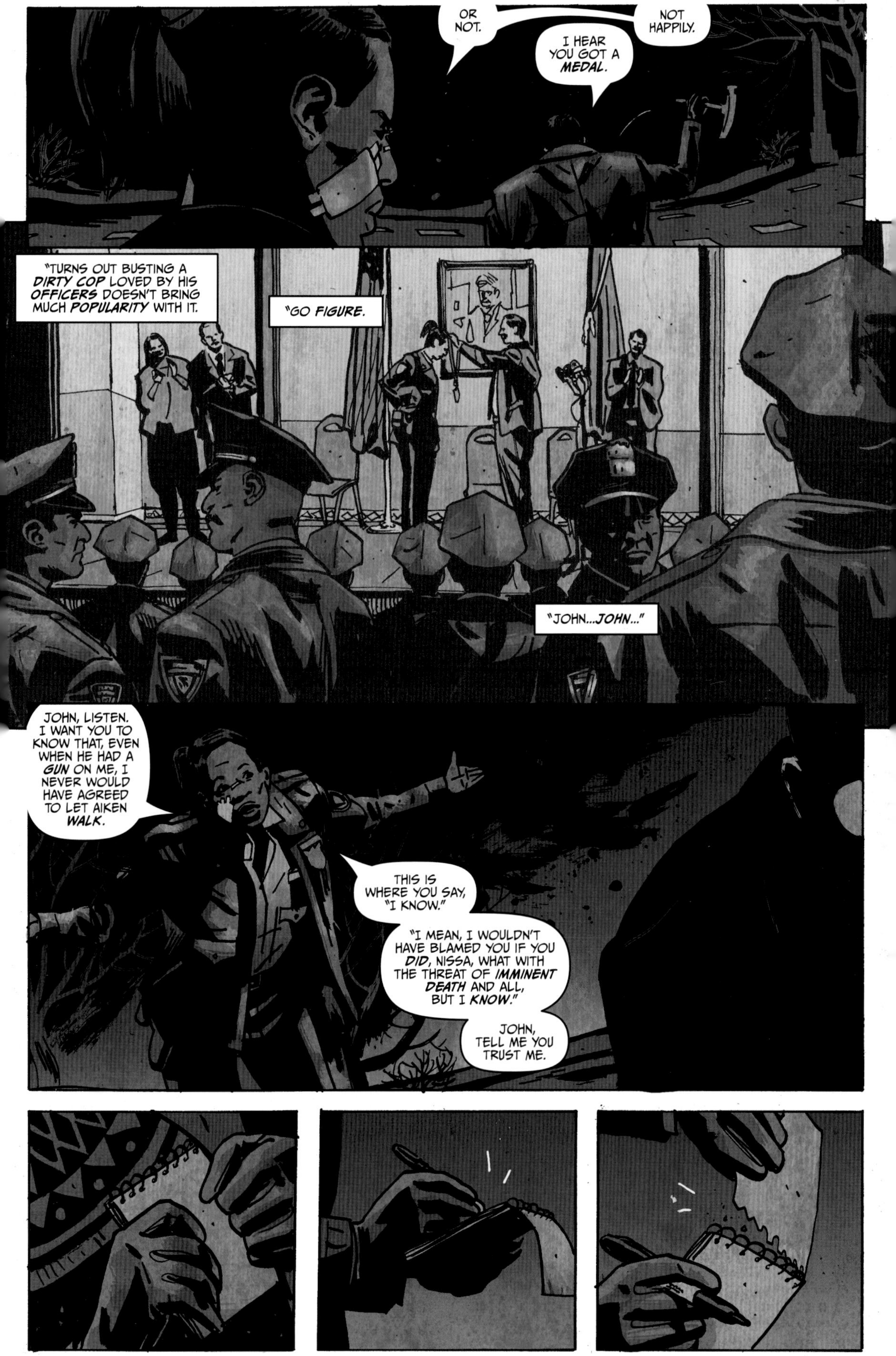

OR NOT.
NOT HAPPILY.
I HEAR YOU GOT A MEDAL.
"TURNS OUT BUSTING A DIRTY COP LOVED BY HIS OFFICERS DOESN'T BRING MUCH POPULARITY WITH IT.
"GO FIGURE.
"JOHN...JOHN..."
JOHN, LISTEN. I WANT YOU TO KNOW THAT, EVEN WHEN HE HAD A GUN ON ME, I NEVER WOULD HAVE AGREED TO LET AIKEN WALK.
THIS IS WHERE YOU SAY, "I KNOW."
"I MEAN, I WOULDN'T HAVE BLAMED YOU IF YOU DID, NISSA, WHAT WITH THE THREAT OF IMMINENT DEATH AND ALL, BUT I KNOW."
JOHN, TELL ME YOU TRUST ME.

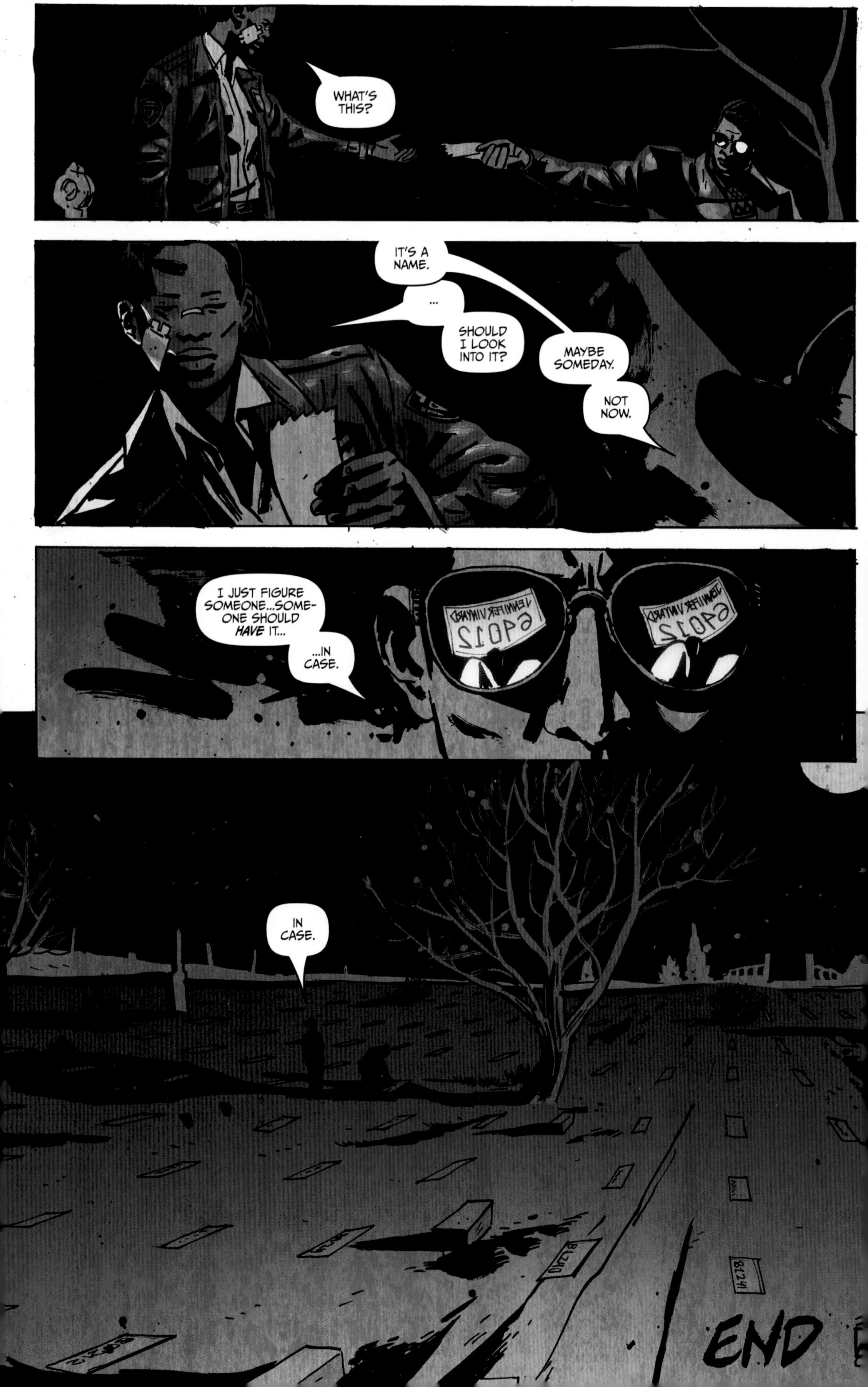
WHAT'S THIS?
IT'S A NAME.
...
SHOULD I LOOK INTO IT?
MAYBE SOMEDAY.
NOT NOW.
I JUST FIGURE SOMEONE...SOME-ONE SHOULD *HAVE* IT...
...IN CASE.
IN CASE.
END

Original "Pilot" 5 page script + "Lost" Steve Yeowell pages.

JOHN DOE:
Script for 5 pages
Mark Waid
First Draft/October 3, 2000

PAGE ONE

PANEL ONE: LONG ESTABLISHING SHOT, POTTER'S FIELD--A SMALL IS-LAND OFF THE COAST OF (BACKGROUND) MANHATTAN. ARTIST, THIS PLACE REALLY EXISTS BUT I CAN'T YET FIND PHOTO REFERENCE, SO FOR NOW, JUST MAKE IT UP, THANKS.

1 CAPTION: New York City, you'll forgive me, is like the screen over a SEPTIC TANK. Not only does the most godawful stuff in the world filter THROUGH it...

2 CAPTION: ...but, worse, sometimes the NASTIER bits and pieces get hung up in the MESH.

3 CAPTION: In the shadow of MANHATTAN, however, there's a much SMALLER island. Crime-FREE. Well-kept LAWN, open to the SUN.

4 CAPTION: You could have a PICNIC there.

PANEL TWO: CLOSER IN ON THE SMALLER ISLAND SO WE CAN SEE THAT IT'S A GIANT CEMETERY FILLED WITH PLAIN GRAVESTONES SHOWING NOTHING BUT A BURIAL DATE. ARTIST, POSITION THESE BURIAL DATES LOW WITH ENOUGH BLANK SPACE ABOVE THEM TO LATER BE FILLED IN, THANKS. WE SEE THE FOOT/LEG OF JOHN DOE IN EXTREME FOREGROUND STANDING BEFORE THE MOST PROMINENT OF THE BLANK HEADSTONES (MARKED WITH BURIAL DATE NOVEMBER 12, 1999).

5 CAPTION: If you were HERMAN AND LILY MUNSTER.

6 CAPTION: POTTER'S FIELD. A CITY CEMETERY--a BIG and very SPECIAL one. It's not for the FAMOUS. In fact, quite the OPPOSITE.

7 CAPTION: It's where the N.Y.P.D. buries the hundreds of UNIDENTIFIED VICTIMS it comes across each year...

PANEL THREE, SMALL: ON DOE'S GLOVED HANDS. HE'S WRITING DOWN THE BURIAL DATE IN A SMALL NOTEBOOK.

8 CAPTION: ...their plain gray headstones marked with the only information about them that's KNOWN:

9 CAPTION: The date their GRAVES were dug.

PANEL FOUR: INTERIOR ESTABLISHING, A NEW YORK TABLOID NEWSPAPER MORGUE--DIMLY LIT, LOTS OF FILING CABINETS, AND ONE DISHEVELED AND UNKEMPT REPORTER--CALL HIM AUGIE--DIGGING THROUGH FILES. FEEL FREE TO MAKE THIS GUY LOOK AS ECLECTIC AS YOU LIKE.

10 CAPTION: My name is AUGIE SHERTZER. You might know my BYLINE from the NEW YORK DAILY SUN. Used to be their TOP REPORTER.

11 CAPTION: "TOPLESS DANCER STUFFED IN GIANT CHEST"? That was mine.

12 CAPTION: If you've MISSED me lately, it's because a surprisingly well-connected ALDERMAN took UMBRAGE when I wrote about his wife's taste in VODKA.

13 CAPTION: By the CASE.

14 CAPTION: Which began my exciting new career as a FILE CLERK in the paper's REFERENCE LIBRARY. That's right...MORGUE duty.

15 CAPTION: But that's when and where a man promised me the INSIDE TRACK on enough EXCLUSIVE STORIES to eventually remake my REP...

PANEL FIVE: AUGIE HANDS A FILE OVER TO GLOVED HANDS WHICH REACH IN FROM OFF TO TAKE IT.

16 CAPTION: ...in return for slipping him the occasional file folder or bit of microfiche, no questions ASKED.

17 CAPTION: What's his NAME? He won't SAY.

PAGE TWO

HALF-PAGE SPLASH: AUGIE'S P.O.V.--A NICE TORSO AND HEAD ESTABLISH-ING SHOT OF JOHN DOE ACCEPTING THE FILE. AS WILL ALMOST ALWAYS BE THE CASE, HE'S SO HARSHLY BACKLIT THAT HIS FEATURES ARE INDIS-TINCT--AT BEST, ALL WE'LL EVER REALLY SEE OF HIS FACE IS A CLOSE-UP OF HIS EYES--SO WHATEVER HE'S WEARING WILL HAVE TO BE HIS IDENTI-FYING TRADEMARK.

1 CAPTION: I call him JOHN DOE.

2 CREDITS: [to come]

PANEL TWO: INTERIOR, POLICE MORGUE. DOE--FACING AWAY FROM US--IS TALKING WITH AN ASSISTANT MEDICAL EXAMINER WHO'S LOOKING AROUND NERVOUSLY AS HE HANDS OVER A MANILA ENVELOPE--CLEAR-LY, THE M.E.'S NOT SUPPOSED TO BE DOING THIS.

3 CAPTION: I'm not the only one who's inked a deal with
          Mr. Anonymous.

4 CAPTION: Carter Hodges is an assistant M.E. whose kid sister VANISHED a couple of years ago without a TRACE.

5 CAPTION: Which is why Carter has to BRACE himself every time he snaps back a SHEET.

PANEL THREE: ON THE CONTENTS OF THE ENVELOPE AS DOE SPILLS THEM ONTO A DESK. THEY'RE PERSONAL EFFECTS, AND NOT MANY OF THEM--A CHEAP WATCH, A SHATTERED PAIR OF EYEGLASSES, AND A MODERATELY DISTINCTIVE MAN'S FINGER RING. WE CAN READ THE WRITING ON THE ENVELOPE.

6 ENVELOPE: VICTIM #856643
                NAME UNKNOWN
                PERSONAL EFFECTS

7 CAPTION: Consequently, Carter and Doe have their OWN understanding...which is why Carter, when no one's LOOKING...

PANEL FOUR: DOE'S HAND PICKS UP THE RING.

8 CAPTION: ...often makes certain items...AVAILABLE.

PAGE THREE

FULL-PAGE MONTAGE. DOE--CROUCHED SO WE CAN'T SEE HIS FACE--IS STUDYING AN OPEN FILE FOLDER WHILE DRAW-ING/RECONSTRUCTING A CHALK OUTLINE ON A BLEAK WATERFRONT DOCK. SURROUNDING THIS ARE MONOCHRO-MATIC IMAGES OF DOE'S "AGENTS": A FEMALE HOMICIDE DETECTIVE (WEARING AROUND HER NECK A POLICE BADGE READING "N.Y.P.D. HO-MICIDE"); AN INTERNET GEEK MANNING A COM-PUTER TERMINAL WHILE DOE STANDS BEHIND HIM; DOE HANDING A TWENTY DOLLAR BILL TO AN ELDERLY HOMELESS WOMAN LIVING IN CARD-BOARD BOXES IN AN AL-LEYWAY.

1 CAPTION: In fact, in the few months he's been active, Doe's established quite a little NETWORK of contacts...

2 CAPTION: ...each with his or her OWN motive for helping Doe with his INVESTI-GATIONS.

3 CAPTION: See, the city's unidentified victims...it's not always that their murders CAN'T be solved...

4 CAPTION: ...just that--given a finite amount of MANPOWER and RESOURCES-- the cops are often pressured to focus on bigger, HIGHER-PROFILE cases.

5 CAPTION: Not Doe.

6 CAPTION: He's decided that NO one should die without a NAME.

7 CAPTION: Without being REMEMBERED.

PAGE FOUR

PANEL ONE ACROSS PAGE TOP: INTERIOR, A BUSINESSMAN'S OFFICE, TASTEFULLY APPOINTED.   WE'RE SEEING IT FRAMED THROUGH THE SPREAD STANDING LEGS OF DOE, WHO STANDS OVER A BLOODIED, UNCONSCIOUS GIGANTIC BRUISER OF A THUG. THE MAN BEHIND THE DESK IS ALARMED. NOTE: A BIG WINDOW SOMEWHERE IN THE ROOM.

PANELS TWO-SIX EQUAL ACROSS MIDDLE OF PAGE:

PANEL TWO: ON THE MAN AS DOE'S HAND, HOLDING HIM BY THE THROAT, SHOVES HIM VIOLENTLY AGAINST THE WALL.

PANEL THREE: THE MAN LOOKS VERY, VERY CONFUSED AND INNOCENT, CLEARLY PLEADING THAT HE DOESN'T KNOW WHAT'S GOING ON--

PANEL FOUR: --BUT HIS EYES GO WIDE AS HE STARES DOWN AT THE FIN-GER RING DOE HOLDS IN HIS OTHER HAND, SHOWS HIM --

PANEL FIVE: --AND, BUSTED, EYES CLOSED, BITING HIS LIP, THE MAN DROOPS HIS HEAD IN RESIGNATION.

PANEL SIX: DOE'S HAND PICKS UP THE TELEPHONE--

PANEL SEVEN ACROSS PAGE BOTTOM: --AND DOE EXITS. WE CAN SEE THE MAN SITTING AGAINST THE WALL, SLUMPED, WEEPING INTO HIS OPEN HANDS, LIT BY THE RED AND BLUE LIGHTS FLASHING THROUGH THE OF-FICE WINDOW.

1 CAPTION: Without being AVENGED.

PAGE FIVE

PANEL ONE: BACK TO THE ISLAND GRAVEYARD. DOE'S CHISELING SOME-THING INTO A HEADSTONE.

1 CAPTION: Forgotten people die the WORST death. They die ALONE. No one to MOURN them. No one to CARE.

2 CAPTION: But John Doe DOES.

3 CAPTION: Why?

PANEL TWO: WE CLOSE IN TO SEE THAT IT'S A NAME.

4 CAPTION: Damned if can tell you.

5 CAPTION: Yet.

PANEL THREE: DOE, HIS HANDIWORK DONE AND VISIBLE IN BACKGROUND,

WALKS OVER TO THE NEXT MOST ADJACENT BLANK HEADSTONE--

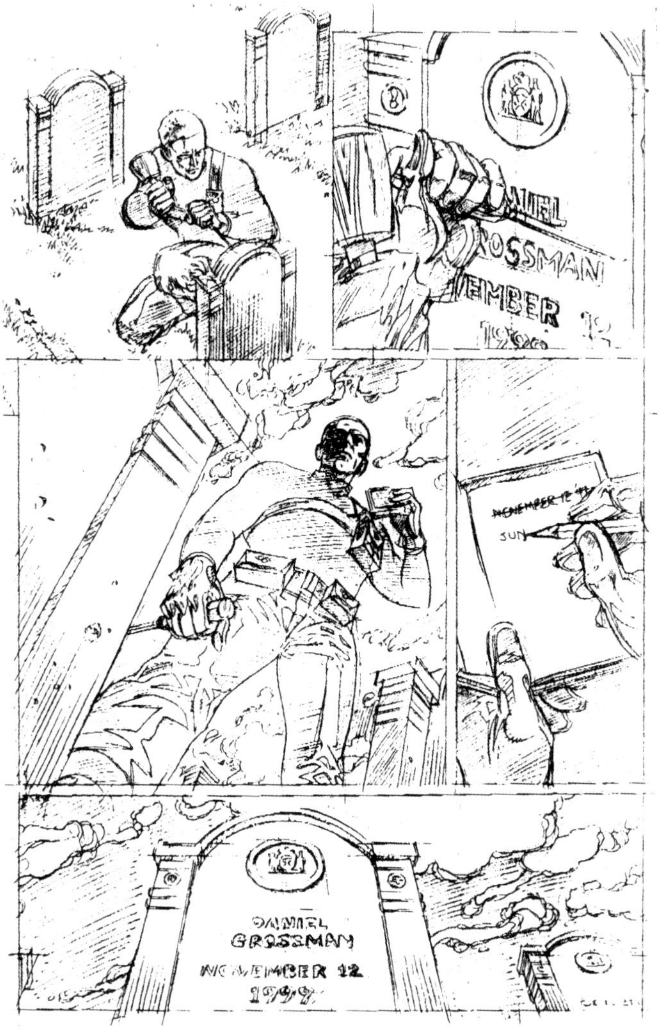
GROSSMAN

6 CAPTION: WHATEVER drives this guy, it drives him HELLAHARD. For every case he digs UP, three more get buried DEEP.

7 CAPTION: Still, he patiently moves from STONE to STONE, never slowing DOWN, never STOPPING.

PANEL FOUR: --AND WRITES DOWN THE BURIAL DATE IN HIS NOTEBOOK.

8 CAPTION: Who is John Doe? What's his story? I wish he'd come OUT with it. A lot of folks, well...

PANEL FIVE: AND WE END WITH ANOTHER LONG ESTABLISHING SHOT OF THE GRAVEYARD, JOHN DOE NOWHERE TO BE SEEN, OFF ON ANOTHER MISSION.

9 CAPTION: ...they're DYING to know.

CHARACTER DESIGNS

BY PAUL AZACETA

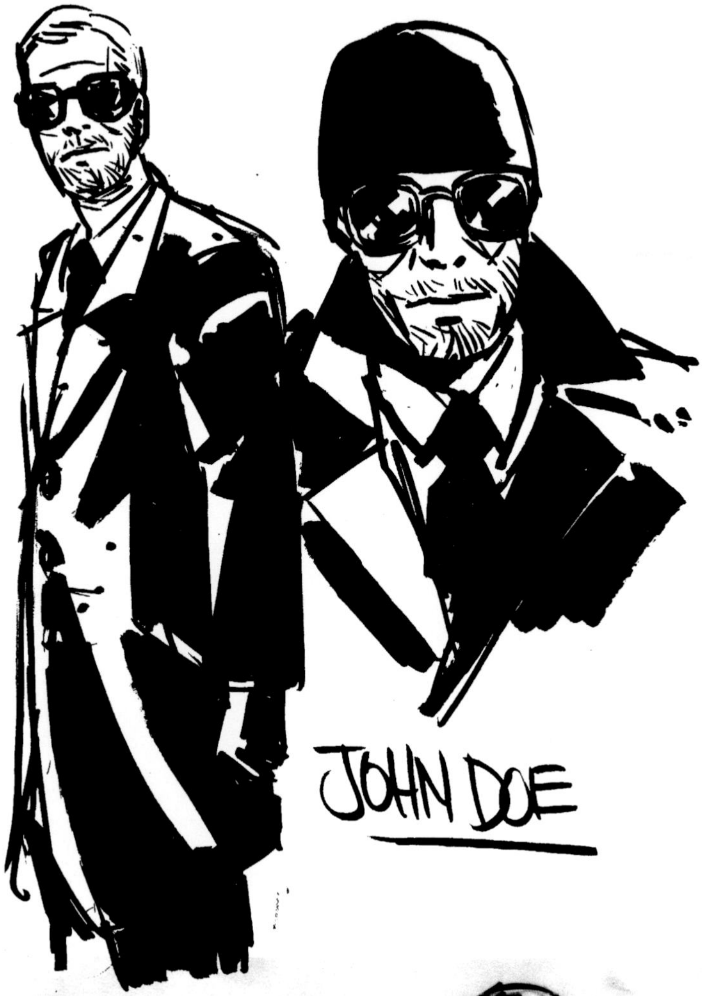
JOHN DOE

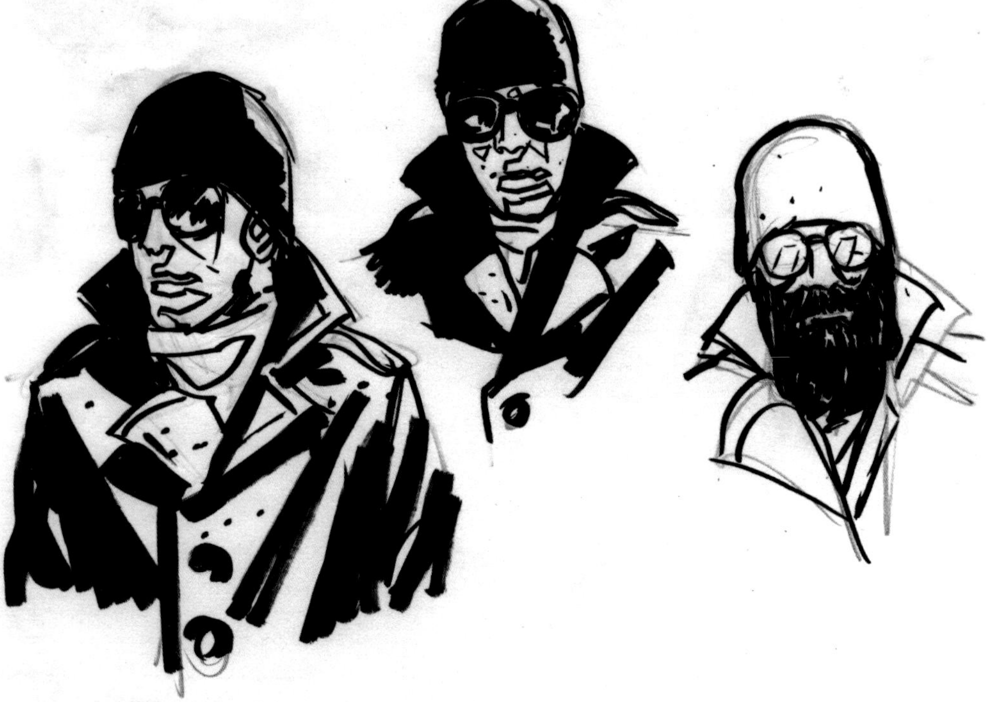

CHARACTER DESIGNS

BY PAUL AZACETA

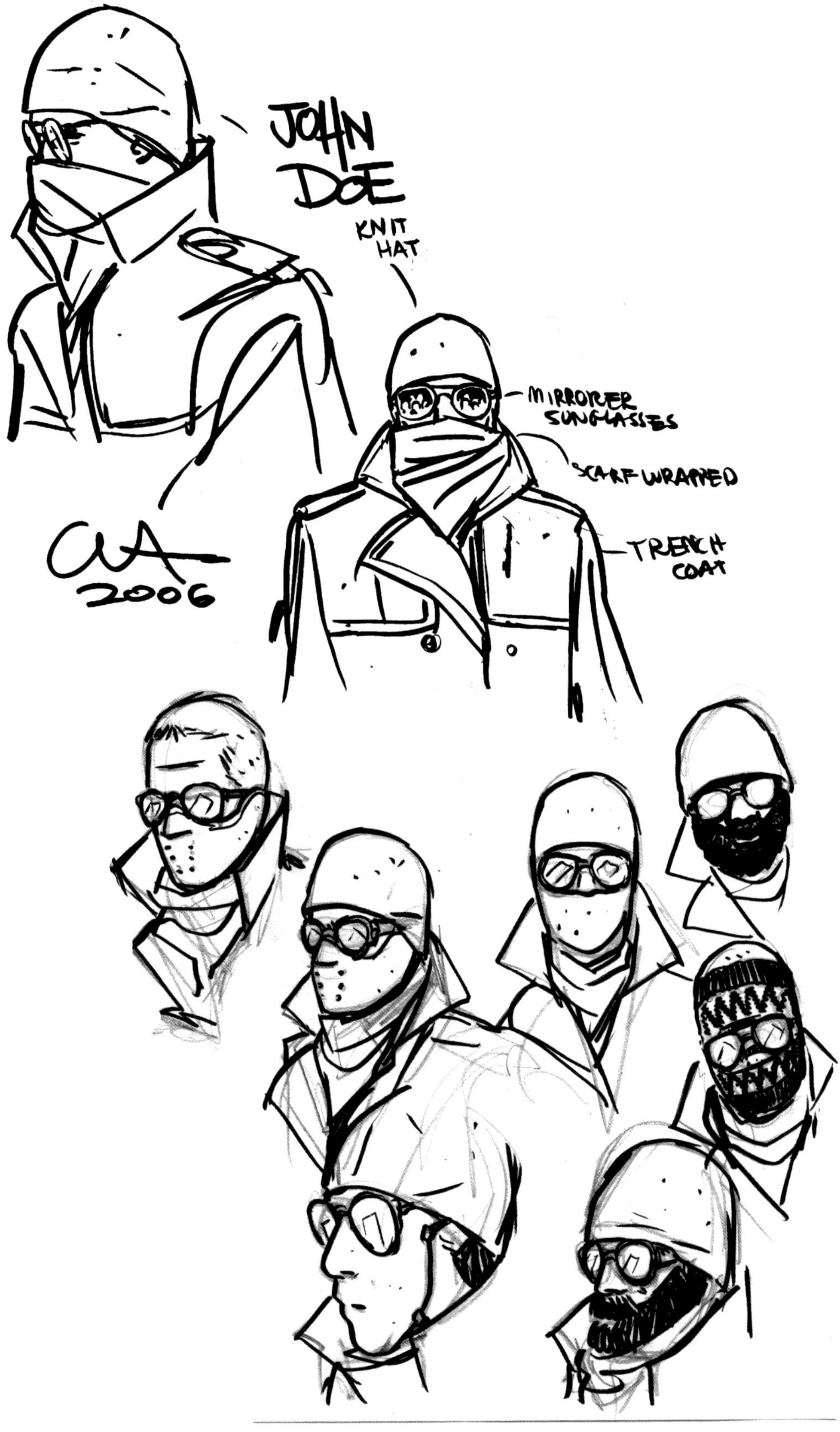

JOHN DOE
KNIT HAT
MIRRORED SUNGLASSES
SCARF WRAPPED
TRENCH COAT
2006